FAMILY MATTERS

The Authors

Karen L. Anderson, King's College, University of Western Ontario
Hugh Armstrong, Vanier College
Pat Armstrong, York University
Janice Drakich, Scarborough College, University of Toronto
Margrit Eichler, Ontario Institute for Studies in Education
Connie Guberman, Scarborough College, University of Toronto
Alison Hayford, University of Regina
Meg Luxton, York University
John F. Peters, Wilfrid Laurier University
Elaine Porter, Laurentian University
C. James Richardson, University of New Brunswick
Geoffrey Tesson, Laurentian University

FAMILY MATTERS: SOCIOLOGY AND CONTEMPORARY CANADIAN FAMILIES

Karen L. Anderson
Hugh Armstrong
Pat Armstrong
Janice Drakich
Margrit Eichler
Connie Guberman
Alison Hayford
Meg Luxton
John F. Peters
Elaine Porter
C. James Richardson
Geoffrey Tesson

METHUEN

Toronto   New York   London   Sydney   Auckland

The television series *Family Matters* was produced by
TVOntario in co-operation with Laurentian Univer-
sity, Wilfrid Laurier University, the University of
Windsor, and the University of Guelph. A contribu-
tion to the television series was also provided by
Methuen Publications, a Division of The Carswell
Company Limited.

Canadian Cataloguing in Publication Data

Main entry under title:

Family matters

Includes bibliographies and index.
ISBN 0-458-81460-1

1. Family — Canada.   I. Anderson, Karen L.

HQ559.F35 1987   306.8′5′0971   C87-095092-4

Printed and bound in Canada

1 2 3 4   87   91 90 89 88

Contents

Acknowledgments

The development of this volume was immeasurably enhanced by the substantial and enthusiastic support we received from numerous individuals. In acknowledging our debts, we thank the contributors, each of whom provided considerable scholarship and an unfailing graciousness in dealing with our many questions. Alison Hayford and Margrit Eichler offered critical insight far beyond the requirements of their task as reviewers. Our thanks are also due to advisory board members Gerald Booth, Sam Luker, John F. Peters, Elaine Porter, and Robert Whitehurst for their ongoing advice and commitment to both the television and the print elements of the project. And we would like to express our heartfelt appreciation to our editor, Lorraine Fairley, who made all things possible.

CHAPTER 1

Outlines of the Family

ALISON HAYFORD

INTRODUCTION

Imagine yourself meeting a rather nosy person for the first time. You might well find yourself answering questions with a statement such as the following:

"My family came to Canada at the beginning of this century from Ireland, but my husband is Québecois and his family has been here since the 1600s. I grew up in a small family, just my brother and me, but my husband is one of ten children. My family is close, though, and every Christmas all the aunts and uncles and cousins get together for a big meal. My husband's family is much more scattered. I have a rather tense relationship with my mother-in-law, because she's bugging me to start a family. She wants us to have a son to carry on the family name. I'd just as soon have a daughter, but in any case we don't feel ready for a family yet."

In this statement the word "family" is used in five different ways. You have no difficulty in understanding what "family" means in each case, because all of these uses of the word are common, everyday ones. We use "family" to mean our ancestors, our brothers and sisters and parents, all of our relations who are currently living, and a vague general sense of identity and relationship, as well as our spouses and children. All of these are important ideas for most of us but, familiar as they are, they are complex and confusing. "Family" is a word most of us never think much about, even though it expresses some of the most important relationships in our lives. It is also one of the most difficult words to define.

DEFINING "FAMILY"

We can see these difficulties when we look at ordinary definitions. Defining "family" is not just a problem for editors of dictionaries. In any society, including our own, understanding how people view and live their family relationships is important, because families play a central role in our social existence. We rely on families to take care of almost all children and a great many old people. We rely on families to provide housing for their members, as well as most food and general care. It is in families that virtually everyone learns to speak, learns cultural values, learns how to function in society. In other words, the family is an institution of central importance. It is also an institution that can be deeply affected by decisions taken in both government and the private sector. For these reasons, knowing how families really work is important, especially since reality can sometimes be quite different from our ideals. This is one reason Statistics Canada produces several volumes of information about families in each census.

In order to collect this information, Statistics Canada has to define what "family" means. This is where they—and we—begin to encounter problems. For example, here's the definition of "census family" that was used in the 1981 census:

> a husband and a wife (with or without children who have never married, regardless of age), or a lone parent of any marital status, with one or more children who have never married, regardless of age, living in the same dwelling. For census purposes, persons living in a common-law type of arrangement are considered as now married, regardless of their legal marital status; they accordingly appear as a husband-wife family in the census family table.

If you think of your own situation in life, you can see some of the problems with this definition. You might be a 30-year-old who's just received a loan from your parents to help with a mortgage—parents you see once a year on a trip home. Maybe you just wrote a cheque to send to your 19-year-old son at university. Or perhaps you share a household and a life with someone you're not related to by any of the terms included in this definition. Whatever your situation may be, your family relationships are likely to be important in the choices you make and the actions you undertake in life—yet some of these relationships may not be covered in the Statistics Canada definition.

No definition of "family" can include all the realities of our family lives. This is one reason Statistics Canada uses different definitions, depending on the information they want to collect and what they want to use it for. Other definitions you'll find in the census or in other surveys such as the labour force survey include "economic family" (which involves a broader range of relationships than the census family) and "household."

Social scientists and politicians also have to establish working definitions of "family." For example, it's important to decide whether you're only going to consider people who actually live together. This isn't as easy as it might seem. Where divorced parents have joint custody of a child, for example, who is living with whom? Many people — perhaps most people — have close and important relationships with relatives they don't actually live with, or they live with different relatives at different times. No single definition can incorporate all the complexities of our family lives.

"Family" is hard to define, because the word reflects a variety of social relationships and all their history. While the word "family" has been a part of the English language for 600 years, its meaning has changed over time as our actual patterns of social relationships have changed (Williams, 1976: 108–111). As Chapter 2 shows, those changes have been profound. The word "family" itself is shown in that chapter to have come from the Latin *familia*, which meant, not "family" in the modern sense, but something more like "household." We first began to use "family" in English in the late 1300s. Before the 1600s, the word referred to households or large groups of kin. It didn't start to take on its modern meaning (of a small group of related people who live together) until the middle of the 17th century; and this meaning didn't become dominant until the 1800s. Words change along with our social structures; the word "family" is a vivid example of this.

What definition will be used in this book? With multiple authors and topics there will be more than one definition. Most often, however, we will use the word in the sense of "nuclear family," since this is the image that usually comes to mind when Canadians talk about the family, and since this is the central concept in so many of our laws and social policies. A nuclear family is usually defined as a two-generation family consisting of parents and their children. We think of this family unit as living together and as being socially and economically interdependent. We also think of it as being set off from the rest of society — as a distinct and identifiable unit, no matter what its relations may be with other people, including other relatives.

Another important concept of the family that will appear in this book is that of the extended family. This means a family that extends beyond the nuclear family—that is, a family of more than two generations, or one that includes a number of adults in the older generation, or cousins as well as sisters and brothers in the younger generation. Often the concept of extended family includes the idea of a shared dwelling space, but in some instances "extended family" refers to meaningful relationships among related people whether or not they live together (Young and Willmott, 1974: 48).

A third important concept that appears in this book and in other works on the family is that of the household. In many cases the household is equivalent to the nuclear family, but this does not hold true for a significant number of people in Canada. For example, nearly 7 percent of Canadians lived alone in 1981 (1981 Canada Census). Single-person households accounted for 20 percent of all households in Canada. These people might have important family relationships, but they don't happen to live in families. Similarly, the 1981 census shows us that about 13 percent of Canadians were counted as non-census family people living in private households, while another 2 percent lived in such collective dwellings as hotels, lodging houses, and military camps. The concept of "household," unlike the concept of "family," focuses on people's living arrangements; it can be as important as the concept of family in describing and understanding people's daily lives.

ELEMENTS OF THE FAMILY

Families vary enormously in their organization and functions, both in what we expect them to be and in how they actually operate. Whatever the organization of any individual family or system of families, we will find certain basic elements. Families are groups of people who are tied together in specific, socially recognized ways. There are, in any family system, two fundamental ways of linking people and of identifying them as family members.

One of the fundamental ways of tying people together into family units is through what today we call "genetic relationships," and what, until recently, would have been called "blood relationships." People are born into these relationships; in our society those between parents and children and among brothers and sisters are perhaps the most important. Other more distant connections may also be important; these include grandparents and grandchildren, cousins and aunts and uncles.

Genetic or blood relationships are important in all family systems, but they are never the only basis of family identity. In any society there is provision for new people to enter families, not by birth, but through some socially recognized arrangement which we might call a contract (although in many societies these arrangements involve much less formality than a legal contract does in modern Canada).

In Canadian society, the most important example of this kind of relationship is marriage, which usually involves a specific legal action, although—as the Statistics Canada definition shows—we now accept that less formal arrangements can involve some of the same obligations that formal marriage does.

The other major form of contractual family relationship is the adoption of children. In some societies this is virtually unheard of; in others it is an accepted and relatively widespread practice. It may involve children who have no genetic relationship at all to the people who adopt them, or children who are already related in some degree but who are not members of the adoptive household. As with marriage, adoption may involve specific formal legal procedures, or it may be a relatively informal, but socially recognized, practice.

THINKING ABOUT THE FAMILY

Because families are so important in our daily lives, we think about them a lot. Ideas of the family are at the centre of a number of public debates. Such current issues as day care, violence against women and children, teen suicide, the problems of old age, child support, divorce, public education, and the changing roles of men and women, all involve ideas about the family. Several chapters in this book deal directly with issues that are currently on our minds: Chapter 4 deals with social policies, Chapter 6 with the relationship of work and home, Chapters 7 and 8 with aspects of divorce, and Chapter 9 with violence in the family.

To some extent, debates about the family arise from problems of definition. Defining the family is not just an abstract academic exercise. We all tend to have strong opinions about families—what they should be as well as what they are. There is no consensus in Canadian society as a whole about either of these things. Public debates about family issues are often fierce, because families are so important to people who have fundamentally different concepts of the family and the values it represents.

Even our strongest and most cherished ideals of the family can be contradictory. We can easily see these contradictions in our everyday experiences. If you walk down an ordinary suburban street, you'll walk by post-World War II houses, almost all of them occupied by single nuclear families. Each house can be freely and legally entered by only three or four or five people out of all the billions on our planet. Each house has a large picture window which faces onto the street; each window is equipped with drapes that cost several hundred dollars; and each set of drapes is left open so that anyone walking down the street can look into the house and see what the inhabitants are doing. Strangers and neighbours can judge the quality of the housekeeping, what television shows people watch, who is visiting, or what the family is eating for dinner. In modern Canadian society, the ideal of the family is that it is private, but at the same time our family lives are supposed to conform to established cultural ideals.

TRADITION AND CHANGE

In many ways this contradiction is typical of concepts of the "traditional" family. We live in an open, flexible society in which people's personal lives are supposed to be their own; indeed, the family is supposed to be the bastion of personal life and individuality. Yet many people also assume that personal lives, including family lives, must conform to certain standards if they are to be of social value. This is the kind of argument made by such groups as REAL Women and politicians who claim they represent traditional values.

We know what people usually mean by "traditional family": a nuclear family household with an adult male who earns money for the family and an adult female who concerns herself primarily with child-care and managing the household. The family has or has had young children; the woman and children are economically dependent on the husband/father. This image of the family is a powerful one which contains a whole range of social assumptions and values. As Chapter 2 shows, however, this kind of family is a relatively recent social form. The "traditional" family has existed for only two or three hundred years, and it has never been universal, even in our own society.

Where it does exist, the traditional family is based on extreme differentiation of social roles. Men and women do not do the same work, inside the household or outside of it. The lines of authority are clear. The adult male is the head of the household, the woman answers to him, and the children are clearly under the control of both. The lines of responsibility are also clear: the father is obligated to provide financial support to family members, at no matter what cost to himself, while the wife and mother has obligations to the members of her family which make it impossible, or at best difficult, for her to do paid work, especially outside the household.

This traditional family is also supposed to be separate, even isolated, from the larger world. Christopher Lasch entitled his essentially conservative work on the modern family *Haven in a Heartless World* to express the idea that middle-class North Americans living through the Industrial Revolution had come to see the family as a refuge (Lasch, 1977). The world of work was brutal and amoral; the pace of social change seemed to threaten every kind of social order.

By establishing the home as a counterbalance to what was going on in the larger society, the middle classes hoped to protect themselves against the threats to social stability created by their own economic activities. For the home to play this role, however, it had to be kept separate from the larger society, and the family had to take on a moral identity that was quite separate from that of the world of work (Ehrenreich and English, 1979: chapter 1). Such a family was the haven in a heartless world.

This separation of family and world is reflected in some of our concepts of adult roles. Adult males within the traditional family are supposed to be part of the larger world, and must understand and share its values, but women are to focus on the household, perhaps even remain ignorant of the values of the larger society. In 19th century terms, the woman was the angel of the hearth, at least if she was middle-class. The traditional family, then, and the women and children within it, are supposed to exist apart from society. Only the man, in his role as breadwinner, must function in the larger world. If he is to be a good breadwinner, he must know how to function well in this amoral world, but he must also have recourse to the moral values represented by the family.

The ideal of the traditional family is reflected in the extent to which Canadian society has come to be segregated by sex. Even though women have entered the paid labour force in great numbers, men and women have remained in fundamentally different occupations, rarely competing directly for jobs (Armstrong and Armstrong, 1978: chapter 2; Wilson, 1986: 118-123). Men and women tend to work in different spaces and to use different routes and methods of transportation in their daily movement (Singell and Lillydahl, 1986). Even our houses reflect an ideal of sex segregation; for example, most kitchens are designed so that it is impossible for two people—wife and husband—to work together at the same time (Hayden, 1984: 40-45, 119-122).

The social ideal of the traditional family has been an important one in North American society. It has been a basic element of many of the social policies discussed in Chapter 4, and in some of the most important social theories of the family, which are discussed in Chapter 3. But one major problem with the concept of the traditional family is that it does not represent reality, either historical or current (Hood, 1986: 349–351). It has been a powerful social ideal, but it has never been an ideal that was shared throughout society, and it has never been economically possible for everyone. Some of the problems the ideal of the traditional family has helped to create are discussed in Chapter 5.

Even in the 19th century, the traditional family was something that only some people could attain; in Canada, it was basically a privilege of middle-class, white, English-speaking people. The family and home could function as a haven only when working men were paid wages adequate to support several people, and sometimes this was in conflict with the ideal of making profits. Even among the middle classes, there were large numbers of women who had no husbands to support them, yet who had to support other family members as well as themselves.

The kind of separation of the sexes and differentiation of social roles that underlie the concept of the traditional family do have a certain basis in reality. But the economic base that would have been necessary for the establishment and maintenance of such families has never been more than partially developed, and today it is attainable for only a small minority of families (Gingrich, 1984: 17). Even where the traditional family can be established, it can also easily break down. It depends essentially on the presence and the breadwinning abilities of one adult male. If he is absent for some reason, or if he cannot earn an adequate living, then the traditional family has no base.

THE FLEXIBLE FAMILY

People who talk about the traditional family appeal to powerful emotions. The word "traditional" seems to refer to all of human history; when we challenge tradition, we are going against human nature, at our peril. In fact, however, as this book will show, families are surprisingly flexible, serving as a means of adaptation to social change as well as a means of social continuity. Chapters 8 and 10 discuss some of the different models of the family that reflect this flexibility.

Families in our society still show the influence of the traditional ideal. For the most part, male and female roles are differentiated: women cook, men take out the garbage; we buy dolls for our daughters and hockey sticks for our sons; most men in the paid labour force earn more than most women. We even assume that women and men have different emotional roles; in many North American families, for example, it is the job of women to maintain family ties through arranging holiday meals, writing letters, and so on (di Leocardo, 1987). A wife may even have the main responsibility for keeping in touch with members of her husband's family. These different household and emotional roles have an effect on economic roles. Women are far more likely to work part-time than men are, and if one family member has to give up a job to accommodate family needs, it is almost certainly the woman who will do so.

Yet at the same time there have been profound changes in our family organization. Even if families aren't always emancipated, they respond to changes in the larger society; sometimes families are even ahead of the rest of society in adapting to changing needs and attitudes. The typical household now has two or more wage earners (1981 Canada Census); if women leave the paid labour force, it is temporarily. In Canada, about half the mothers of pre-school children work at least part-time for pay. Furthermore, at least one quarter of Canadian women can expect to spend a part of their adult lives as single mothers of young children, either because they have never married or because their marriage has ended. There are also strong social pressures on men to become more involved in housework and in the care of their children (Boyd, 1984: 37-41; Lamb, Pleck, and Levine, 1986:67-68). Changes in family patterns have made the question of how we raise our children a perplexing one; as Chapter 5 shows, some of our most contentious social issues are those which arise out of the problems of parenting.

Families have to be flexible, because society itself is constantly changing, and because the various components of family membership can never be rigid and fixed. People don't stay the same, if only because they age, and with changes in the individual come changes in family composition and relationships. Even the ideal traditional family represents only a part of the life cycle; as children grow up and parents age, relationships and living arrangements change. Families are also often the centres of our strongest feelings, both love and hate, and feelings rarely remain constant. Changes in the structures of family life don't necessarily represent the breakdown of a basic institution. We can see them instead as evidence of the family's ability to adapt to changing social conditions, and of its ability to help us adapt to change as individuals.

CANADIAN FAMILIES IN THE 1980s

A lot of discussion and debate about families takes place in something of a vacuum, because most of us don't have a very clear picture of families in general. We tend to assume either that our own family experiences are typical or that other families approach some kind of ideal and our own is an exception. Public debates about family life and issues affecting the family are often based on unrealistic assumptions about both the past and the present. One of the major aims of this book is to describe certain aspects of contemporary Canadian families so that we can make some sense of the issues surrounding the family.

Patterns of family life are often sensitive to larger social forces. Rates of birth, marriage, death, and divorce are all responsive to cultural ideals, economic realities, and other factors of our existence. In our society the family is the realm of our personal lives, but it is also the realm where we come to grips with powerful social forces that are beyond the control of any individual. Through looking at statistical information on family life we can gain a sense of the interactions between families and the larger society, and we can place our debates in a meaningful context.

The birth rate tends to be sensitive to social forces, even in societies with no knowledge of modern techniques of birth control. We know of no society whose birth rates have reached the maximum that is biologically possible (although 17th century Quebec came as close to it as any society for which we have reliable information). The factors that affect fertility are complex. We know that fertility rates often reflect economic conditions; in Canada, for example, the 1930s saw not only an economic depression, but a depression in birth rates as well (*Fertility in Canada*: 13) — even though birth control information was illegal in Canada at that time (McLaren and McLaren, 1986: 9). But levels of prosperity are clearly not the only factors at work. The late 1960s saw a dramatic and unpredicted decline in fertility in western countries, including Canada, yet this was a period of general prosperity. It was also, however, a period of increasing female labour force participation, of a new birth control technology which seemed safe and was legal, and of rapidly changing social and cultural attitudes (McLaren and McLaren, 1986: 139–145).

In 1985, the general fertility rate for Canadian women in the 15–49 age group was 55.1 per 1,000 women (89.9 per 1,000 married women) (Vital Statistics 1985: 8, 10). This means that slightly more than one woman in twenty in this fertile age group actually gave birth. Most births are concentrated among women in the 22–31 age range but in 1985, 998 girls of 15 or younger had babies, along with 83 women of 45 or over (Vital Statistics 1985: 6). While there is a great deal of public concern about births out of wedlock, and political statements by such groups as REAL Women often give the impression of a great tide of illegitimacy, in fact most babies — 82 percent in 1985 — are born to married women (Vital Statistics 1985: 11). In addition, some unknown proportion of the remaining 18 percent is born to women in stable relationships. While births to unmarried mothers are a serious issue in some communities, we need to remember that the great majority of babies are born into recognized families.

Canadians do have small families. In 1981 the average Canadian two-parent family had 3.4 members; single-parent families were slightly smaller, averaging 2.7 members (1981 Census of Canada). It's important to remember that an average doesn't represent the actual behaviour of any particular family; the 1981 census showed that nearly 38 percent of Canadian families had only two members, while nearly 16 percent had five or more members. Most families — 68 percent — include at least one child but, in nearly 19 percent of them, all the children are 18 years of age or older (1981 Census of Canada).

Canada also has a large number of lone-parent families. In 1981, 713,815 families, 11.3 percent of all families, were headed by single parents; nearly 83 percent of them were headed by women (1981 Census of Canada). By definition, all of these lone-parent families included children; in about 13 percent of lone-parent families all the children were under six, while in a third all the children were 14 or under. Nearly 240,000 Canadian children 14 and under lived in such families in 1981. The large number of female-headed lone-parent families has important implications for the economic welfare of women and children. People living in these families are usually relatively poor, and the large number headed by single women is one reason that Canadian women and children tend to be poorer than Canadian men (Abowitz, 1986).

Divorce, which is the major cause of lone parenthood, is another area of concern. Issues surrounding divorce are discussed in detail in Chapters 7 and 8, so it is not necessary to go into detail here. Nonetheless, it is useful to introduce a few figures to show how divorce rates, like birth rates, respond to what is going on in the larger society. The end of the 1960s saw an enormous jump in divorce rates in Canada, from 54.8 per 100,000 persons in 1968 to 124.2 per 100,000 persons in 1969 (McKie, Prentice, and Reed, 1983: 59). This jump does not reflect a massive decline in morals, however, but the fact that the 1968 federal Divorce Act made divorce a great deal easier to obtain. The almost immediate jump in rates suggests that when divorce became easier people rushed to take advantage of it, to end marriages that had already broken down.

By the late 1970s experts were predicting that some 40 percent of all Canadian marriages would end in divorce (McKie, Prentice, and Reed, 1983: 60). This prediction was based on the assumption that divorce rates would remain steady. By the middle 1980s, however, changes had begun to appear. Divorce rates reached a peak of 285.9 per 100,000 people in 1982, but by 1985 the rate was down to 244.4, a decrease of 14.5 percent in three years (Vital Statistics 1985: Table 10). This decline took place before any changes in heterosexual habits that might result from concern over AIDS. While divorce rates are still high, they vary among regions and can change rapidly in short periods of time.

The 20th century has seen significant changes in Canadian marriage patterns. At the end of the last century, in 1891, the average age at first marriage in Canada was 26.1 for women and 29.2 for men (Basavarajappa, 1983: 71). By 1956 the average age at first marriage had dropped substantially, to 21.8 for women and 25 for men (ibid.), and by 1985 these ages had risen to 24.6 for women and 26.7 for men (Vital Statistics 1985: Table 1). The age gap between husbands and wives had also decreased, from three to two years. At current rates, over half of these marriages will not end in divorce; of those that do, the average length of the marriage will be about 12.5 years (ibid.) Slightly over half of all divorces involve dependent children (ibid.: Table 19).

Canadian marriage patterns have been shaped by a number of social forces. Western European society traditionally showed high ages at marriage; immigrants in Canada have tended to marry at later ages than Canadian-born people; also, people tend to marry at younger ages when times are prosperous. Our strong cultural preference for men to be older than their wives is quite flexible.

Perhaps the most striking changes in Canadian family patterns are those in the labour force participation of married women. In 1984, females made up 51.1 percent of the Canadian population and 42.2 percent of its labour force (Labour Canada, 1986); 52.6 percent of Canadian women participated in the labour force at least part-time in 1983. Thirty years earlier, in 1953, only 23.4 percent of women were in the paid labour force, compared with 82.9 percent of men. The 20th century has seen a general increase in female labour force participation rates; at the turn of the century, in 1901, only 16.1 percent of Canadian women aged 14 and over were in the labour force (Denton and Ostry, 1967: 29).

By the 1980s, the typical Canadian family had two or more persons working for pay. The rate of change has sometimes been extremely rapid. For example, while in 1973 nearly half of Canadian families — 46.1 percent — reported that the wife had done no work for pay during the year, only six years later the proportion had dropped to 32.6 percent (Gingrich, 1984: 17).

Since the early 1970s, most Canadian families have been able to maintain their standard of living only by sending more of the family out to work. While substantial numbers of teenagers work for pay, the most significant secondary income is that of the wife. Though women still contribute a relatively small proportion of total family income (about a quarter of it), this contribution is essential to the maintenance of the family. The real wages of men have declined since the early 1970s, and without women's earnings most families would suffer a decline in their spending power and in their standard of living.

The figures in this section give only a brief sketch of some aspects of the contemporary Canadian family. While the picture is by no means complete, we can see the broad outlines of the place of the family in our society. Most people marry — sometimes more than once; most people have children, though few have more than two or three; a lot of people divorce, but most people do not; and the great majority of people spend most of their adult lives in the paid labour force. These are the shared experiences of most Canadians that shape our family lives. But within these experiences we find a great deal of variation which reflects cultural expectations, economic forces, conditions of the immediate community, and differences among individuals. To understand how our families work we must go beyond statistical evidence, important as that is, and develop some broader concepts of the forces that create families.

FORMAL THEORIES OF THE FAMILY

Academic theories about families, which are discussed in more detail in Chapter 3, are usually a part of some larger theory of society. Until recently the family was often taken for granted, and some important social theories paid almost no attention to the family as a social force.

Perhaps the most significant example of this omission is in Marxist thought. Other social theories pay more attention to the family, but there often tends to be a strong normative component to traditional analyses: in other words, these theories go beyond analysis and state what the family ought to be. Perhaps the most significant example of this is the structural functionalist theory that dominated mainstream social science for so many years, up until the 1970s.

With the rise of the women's movement in the 1960s, as well as the other major social changes that have been taking place in our society, social theories have begun to change as well. No one academic perspective on the family can now be said to dominate but, overall, our concepts of the family have become more flexible as we have recognized the flexibility of the family as an institution.

In general, earlier mainstream theories stressed two things: social norms and social consensus. Proponents of these theories tended to argue that there are forms of behaviour which are normal (and, by implication, others which are not normal), and that members of society generally agree upon concepts of normality (thus people who don't agree with these concepts might be "abnormal"). These earlier theories also often treated the family as an institution whose social form was pre-determined by biology, and therefore not open to question or analysis.

Some of the earlier theories of the family were also linked to concepts of social health. Where social scientists don't want to use the concept of norms, they often substitute the concept of health. The implications are much the same. Whether we talk about norms or health, we are suggesting that, while people who live in an egalitarian democracy have choices, not all of these choices are equal. Thus some mainstream theories argued, in effect, that if we want to be mentally healthy, we should be sure to live in a family that provides for the right differentiation of roles and obligations. Twentieth century social scientists don't usually call upon divine power to justify their assertions, but the health argument is almost as powerful. For a large part of the 20th century, ideas based upon the psychoanalytic theories of Sigmund Freud have been central to our concepts of healthy individuals, the families that produce them, and the societies they form. These concepts of health left little room to accept either differences among families or changes in them, over time.

Normative, prescriptive, social theories are especially inadequate during times of social change. We have been living in such a time, and mainstream theories of the family have become increasingly outdated. We know from experience that many people survive family disruptions without becoming mentally unhealthy or being bad people; we know from experience that the children of stay-at-home fathers or working mothers can turn out just fine. Theories which see only one kind of family as being healthy clearly don't describe our real experiences.

More recent theories of the family tend to stress the idea of the family as an element of a conflictual society (for example, Barrett and McIntosh, 1982). Marriages break up, women have children outside of marriage, and the economic basis of the family is uncertain, but these disruptions arise less because of personal choices people make or their individual failures than because of the effects of powerful social forces. Current theories are also more concerned than earlier ones with seeing differences among families as the result of the complexities of larger social forces, and not as deviations from a single social norm.

Some current theories see the family as a major means of transmitting social values, including negative values of inequality and hierarchy; other theories stress the importance of the family as a means of adapting to or resisting social pressures and uncertainties. While the normative social vision of structural functionalism dominated theories of the family in the 1950s, in the 1980s there is no one single theoretical vision that could be said to dominate. The main thrust of more recent theories, however, has been to understand change, since change has been the main condition of our family lives for most of this century.

RECOGNIZING CHANGE

Societies change at different rates, and ideas don't always change as fast as social realities. This is the case with the family. Much family law and policy is still based on concepts of the traditional family and on the scientific justifications provided by earlier theories (Dranoff, 1977; Sloss, 1985). It is difficult for a society to give up the moral certainties of a normative theory for the relativism of a more analytical one, but real problems arise when social practices change and laws do not. We have seen this happen in Canada; many of us have experienced the effects of inconsistent rates of change in our own lives.

While there is no one body of laws and regulations in Canada which constitutes a family policy, we nonetheless have many laws which do directly affect the ways we live our family lives. Governments respond to families and their needs in a piecemeal fashion, but the total impact of laws and regulations that concern families has the effect of a family policy. This policy is based both on certain cultural assumptions about the nature of family life and on academic theories and research. The impact of this *de facto* policy is discussed in Chapter 4.

Laws are often out of step with the real needs of people's lives. This is especially true in the case of laws and policies affecting families; some of the greatest social changes in recent years have involved women and children, but politicians tend to belong to neither of these groups. Yet laws and policies affect all of our lives profoundly, so they, and the academic research that is used to justify them, are of immediate importance to all of us.

The laws that we may be most aware of are those governing marriage. Governments determine whether people may marry; they also determine if and when marriages may be terminated, and what kinds of provisions may be made for property and children in the event of a separation or divorce. Traditionally, the state has made a distinction between children born within marriage and those who were not. It has even regulated the sexual relations of marriage partners and their decisions to have children; until 1969, it was illegal in Canada for anyone to disseminate information on birth control or to provide or prescribe birth control devices. Governments determine what a married woman's legal residence is; in most Canadian jurisdictions it is that of her husband, although, now that we have the Charter of Rights, these kinds of laws will have to change (Day, 1985: 41). Governments closely regulate that personal, private relationship we call marriage, and much of this regulation has had as its goal the establishment and maintenance of families on the traditional model of the male breadwinner and the dependent female.

Other laws may affect family life less obviously, but are no less important. Some have become areas of serious social conflict. For example, Canadian provinces have had laws requiring compulsory schooling since the late 19th century. That these laws have implications for family life was clear when they were first passed, since some of the debates in Parliament dealt with the extent to which compulsory education undermined the authority of the father. Over a period of several generations, however, most of us have stopped thinking about this aspect of these laws. We take for granted the idea that children cannot learn everything they need to know within a family, and that society owes something both to children and to itself which can be provided only through public education.

In the last few years, however, this idea has been under attack. Few parents or politicians would argue against the idea of education, but increasingly some are disputing the idea that professional educators are the best people to determine the content of education programs. Most of the recent debates over public education have been initiated by parents who argue that they should have the main voice in determining the content of their children's schooling, or that certain subjects, most notably sex education, should be taught only in the family and not in the schools at all.

In general, the position of children in Canadian society, like that of their parents, has been changing radically. Until the end of the 19th century, children had virtually no citizenship rights. This meant that they were under the total authority of their parents, and in particular their fathers. Children had no independent right to an education, to health care, or to freedom from physical harm. As we have gradually developed the concept that children have citizenship rights, governments have had to act more and more directly on their behalf, to protect them from abusive or neglectful parents and to ensure children's access to social opportunities. Because children are not fully capable of taking charge of their own lives, this change in the status of children has created serious problems. Who determines when a child's rights are in conflict with those of the parents or the larger family, and who intervenes to resolve any conflicts? What happens when parents' obligations conflict with parents' rights? All of us have been affected by our society's formal and informal responses to these questions and to others that arise from the situation of children. The changing legal and social position of children is one more indicator of the profound ways in which families can change.

One way and another, our family lives are tied into a web of decisions that affect us directly and indirectly. It's important to understand the basis of these laws in our culture and in the formal research that lawmakers draw upon to support and justify their decisions. The study of the family helps us to understand the conditions of our own lives, including the ways in which our personal lives and individual experiences are intertwined with our society as a whole. As this book will show, perhaps the most important thing we can bring to a study of the family is an open mind and a willingness to accept that our own strongly held ideals of family life represent one truth, but not all truth.

REFERENCES

Abowitz, Deborah A. 1986. "Data Indicate the Feminization of Poverty in Canada, Too." *Sociology and Social Research* 70:30 (April) pp. 209–213.

Armstrong, Pat, and Hugh Armstrong. 1978. *The Double Ghetto*. Toronto: McClelland and Stewart.

Barrett, Michele, and Mary McIntosh. 1982. *The Anti-Social Family*. London: Verso.

Basavarajappa, K. G. 1983. "Trends and Differences in Mean Age at Marriage in Canada." In K. Ishwaran, ed. *Marriage and Divorce in Canada*. Toronto: Methuen, pp. 70-88.

Boyd, Monica. 1984. *Canadian Attitudes Toward Women: Thirty Years of Change*. Ottawa: Women's Bureau, Labour Canada.

Census of Canada, 1981.

Census of Canada 1971 — Profile Studies: *Fertility in Canada*. 1976. Ottawa.

Day, Shelagh. "The Charter and Family Law," in Sloss (cited below), pp. 27-61.

Denton, Frank T., and Sylvia Ostry. 1967. *Historical Estimates of the Canadian Labour Force*. Ottawa: Dominion Bureau of Statistics — 1961 Census Monograph Programme.

di Leocardo, Micaela. 1987. "The Female World of Cards and Holidays: Women, Families and the Work of Kinship." *Signs* 12:3 (Spring), pp. 440-453.

Dranoff, Linda Silver. 1977. *Women in Canadian Law*. Toronto: Fitzhenry and Whiteside.

Ehrenreich, Barbara, and Deirdre English. 1979. *For Her Own Good: 150 Years of the Experts' Advice to Women*. Garden City: Anchor.

Gingrich, Paul. 1984. "Decline of the Family Wage," *Perception*, 7:5 (May/August), pp. 15-17.

Hayden, Dolores. 1984. *Redesigning the American Dream*. New York: W. W. Norton.

Hood, Jane C. 1986. "The Provider Role: its Meaning and Measurement." *Journal of Marriage and the Family* 48:2, pp. 349-359.

Labour Canada. 1986. "Women in the Labour Force," 1985-1986 edition. Ottawa: Women's Bureau, 16.

Lamb, Michael E., Joseph H. Pleck, and James A. Levine. 1986. "Effects of Paternal Involvement on Fathers and Mothers." *Marriage and Family Review* 9: pp. 3-4, issue on "Men's Changing Roles in the Family."

Lasch, Christopher. 1977. *Haven in a Heartless World*. New York: Basic Books.

McKie, D. C., B. Prentice, and P. Reed. 1983. *Divorce: Law and the Family in Canada*. Ottawa: Statistics Canada.

McLaren, Angus, and Arlene Tigar McLaren. 1986. *The Bedroom and the State: the Changing Practices and Politics of Contraception and Abortion in Canada, 1880-1980*. Toronto: McClelland and Stewart.

Singell, Larry D., and Jane H. Lillydahl. 1986. "An Empirical Analysis of the Commute to Work Patterns of Males and Females in Two-Earner Households." *Urban Studies*, 23:2, pp. 119-129.

Sloss, Elizabeth, ed. 1985. *Family Law in Canada: New Directions*. Ottawa: Canadian Advisory Council on the Status of Women.

Vital Statistics 1985, Vol. I. 1986. Ottawa: Statistics Canada.

Williams, Raymond. 1976. *Keywords*. Glasgow: Fontana.

Wilson, S. J. 1986. *Women, the Family, and the Economy*, 2nd edition. Toronto: McGraw Hill-Ryerson Ltd.

Young, Michael, and Peter Willmott. 1974. *Family and Kinship in East London*. Harmondsworth: Penguin Books.

CHAPTER 2

Historical Perspectives on the Family

KAREN L. ANDERSON

INTRODUCTION

It is a commonly held belief that for the most part, the family is a stable structure that has varied little in the course of human history. This view is largely based on what seems to be self-evident, that women and men get together to conceive and provide for children. Families, then, appear to constitute an irreducible unit. They seem to be an aspect of human life governed by immutable natural laws.

Indeed, until recently, even social scientists accepted this view of the family as a universal form of social organization, basic to all human societies. Although he did not agree with them, the French anthropologist Claude Levi-Strauss referred to anthropologists who believed that "the family, consisting of a more or less durable union, socially approved, of a man, a woman, and their children, [was] a universal phenomenon, present in each type of society" (Levi-Strauss, 1971). Disputing this line of reasoning, Levi-Strauss pointed to cross-cultural and historical examples of a variety of family forms. For example, amongst the Nayar living on the Malabar coast of India, marriages were largely symbolic. Warfare kept men away from their homes for long periods of time; during those absences, Nayar women would take lovers. Any child of a Nayar woman was reckoned to be a member of its mother's clan, and descent was only through the mother's line.

Levi-Strauss also noted similar familial arrangements among the ancient Spartans, whose men spent most of their adult lives in military barracks. Children lived with their mothers, paternity was not an important issue, and same-sex love relations were encouraged (Kelly, 1986:111–112).

Families exist in all societies, but there are great variations in their composition, patterns of residence, and patterns of descent-reckoning, as well as in their economic, social, and emotional functions. Moreover, as historians of the family, anthropologists, and sociologists have recently shown, not only do families differ from society to society, they have also changed over time.

Studying the social history of the Western family is a relatively recent undertaking for social scientists. Most of the literature on the subject has been written since 1970. The newness of the subject makes it both exciting and fraught with difficulties. One of the major problems with constructing a history of the Western family lies in the diversity of family forms that have came into existence over the last several centuries. Moreover, several different family forms, functions, and attitudes to family relations have existed in the same society at the same time. As Michael Anderson has noted in his seminal work, *Approaches to the History of the Western Family 1500–1914*:

> Peasant families have typically differed markedly from merchant families and labouring families from aristocratic families. Peasants in eighteenth-century north-west France differed from peasants in central France, and in Germany or Sweden marked differences could be found even between neighbouring communities. England perhaps alone appears to have been much more homogenous [sic] yet even here illegitimacy in one area could occur twice as frequently as in another. Everywhere, certain groups—large like French Canadians or small like Hutterite communities—had behaviour which differed markedly from the rest of the society in which they lived . . . (Anderson, 1980:14).

Anderson concludes that "[t]here is, except at the most trivial level, no Western family type" (1980:14).

In contrast to the extensive amount of research now being down on the Western European family, to date few historians and even fewer sociologists have paid much attention to studying the Canadian family. However, those who have begun the task of analyzing changes in the structure of the Canadian family have noted significant variations across provincial boundaries (Darroch and Ornstein, 1984). Thus it is doubly difficult to discuss the history of the Canadian family in general terms; first because of the paucity of information on the history of the

Canadian family, and second because of the wide variations in family composition, structure, and functioning within Canada. Because of these problems, the history of the Canadian family must still be discussed in terms of the history of changes in the structure and functioning of the Western family in general.

Within the last 15 years much has been written about the transformations the family has undergone over the last four or five centuries of Western history. In general, current work on family history can be grouped under three headings: work concerned with demographic changes, work which examines changes in the economic functioning of the family, and finally, work which traces changes in the emotional lives and the sentiments of family members.

THE CONCEPT OF THE FAMILY

A survey of changes in dictionary definitions of the word "family" provides us with a point of departure for discussing some of the important transformations the Western family in general and the Canadian family in particular have undergone in the three areas of demography, the economic functioning of the family, and the emotional side of family life.

In contemporary Western usage, the word "family" is most often employed in one of two ways: either to refer to those related people who live together in a single household — usually parents and their dependent children — or to refer to a larger, less well-defined set of biological relations and in-laws. *Webster's New World Dictionary* (1982) defines its current meaning as "a social unit consisting of parents and the children that they rear," or, alternatively, as "a group of people related by ancestry or marriage; relatives" (1982:505).

Yet, if we step back in time, we discover that this usage emerged only recently (Flandrin, 1979:9). During the Middle Ages, for example, no term existed to signify that grouping of parents and children which we now find defined as the "family" in contemporary dictionaries. Instead, a much larger circle of persons were regarded as members of this social group (Mitterauer and Sieder, 1982:6).

The *Oxford English Dictionary* (1981) tells us that the word "family" has the same root as the Latin "familia," meaning "household," and "famulus," meaning "servant." Thus "familia" originally referred to "the total number of people living in a house, including domestic servants, and slaves." Indeed, it is the notion of co-residence that underlies the definition of family in the older English dictionaries. In a survey of the definitions of the word "family" found in 17th to 20th century French and English dictionaries, Jean Louis Flandrin notes that the dictionary of Samuel Johnson (1755) gives

> 'those who live in the same house', and as a synonym, 'household'. Abel Boyer, in the first edition of his *Dictionnaire royal francoys et anglois*, understood by the word 'famille', 'all those who live in the same house, under the same head; and he gave as English equivalents 'family' and 'household'. Similarly, Cotgrave, writing in 1673, translated famille as 'a family or household', and 'family' as 'famille, maisonnée'. . . . Not one of these dictionaries restricted the concept of the family to those who, living in one house, are united by ties of kinship. Moreover, usage confirmed the fact that the servants and other domestics were part of the family. Thus Samuel Pepys wrote in 1660, at the beginning of his famous *Diary*, 'I live in Axe Yard, having my wife, and servant Jane, and no more in family than us three' (Flandrin 1979:5).

It was not until the 19th century that dictionaries began to unite the concept of residence with that of close kinship into a definition of "family" (Flandrin, 1979:5).

In their study, *The European Family*, Mitterauer and Sieder list four factors influencing this change which occurred between the mid-16th and the mid-19th centuries: the separation of work from the place of domicile, a restructuring of relations between parents and children, the release of servants from the community of the household with the emergence of wage labour and, finally, the emergence of the family in the modern sense of the term, as the basic unit of residence (1982:7). As we will see, these changes to the family took place within the context of a major transformation in social relations among members of society. Specifically, those changes included the gradual replacement of the family as the basic unit of production by wage relations and capitalism, changes in marriage patterns, fertility, and family composition, and a revolution in emotional life and sentimentality.

FAMILY SIZE

Many social thinkers of the 19th century had an evolutionary view of society in general, and of the family in particular. For social theorists, such as Bachofen, Maine, Morgan, and McLennan, human history consisted of a necessary succession of familial forms, from the most primitive to the most civilized. Summarizing the work of these early theorists, Peter Laslett noted that they were:

deeply impressed with the Darwinian theory of the descent of man from the animals, and assuming a time scale which we know now to have been woefully abbreviated, had to face the problem of explaining how civilised, monogamous man evolved from his Simian predecessors. They felt they had to account for the emergence from the 'primeval horde' of the familial group which they themselves experienced and admired. They showed a strong disposition to moralise as well, and this seems to have been less successfully overcome by those who have come after than the evolutionary bias. The family was regarded as fundamental to society not only as its final structural unit, but as the receptacle of its values (Laslett, 1972:4).

One of the assumptions of the earlier theorists was that family groupings of the past were both larger and more complex than contemporary ones. This stereotypical view has made its way into present-day, popular thought in which it is often taken for granted that pre-industrial households were large and complex, frequently containing three consecutive generations, as well as an assortment of other blood relatives (Mitterauer and Sieder, 1982:24; Anderson, 1980:22; Laslett, 1972:4). The classical family of Western nostalgia was thought to have been characterized by "large aggregations of kin who lived together in large houses or stayed together geographically; infrequent marital breakup; and general family stability and happiness" (Nett, 1981:241).

Until the mid-1960s, the ideas of the 19th-century French sociologist Frederic Le Play, called "the founder of empirical family sociology," (Mitterauer and Sieder, 1980:24) dominated thinking on the pre-industrial family. Le Play characterized three "ideal types" of families: patriarchal, stem, and unstable families. Patriarchal and stem families, according to Le Play, emphasized authority, tradition, and lineage, while "unstable families" were a symptom of the moral decline occurring under the influence of industrialization.

According to Le Play's typology, patriarchal families resulted in large domestic groupings containing all the male descendants of a given patriarch. Stem families usually restricted co-residence to the patriarch and one of his sons, chosen to inherit the property. Le Play believed the family form characteristic of urban manufacturing populations, that is, the nuclear family, to be unstable, because it was brought into existence with the marriage of two independent people, and ended with their deaths, the children having been sent out into the world to fend for themselves (Anderson, 1980:23; Mitterauer and Sieder, 1980:25).

It was Le Play's opinion that, in former times, a woman might have given birth to between 15 and 25 children during her reproductive career. Le Play's assumptions went pretty much unchallenged until the mid-1950s. It was only then that French researchers such as Pierre Goubert (1977) began their laborious attempts at reconstructing family demographic parameters. In England the members of the Cambridge Group for the History of Population and Social Structure, working since the mid 1960s, as well as other social historians and demographers, have done much to dispel the "myth" of a major transition in family size from large to small family units during the Industrial Revolution.

The work of several researchers, extending back to the 17th century, has indicated that, on the whole, European women and men married quite late: between 24 and 26 for women and 27 or 28 for men (Anderson, 1980:18, Flandrin, 1979:53). Furthermore, there is very little evidence of any major long-term changes in pattern over the period 1600–1850 (Anderson, 1980:18; see also Gaskin, 1978 and Smith, 1977). This late age for marriage had a dampening effect on fertility rates and, combined with a relatively long interval between subsequent births, held the birth rate down in most areas to somewhere between 5 and 8 (Anderson, 1980:19; Flandrin, 1979:53). Moreover, a good portion of those children born in the 16th to late 19th centuries would not have survived to adulthood, given high rates of infant mortality and other factors influencing life expectancy. Often fewer than one-half the children born survived to the age of twenty (Flandrin, 1979:53).

In a paper published in 1969, Peter Laslett demonstrated that, at least for England between the mid-16th and early 19th centuries, mean household size remained about constant at 4.75 persons. Other writers have made the same point. Richard Wall (1983), a colleague of Laslett's, has recently shown that, in the pre-industrial era, households were small, with fewer than five members, and few households contained three or more generations. In general, the same conditions prevailed throughout Europe, with families averaging four to six persons (Flandrin, 1979:55).

Like their European counterparts, Canadian sociologists and historians have also, until just recently, espoused a version of family history which argued that in former times Canadians lived in large, economically self-sufficient, and stable familial groupings (Nett, 1981:241). Elkin, for example, maintained that early Canadian families were "almost self-sufficient units of production and consumption." In the colonial period, he argued, ". . . the family's activities were still home-centred and each member of the household, including grandparents, had tasks to perform which were vital to the maintenance of the family" (Elkin, 1968:12 cited in Nett, 1981:241).

Disputing this image, in her ground-breaking study of Canadian families, Emily Nett maintains that the historical record available to us leaves little doubt that regardless of geographical location or urban or rural setting, most Canadians lived in nuclear or "simple" family households (Nett, 1981:242). "There is nothing in the accounts," she concludes, "to dispute the fact that the two-generation family household was the norm for most colonists and pioneers" (Nett, 1981:243).

Nett also disputes the notion that in former times the Canadian family was much more "integrated, more cohesive, and subsequently more moral" than the contemporary Canadian family. According to Nett, "[t]he failure to investigate the occurrence and frequency of illegitimacy, premarital and extramarital sex, alcoholism, rape, incest and child abuse occurring in families prior to the middle of this century has contributed to the myth of the happy family of the past" (Nett, 1981:242).

In a recent study analyzing the 1871 census data, Darroch and Ornstein found that, as was the case in Europe, the majority of Canadians lived in nuclear families: "fully 75 percent of all households were nuclear in structure and the great majority, 67 percent, contained married couples alone or with unmarried children" (Darroch and Ornstein, 1984:162–163). However, Darroch and Ornstein were surprised to find that close to 11 percent of the population lived in households containing two families with different surnames, and 2.6 percent of the population lived in three- or four-surname households (Darroch and Ornstein, 1984:164). People living in Nova Scotia, New Brunswick, and Quebec were much more likely to live in such households than those living in Ontario. The most likely explanation for such differences lies in the connection between the social and economic networks of support and subsistence that obtained during the late 19th century. According to Darroch and Ornstein,

> Household-centred networks were associated with local, recurrent migration and were common in marginal economic circumstances where families engaged in a variety of productive activities, often combining seasonal wage labour with various subsistence activities. . . . Relatively stable wage labour markets and commercial farm production, on the other hand, fostered nuclear households—as in the case of

Ontario. Specifically . . . the economy of Ontario in 1847 was most likely to provide options for individuals and families for earning a living in a farm market economy and in non-farm pursuits (Darroch and Ornstein, 1984:173-174).

Moreover, Darroch and Ornstein found the average size of the nuclear household headed by a couple to have been 5.9 persons in 1871. This figure is higher than comparable figures for other countries, suggesting that late 19th century Canadians lived in rather cramped quarters (1984:163). This figure, too, includes domestics, servants, and boarders. The tendency for such people to reside with a married couple varied with economic conditions and immigration (Nett, 1981:244). Thus, the fact that Canadian households of 1871 tended to contain more people, on average, than did European households of the same period, may in part be attributed to the presence of large numbers of new immigrants who had not yet settled in their own households.

The reasons for such a predominance of nuclear families over extended ones are numerous, both in Europe and in Canada. For one thing, neither available living space nor material resources would have been sufficient for most families, especially poor ones, to support more than a few dependents. Peter Laslett's study of Goodnestone-next-Wingham in Kent (1971) showed that out of the 277 inhabitants, 52 were domestic servants, almost every one of whom worked in the manor-house or in the houses of yeomen. Moreover, the poor had considerably fewer children than did the gentry and yeomen, for the households of the poor "were generally former households of labourers which had sunk into poverty on the death of the father of the family," and poverty invariably increased infant mortality. (Flandrin, 1979:58) In Canada infant mortality rates were also high. On average, Canadian families in 1871 had only two more children than families in 1971, although each woman in 1871 would have given birth to between six and seven children over her entire fertile period (Nett, 1981:243).

Secondly, life expectancy was low, and since, as has been stated, age at marriage was relatively high, it made it unlikely that many grandparents and grandchildren would have been alive and occupying the same household at the same time. Finally, few children of the poor remained for long in their parents' homes. They either left to become domestic servants in the household of another, or they set up their own household away from their parents. (Wall, 1983; Mitterauer and Sieder, 1982).

Olwen Hufton's (1981) study of young women in 19th century France is an excellent case study of life-cycle history in relation to family formation, size, and living conditions. According to Hufton "[t]he largest category of women in eighteenth-century France was that of the daughters of smallholders or of agricultural labourers, village artisans and casual odd job men" (1981:187). These young women had the misfortune to live in a society where between 50 and 90 percent of all farms and other artisanal enterprises were unable to provide for the support of even two or three children. Agricultural labourers were often unemployed, and industrial wages, when they existed, were not sufficient to support a family. Hufton estimates that as many as one-third of the population lived under the threat of imminent destitution, while another fifth suffered from chronic hunger (1981:187).

Under such circumstances a young girl would most likely have started to work at around age 12, as an illiterate, undernourished victim of vitamin-deficiency disease. She would have begun her working life, too, with the absolute knowledge that she alone would provide for her future, as bleak as it might be (1981:187–188). Once employed in a household, a young girl could expect to be required to do a variety of chores, including spinning, making lace, washing raw cotton or wool, and embroidering ribbons. If she worked on a farm, her work might include foraging for and feeding the livestock, gathering firewood and edible foodstuffs, looking after children, or cooking (1981:187–188).

With her earning power restricted (wages rarely allowed her to do more than feed and clothe herself), any young woman who aspired to some sort of economic security in later life needed to marry. To marry she needed a dowry. As Hufton describes it,

> The obstacles which lay between a girl and the realization or her coveted dowry were legion. She might fall sick and be unable to earn. She might be the victim of slump. She might become pregnant. The commonest recruit to the ranks of the unmarried mother was the servant-girl. Distant from her family, lodged in an attic, a cupboard or even expected to sleep on the kitchen floor, she was prey for both master and apprentice (1981:194).

Although such a girl's brothers might fare a bit better, in that at least one of them could expect to inherit parental property, they too could be forced out of their parents' home at an early age, usually to work in the household of others.

Like their European counterparts, young Canadian women of the 18th and 19th century were also employed in domestic service. Indeed, domestic service was a common experience of young women in Acadia, New France, and Upper Canada until Confederation. Only those girls from "the most fortunate circumstances in the towns and cities" escaped this fate (Nett 1981:247). Often too, in Canada, the search for and employment of young women as domestic servants was closely related to the search for wives for the unmarried men of the colony.

THE EFFECTS OF WAGE LABOUR AND INDUSTRIALIZATION

Changes had been slowly taking place in both Europe and North America which eventually led to the widespread decline of the household as the basic unit of production in society. Those changes centred on the extensive use of wage labour as the dominant source of income, a phenomenon associated with industrialization under capitalism. Most importantly, by the turn of the 19th century, the demand for wage labour had enormous consequences for family life.

As we have seen, prior to industrialization, not just agriculture, but crafts, too, were organized around the household as the economic unit. Mining and building were perhaps the only enterprises to be organized on a larger scale (Zaretsky 1976:38; Mitterauer and Sieder, 1982:39–40).

Children also provided useful labour power. For peasants and yeoman farmers, family needs could be met only if all members of the household were continually engaged in agricultural labour or craft production, or in some other domestically focused activity (Anderson 1980:70). One of the ways in which these families survived as producing units running farms or workshops was to supplement their own labour by bringing in maids and men-servants, apprentices, journeymen, and labourers when they needed them. Lodgers and boarders also formed part of the pre-industrial family. In the pre-industrial era, between 7 and 15 percent of household membership consisted of domestic servants (Mitterauer and Sieder, 1982:41). Peasant families had to constantly keep a balance between labourers and resources, making sure to have enough workers available to supply household needs, while keeping demands on family resources to a manageable level (Anderson, 1980:70).

Among peasant households, labour was divided on the basis of sex and age, making marriage mandatory if the farm was to be an economically viable unit (Lofgren, 1977:30). Since the means of production, including land and equipment, were usually acquired through inheritance, parents exercised a great deal of control over whom and when their children could marry. That control was somewhat lessened, however, by the inheriting son's commitment to support aging parents once he and his wife took over the holding. Often the parents' old-age security had to be guaranteed by legal contract (Anderson, 1980:73).

From the 17th century onward (earlier, in parts of England), two other forms of work organization became increasingly important: the employment of the landless labourer and the "proto-industrial labourer," employed in the emerging manufactories. In both cases individuals worked, not for a household enterprise, but for the interests of employers. Unlike smallholders of productive property, those who worked only for a wage had little means of inducing their children to support them in their old age. Thus, as wage relations spread with the growth of capitalism and industrialization, the family began to lose its status as the basic unit of production in society; its members (whether related or not) sought employment outside its boundaries. As a direct result, the family was transformed from a property-holding unit engaged in economic activity to one whose function lay largely in producing the next generation of wage labourers (Medick, 1976:303).

Faced with the possibility of being independent of the control of the household, although without any inheritance to provide them security, wage labourers began work at an early age, and were thus free to marry independent of the needs of their parents and the family economy.

Mitterauer and Sieder (1982) have noted a major difference in family strategy between families whose households engaged in productive functions and families whose existence was supported by wage labour. In the former case, incomplete families could not exist over any period of time. A son inheriting from his aging parents had to marry and have children if the family economy was to be kept going. Not so for the wage worker: single persons, single parents, or childless households could exist without "much compulsion to complete them" (Mitterauer and Sieder, 1982:40).

The work of Darroch and Ornstein suggests that, among wage labourers in Canada, differences in family strategies depended on economic circumstances. When wage workers faced unstable economic situations, or situations of recurrent migration like seasonal employment, the tendency was for more than one unrelated family to share a household.

These households often formed the central hub of a network of "mutual aid and support . . . providing for individuals, especially in times of economic crisis, illness and old age" (1984:173). On the other hand, stable economic circumstances and wage labour markets fostered nuclear households (1984:173). Moreover, Darroch and Ornstein suggest that networks of social exchange centring around the complex household may have been more common in urban settings, especially among manual workers, while farmers and commercial or "white-collar" workers would have had less need for such support networks (1984:174–175). Marriage for people living in rural Ontario during the 19th century was dependent on the ability of the couple to set up their own independent household, (Gaffield, 1979) while workers in cities such as Montreal or Hamilton began their married lives as renters in the households of others to whom they were not related (Nett, 1981:243).

Prior to industrialization, farm labourers and other domestic servants were subjected to the patriarchal authority of the head of the household, but the possibility of working for wages freed many people from this discipline. With the growth of capitalism, as increasing numbers of people were drawn into the wage economy and out of households engaged in petty-commodity production, the decision to marry could be made in response to individual needs and not necessarily in response to community expectations and the social controls exercised by the male head of the household (Levine, 1983:29).

With more control over making their own decisions, "this plebeian army of proto-industrialists," as David Levine (1983:29) calls them, were able to marry at younger ages and without amassing the sum of money they had formerly needed to set up independent households. A drop in the age of marriage generally meant an increase in the number of years a woman was able to bear children. This, combined with a slight rise in marital fertility, contributed to higher population growth, at least in England during the latter half of the 17th century (Levine, 1983:30).

As the family lost most of its production functions, an important change began to take place in parent/child relations, as well as in relations between husbands and wives.

THE FAMILY AND EMOTIONAL LIFE

The family of the 16th and 17th centuries, engaged as it was in a common economic enterprise, and composed of children, parents, servants, journeymen, and others, was characterized by "strong elements of deference, patriarchy and authoritarianism" (Anderson, 1980:43). The father, as head of the household, was solely responsible for both the economic and spiritual control of all members of that household. Moreover, male heads of households were not just given the right to impose their will over all other members of their household; they were compelled under force of law to carry out that role (Flandrin, 1979:123–126).

Church doctrine of this period clearly viewed women as inferior to men, and in constant need of chastisement and control. According to the 16th century church moralist, Benedicti,

> A wife who does not wish to obey her husband in matters touching the government of the family and of the house, and those concerning virtues and good morals, sins. For the wife is obliged to carry out the commandments of her husband. If, on the contrary, she tries to assume the government of the house, pertinaciously and against the will of her husband when he forbids it for some good reason, she sins, for she must do nothing against her husband, to whom she is subject by divine and human law (Benedicti, nos. 34 and 35, cited in Flandrin, 1979:126).

Although men were enjoined not to beat their wives "cruelly or atrociously," the husband had a clear duty to correct or chastise his wife, and this could involve some measure of violence (Flandrin, 1979: 128–129). If a wife went on to "commit some mortal sin because he [her husband] has not kept her on a close rein, he [her husband] shares in her sin" (Benedicti, no. 28, as cited in Flandrin, 1979:128). As the husband ruled his wife, so did he rule his children and servants. It would appear that domestic relations of the 16th and 17th century were more often than not characterized by respect, deference, obligation, and fear than by sentiment and attachment (Flandrin, 1979:118–173; Anderson, 1980:43).

This structured, hierarchical, patriarchal family was gradually replaced by a more egalitarian set of relations, in which family life was centred largely around emotional issues. Most scholars agree that the process of change took several centuries; that gradually the centre of power shifted out of the producing family, and into the hands of individuals (Zaretsky, 1976:57).

As wage relations came to dominate the economic lives of most members of society, there emerged both an increasing differentiation of the family as a separate social unit and an increasing emphasis on individualism (Zaretsky, 1976; Flandrin, 1979; Anderson, 1980).

According to Zaretsky, it was the rise of industrial capitalism, with the spread of wage labour, that "progressively removed goods production from the home" (1976:78). With this removal, the family came to be viewed as separate from the economy, and personal life became ". . . a separate sphere of life divorced from the larger society." Sentiment and consideration became new defining characteristics for familial relations. The world became divided into the outside, objective, social world, which increasingly took little notice of the individual, and the family, shut off from the harsh reality of business and technology: a protected island of subjectivity.

Not only did changes in the economy of western Europe help to lay the groundwork for changes in family structure, changes in religious life also contributed to the transformation of the family. From the 16th century onward, Protestant reformers stressed that marriage was a partnership. Reformation theology viewed marriage as a companionate relation between husbands and wives, and urged that marriages be founded first and foremost on love (Stone, 1975:26–27).

Parent-child relations, previously characterized by a kind of callousness, took on increasing concern for the child's physical and emotional well-being (Aries, 1962:403). Evidence exists to indicate that during the 16th and 17th centuries, adults in charge of children felt it their duty to break the child's will and to subject the child to the absolute authority of elders and superiors (Stone, 1975:36). In the 17th century, according to Lawrence Stone, "the early training of children was directly equated with the breaking in of young horses or hunting dogs." Physical punishment, flogging, and whipping were common methods of discipline throughout society, and children in particular were singled out for this kind of treatment (Stone, 1975:40).

Although Reformation theology may have laid stress on companionate relations between husband and wife, it did little to improve relations between parents and children. Calvinist moral philosophers became more and more concerned about the sinfulness of children. "A new-born babe," wrote Richard Allestreed in 1676, "is full of the stains and pollutions of sin, which it inherits from our first parents through our loins" (cited in Stone, 1975:42). In the companionate marriage, the mother was enjoined to assist her husband in breaking the stubborn will of the sinful child in the hopes of creating a person who would always be compliant to a parent's demands.

In his study, *Children in English-Canadian Society*, Neil Sutherland contends that, in the late 19th century, "English Canadians showed little awareness of children as individual persons; . . . saw nothing of the inner, emotional life of youngsters" (1976:6). According to Sutherland, children were viewed as "partially formed and potential adults[s]." They were "a resistive, refactory, . . . but nonetheless basically plastic raw material. Out of this tough matter, parents and other adults could, if they were persistent enough, fashion moral, hardworking, productive adults" (Sutherland, 1976:11). Sutherland goes on to say:

> With the help of the church and the school, the family was the main instrument for this essential but not necessarily pleasant social task. In the context of these basic assumptions, most people evaluated the events which went into the years between infancy and adulthood almost solely as to how they thought that each would serve as a means towards the achievement of their clearly defined end. While they hoped that parents would provide children with a satisfactory though preferably Spartan physical environment — wholesome food, sufficient but often uncomfortable clothing, and basic shelter — they did not consider these nearly as important as other elements of a good upbringing. Most of all, they expected parents to inculcate morals and good work habits. Both of these virtues were achieved, they believed, by precept repeated at home, at school, in Sunday school, in books and in papers, and by the example of their parents and other adults. Christ's youth suggested a number of practical lessons to Canadian young people: 'submission to parents,' the 'dignity of labour,' the need for 'personal improvement,' and, finally, 'submission to the Divine will' (Sutherland 1976:11).

Yet important changes had begun to take place in the bonds that could develop between husbands and wives or parents and children, even by the late 18th century. With the rise of wage labour, the family community had been reduced to parents and children, a transformation which would have been impossible without the family being relieved of its production functions (Mitterauer and Sieder, 1982:53). Because families no longer had to send children away, and smaller groups of people could live together over longer periods of time, the emotionalism and sentimentalism of family life had a chance to flourish (Aries, 1962:403; Mitterauer and Sieder, 1982:60).

The reduction of the family from a household containing parents, children, servants, journeymen and others to a grouping of parents and children truly encouraged the development of a "private life," that is, a life that could be hidden from public scrutiny. As children no longer were the key to their parents' well-being, parents became identified more and more as the custodians of their children's happiness and well-being, at least during their early years of life. The health, moral life, and education of children became their parents' central concerns.

Moreover, as data from the 1871 census show for Canada, the likelihood of living in a nuclear family varied little across occupational categories. In Canada, in 1871 over 75 percent of all families whose household head was a merchant or manufacturer lived in nuclear households, with similar figures for the families of semi-skilled labourers and farmers: 74.6 percent and 75.8 percent, respectively (Darroch and Ornstein, 1984:170). This would suggest that, in spite of class differences, all segments of Canadian society were experiencing the effects of the privatization of the nuclear family.

Isolated, separated from the often impersonal world of wage labour, the family of the mid-19th century came to be venerated as a retreat, a place where individuals could truly express their innermost being (Anderson, 1980; Zaretsky, 1976). Women, too, came to be venerated in their roles as homemakers and mothers. With domesticity now associated with sex-specific roles, work performed away from the home became almost exclusively the sphere of men, leaving household concerns wholly the sphere of women.

CONCLUSION

The family as we have come to know it really only emerged as the "norm" in Western societies in the 19th century. In Britain, for example, its emergence was hastened by social legislation passed during the early decades of that century. This legislation was aimed at getting women and children out of the labour force and at providing a "family wage" for the male members of the "respectable working classes." In this way the British working classes sought to ensure themselves a protected home-life. Ideally it was to provide "companionate marriage," a child-centred household, and a warm domestic refuge safe and secure from a "cold and competitive society" (Lasch, 1977:6).

Yet there are many contemporary theorists of the family who would argue that the "good old days" never existed, especially for women and children. Pointing to child neglect and abuse, unequal and abusive relations between husbands and wives, and a system of organizing emotional life which places responsibility on the shoulders of women, numerous writers have called, not just for changes in the family, but also for changes in the society which helps to structure the family (Barrett and McIntosh, 1982). Although it is not clear exactly what the future holds for the Canadian family, it is clear that, for many Canadians, the family as a "child-centred household, and warm domestic refuge," is still an unrealized dream.

REFERENCES

Anderson, Michael. 1980. *Approaches to the History of the Western Family*. London: Macmillan.

Aries, Philippe. 1962. *Centuries of Childhood: a Social History of Family Life*. New York: Vintage Books.

Barrett, Michele and Mary McIntosh. 1982. *The Anti-social Family*. London: Verso.

Darroch, A. Gordon and Michael Ornstein. 1984. "Family and Household in Nineteenth-Century Canada: Regional Patterns and Regional Economies." In *Journal of Family History*, Summer.

Flandrin, Jean-Louis. 1979. *Families in Former Times: Kinship, Household and Sexuality*. Cambridge: Cambridge University Press.

Gaffield, Chad. 1978. "Canadian Families in Cultural Context: Hypotheses from the Mid-nineteenth Century." In *Historical Papers*, Canadian Historical Association.

Gaskin, K. 1978. "Age at First Marriage in Europe before 1850." *Journal of Family History*, III.

Goubert, Pierre. 1977. "Family and Province: a Contribution to the Knowledge of Family Structure in Early Modern France." In *Journal of Family History*, 2.

Hufton, Olwen. 1981. "Women, Work and Marriage in Eighteenth-Century France." In R. B. Outhwaite, ed. *Marriage and Society: Studies in the Social History of Marriage*. London: Europa Publications Ltd.

Kelly, Joan. 1986. *Women, History and Theory*. Chicago: University of Chicago Press.

Lasch, Christopher. 1977. *Haven in a Heartless World*. New York: Basic Books.

Laslett, Peter. 1969. "Size and Structure of the Household in England over Three Centuries." *Population Studies*, 23.

——. 1971. *The World We Have Lost*. London: University Paperbacks.

——. 1972. "Mean Household Size in England Since the Sixteenth Century." In Laslett and Wall, eds. *Household and Family in Past Time*. Cambridge: Cambridge University Press.

Laslett, Peter and Richard Wall. 1972. *Household and Family in Past Time*. Cambridge: Cambridge University Press.

Levine, David. 1983. "Proto-Industrialization and Demographic Upheaval." In Leslie Moch and Gary Stark, eds. *Essays on the Family and Historical Change*. Arlington: University of Texas Press.

Levi-Strauss, Claude. 1971. "The Family," in H. Shapiro, ed. *Man, Culture and Society*. London: Oxford University Press.

Lofgren, O. 1977. "Family and Household among Scandinavian Peasants." *Ethnologia Scandinavia*, II.

Medick, H. 1976. "The Proto-industrial Family Economy: the Structural Function of Household and Family during the Transition from Peasant to Industrial Capitalism". *Social History*, I.

Mitterauer, Michael and Reinhard Sieder. 1982. *The European Family*. Oxford: Basil Blackwell.

Moch, Leslie and Gary Stark. eds. 1983. *Essays on the Family and Historical Change*. Arlington: University of Texas Press.

Nett, Emily. 1981. "Canadian Families in Social-historical Perspective." In *Canadian Journal of Sociology*, 6(3).

Outhwaite, R. B., ed. 1981. *Marriage and Society: Studies in the Social History of Marriage*. London: Europa Publications Ltd.

Rosenberg, Charles E., ed. 1975. *The Family in History*. University of Pennsylvania Press.

Smith, D. S. 1977. "A Homeostatic Demographic Regime: Patterns in Eastern European Family Reconstitution Studies." In R. D. Lee, ed. *Population Patterns in the Past*. New York: Academic Press.

Stone, Lawrence. 1972. *The Family, Sex and Marriage in England 1500–1800*. New York: Harper & Row.

——. 1975. "The Rise of the Nuclear Family." In Charles E. Rosenberg, ed. *The Family in History*. University of Pennsylvania Press.

Sutherland, Neil. 1976. *Children in English-Canadian Society: Framing the Twentieth-Century Consensus*. Toronto: University of Toronto Press.

Wall, Richard. 1972. "Mean Household Size in England from Printed Sources." In Laslett and Wall, eds. *Household and Family in Past Time*. Cambridge: Cambridge University Press.

——. 1983. "Introduction." In Wall, Robin, and Laslett, eds. *Family Forms in Historic Europe*. Cambridge: Cambridge University Press.

Zaretsky, Eli. 1976. *Capitalism, The Family and Personal Life*, New York: Harper & Row.

ANNOTATED BIBLIOGRAPHY

Anderson, Michael. 1980. *Approaches to the History of the Western Family 1500–1914*. London: Macmillan. This short book is an excellent guide for students to the various approaches that scholars have recently taken in studying the Western family. The book provides a concise and clearly written summary of some of the major controversies in the field of the history of the family.

Mitterauer, Michael and Reinhard Sieder. 1982. *The European Family*. Oxford: Basil Blackwell. In this well-written history of the European family, Mitterauer and Sieder trace the change in the role of the family from the social unit in which production and consumption took place, to its contemporary role, largely devoid of involvement in production. Through-out the book they are concerned with authority relations both between husbands and wives and parents and children.

Nett, Emily M. 1981. "Canadian Families in Social-Historical Perspective." In *Canadian Journal of Sociology*, 6(3). Emily Nett's article examines some of the more persistent "myths' about the Canadian families in the past. Nett debunks a number of these myths, thus providing a good basis for further research on the Canadian family in an historical context.

Rosenberg, Charles. 1975. *The Family in History*. University of Pennsylvania Press. This book contains a good collection of essays from a social-historical perspective, examining the relationship between social change and changes in ideology as it has affected the family.

Zaretsky, Eli. 1976. *Capitalism, the Family and Personal Life*. New York: Harper & Row. Zaretsky offers a short, readable account of the historical processes that brought about the division between private and public life in Western society. The account is phrased in terms of the impact of capi-talism on the traditional, patriarchal family on the one hand, and the rise of subjectivity and personal life on the other.

CHAPTER 3

Conceptual Frameworks for Studying Families

ELAINE PORTER

INTRODUCTION

Historical and anthropological data document variations in family beliefs and practices over time and across cultures. Conceptual frameworks in sociology classify and organize these data; they also seek to define the essential characteristics of families and determine what it is that family members do for one another and, depending on the framework, for society as a whole. The efforts of family sociologists to develop tenable explanatory frameworks is constantly being challenged, however, by the rapid pace of family-related technological and social change. The practice of surrogate motherhood, for example, raises a complex set of legal and moral issues which require for their resolution a sound conceptual basis for distinguishing between biological and social parenthood. All of us engaged in the study of the family are clearly called upon to go beyond our taken-for-granted reality to ask new questions about the meaning of family life.

It was the challenge presented by changes in families and in social life a hundred and fifty years ago that produced the three classical sociological conceptual frameworks examined in this chapter. They evolved from the efforts of social scientists to understand the large-scale social changes taking place in industrializing Europe and the United States during the early 19th century. Each framework contains its own set of assumptions about which aspects of social reality are important to study and the kinds of data that should be collected. Each also represents an intellectual heritage which has been modified and expanded through the intervening years by many contributors. In some cases, these revisions have led to the development of separate frameworks such as the two newer perspectives that we will examine: feminism and the family developmental framework.

By rigorous scientific standards, a theory consists of a set of systematically interrelated concepts which are empirically testable (Tiryakian, 1963:11); yet, zealously applied, these standards would exclude most theorizing within the social sciences as a whole. In contrast, a minimal definition refers to any statement connecting at least two ideas; in this respect, a number of "theories" on the family are partial or substantive theories applied to specialized topics in various aspects of family behaviour. A "conceptual framework" falls somewhere in between; as a set of loosely interrelated concepts, this term characterizes the state of theory-building in family sociology at this time.

Despite differences in the content of their theorizing, theorists share an orientation toward thinking about families which is quite different from our everyday understanding of them. Although our more reflective questions about the family might touch on theoretical issues, they are more likely related to our personal goals. In contrast, sociologists ask their questions within a theoretical framework so as to broaden the scope and range of the ideas considered. Their discussion must meet public scrutiny from their peers as published work or papers presented at professional meetings.

There are three theoretical frameworks of long standing, structural-functionalism, conflict theory, and symbolic interactionism, and the two newer theories, the feminist and the family developmental. All will be discussed in detail in this chapter.

Theorists are divided over whether it is possible or desirable for conceptual frameworks to be value-free. Since "conflict" theorists view the social scientist's value-biases as inevitable, they recommend the virtues of openly stating them and using them as the basis for a critical analysis. Although "structural functionalists" promote the ideal of value-neutrality, functionalist analysis has nevertheless been plagued by its hidden bias toward supporting the status quo in North American society.

Whatever their assumptions, conceptual frameworks are indispensable tools for sifting through the incredible diversity of "home-grown" family life. To "see the forest from the trees" requires development of concepts which set out the central features of families. Moreover, families live in a larger environment that includes the social class structure and norms for such family behaviour as cohabitation and childcare. What the structural-functionalist and conflict frameworks provide is the advantage of viewing families from a broad, (macro-level) perspective.

Following a discussion of their major ideas, the three classical and two newer conceptual frameworks will be examined from an historical perspective and their strengths and weaknesses assessed. Having originated in conflict theorizing during the 1960s, feminism will be discussed in the section on the conflict perspective. The developmental framework, since it is a combination of two classical perspectives, will be given a short section of its own.

I. THE STRUCTURAL-FUNCTIONALIST FRAMEWORK

A. Definition and Description

According to the influential definition provided by the functionalist anthropologist, George Murdock:

> The family is a social group characterized by common residence, economic cooperation, and reproduction. It includes adults of both sexes, at least two of whom maintain a socially approved sexual relationship, and one or more children, own or adopted, of the sexually cohabiting adults (1949:1).

The nuclear family, a special subset of this more inclusive definition, refers to ". . . a married man and woman with their offspring, although in individual cases, one or more additional persons may reside with them." Murdock's thesis, once widely accepted, considers the nuclear family to be a universal phenomenon, since it is analytically separable in every society.

Talcott Parsons, the most widely known of the functionalist theorists, viewed the family as a sub-system within any society; society, in turn, he conceptualized as a social system in which all parts are interrelated. Because the patterns of behaviour associated with the family are pervasively accepted and contribute significantly to the framework of values in a society, the family is considered an institution. In this view, the other four basic institutions, the political, the economic, the educational, and the religious work together with the family to maintain a society in a state of equilibrium.

The "structural" dimension refers to the way in which the family is organized. The nuclear family is structured around the three statuses of husband/father, wife/mother and child. Each family status carries a set of role expectations concerning appropriate behaviour. The division of labour within the family, another structural feature, sees the husband in the role of task specialist with an instrumental role; this designation refers to his responsibilities as economic provider. The wife, on the other hand, is expected to play the role of the family's emotional specialist, in an expressive role (Parsons and Bales, 1959).

Long-term societal development, for Parsons, consists of the dual evolutionary processes of functional specialization and structural differentiation. The Industrial Revolution is held responsible for differentiating the family structurally into a nuclear type, and for removing the workplace from the household to create the basis for specialized functions.

Structural isolation from the family's kinfolk also increased with industrialization, a factor both contributing to and resulting from geographical and social mobility. Parsons' statements on the isolation of the nuclear family were originally interpreted to imply a lack of contact between adult children and their parents, and stimulated researchers to "discover" the existence of close, important ties between the generations (Adams, 1971). Apparently Parsons actually meant that grandparents no longer lived with their children, i.e., were structurally isolated, though his generalization is based on the erroneous idea that parents had lived with their adult offspring in the past.

Industrialization accelerated the gradual loss of functions that the family performed for a society; these losses, however, were balanced by the family's gain of new functions on which great importance was placed, sociologically. According to Parsons, families in modern industrialized societies are called upon to perform two basic functions: 1) the socialization of the young; and 2) tension management. Children need to grow up having internalized the appropriate values required to function as adults in an achievement-oriented society. However, the emotionally intense setting of the nuclear family tends to encourage dependency in children. Parsons' resolution of these tensions relies on Freud's notion of the oedipal complex; this process is seen as crucial for transforming eroticized feelings into healthy identification with the same-sex parent, thereby fostering internalization of societal values.

It is the "tension management" function which epitomizes the "home as haven" concept, a place for love and acceptance as a person, ungoverned by the impersonal criteria of the business world. Notice that both this function and much of the socialization function are assigned to the wife/mother. The husband/father does participate in childrearing, but only through his occupational role outside the family. By being a worker, he fulfills both his family responsibilities and the needs of the economic system. The wife, in contrast, takes the responsibility of the family roles, and contributes to the economy only indirectly, by giving emotional support to her husband/worker and raising her child to be occupationally successful.

B. Historical Development

This perspective can be traced to early attempts by August Comte (1798–1857) and Emile Durkheim (1858–1917) to establish the study of society as a science. Both Comte and Durkheim saw the family as the bulwark of moral values and sentiment, but gave little attention to studying it. Frederic Le Play (1866) was among the first to actually conduct field studies on families. He examined the adaptiveness of various family types in different areas of industrializing 18th century Europe. Since the stem family defined only one adult child, usually the married first-born son, as the inheritor of the family farm, the landholdings remained large enough to be economically productive, and fathers retained patriarchal control over the family. All other children were freed up to seek employment in urban areas.

The earliest functionalist theorists to focus on the family were British anthropologists, Bronislaw Malinowski (1884–1942) and A. R. Radcliffe-Brown (1881–1955); their ethnographic studies of "primitive" societies were conducted so as to discover universal features of family life. During the 1920s, Malinowski (1964) declared the "principle of legitimacy" as the universal basis for the family's existence; for the sake of society, each child's social paternity had to be established. Legitimacy is seen as the sociological mechanism for ensuring that a child acquires a place in society as an adult. This is achieved through the father's provision of social status and economic support by way of inheritance rights.

The two earliest functionalist sociologists were William F. Ogburn, who wrote between 1922 and 1955, and Talcott Parsons, referred to earlier, whose career stretched from 1937 to 1978. They argued against the position, expressed from time to time since the 1920s, that a loss of family functions implied eventual disintegration of the family. Instead, Parsons argued that the two functions for which the family is responsible, socialization and tension management, give the family even more importance than in the past. These and other functionalist ideas pervaded all aspects of sociological thinking from the late 1930s until they were challenged by conflict theorizing in the late 1960s.

C. Evaluation of the Structural-Functionalist Framework

Today, functionalist ideas are incorporated into other conceptual frameworks such as family developmentalism, but are seldom applied on their own account. The normative bases of the functionalist framework, may, however, still guide research. For example, the intensive research activity of the 1970s, centred on the effects on children of their mothers' employment, was influenced by this framework. Functionalist thinking operates wherever the assumption is made that people need to be guided by norms. A functionalist interpretation of remarriage, for example, assumes that it is a sign of continued support for the institution of marriage. (It may, however, represent a lack of viable alternatives.)

Gouldner (1970) credits much of the initial success of this framework to its compatibility with the ideals of middle-class family life and its elitist notions of the welfare state. By institutionalizing the nuclear family, the functionalist perspective sets the stage for the development of social policies which single out as deviant other family forms such as one-parent households, and consequently offer social services on that premise.

One of the reasons for the disuse of functionalism today is its failure to cope conceptually with the processes of social change. Although Parsons recognized the existence of strains in the family, he tended to play down their contribution to change. For instance, in Parsons' view, women's roles in the family are under strain because, as children, they were encouraged to compete with boys in the educational system but, as adults, they have been unable to use their educational attainment to acquire their own status. Parsons' solution was to have women get involved in volunteer work or gourmet cooking, any endeavour to minimize status competition with their husbands. Not surprisingly, functionalists were unable to explain the growth of the women's movement and its relationship to family changes.

The tendency for functionalists to rationalize the status quo is evident from their assignment of functions to the family. Functionalists such as Murdock (1949) state, for example, that since economic co-operation fulfills a societal need and the family performs this function in all societies known to the theorist, economic co-operation is necessarily a function of the family. Critics of structural functionalism have proposed, based on anthropological data, that all functions assigned to the family except that of nurturant socialization could be done by other institutions (Reiss, 1965). In communal groups, the unit of economic co-operation is not the family, but the larger unit, as with the kibbutzim in Israel.

The conceptual categories used by functionalists also raise a number of problems. Their great degree of abstraction produces such high-level generalizations that it obscures important differences between families. Parsons' grand-scale theorizing proves to be a sterile approach to producing researchable ideas. Cultural and historical data provide the richness for his "empty" categories. Social historians have documented the existence of the nuclear family in England long before the Industrial Revolution (Laslett and Wall, 1972), and question whether the nuclear family always functions better than some other family arrangement (Sennett, 1970).

The degree of functional specialization that occurs in families has been called into question on several accounts. More recent research by Bales (1970), whose original data were cited by Parsons, shows overlap in both tasks and emotional roles. George Levinger (1964) notes that, in such a small group as the family, emotional specialization is an unlikely division of labour. Also, to regard a wife's role as primarily expressive (emotional) is to overlook its many aspects which are task-oriented, such as bill-paying and cooking.

Parsons is respected more today for what he attempted than for his actual accomplishments. The wide scope of the variables he included, from the level of the personality through to the level of the social system, his efforts to tap and integrate several classical theoretical traditions, and his work in systematizing a set of important societal values have earned him a permanent place within the profession.

Perhaps the greatest "success" of structural functionalism lies with the research and critical commentary that it provoked. Without the concept of "the isolated nuclear family," for example, there might not have been as much interest in examining intergenerational relations. Besides, the criticisms have led to the crystallization of other frameworks, most notably that of the conflict perspective.

II. THE CONFLICT FRAMEWORK: ECONOMIC AND GENDER RELATIONS

A. Definition and Description

The following family definition reflects this framework's concentration on important cleavages criss-crossing all levels of a society, including families:

> Any unit in which there exists a sharing of economic property, mutually held, and relatively permanent rights of sexual access between sexual partners, a sense of commitment to or identification with the other members, and including any children born or raised by members. The many forms include: nuclear, extended, single-parent, communal and homosexual (Collins, 1985:478-479).

Such emphasis on materialist forces which lead to differences in ownership and power contrasts starkly with the sentimental family form of structural functionalism.

Although both functionalists and conflict theorists examine societal-level factors, their views of how a society is held together are quite different. The functionalist view of a society as one organic whole suggests the application of an invisible homeostatic device with the job of maintaining society in equilibrium. In contrast, conflict theorists point to the uneasy tension existing in a society that is dominated by capitalists who own the means of production (factories, businesses, etc.) and therefore control the society in their own interests.

Both functionalism and the conflict framework use macro-level variables to define the societal factors which affect the family, though there are important differences in the emphasis they give. For example, membership in a social class, not incorporated conceptually into functionalism, is seen within the conflict framework as a major factor conditioning a family's acquisition of the material basis for a satisfactory life. The family, rather than providing a haven from the world, reflects and even intensifies the structural conflicts of the society around it (see also Chapter 6).

Marxist analysts have generally given relatively little attention to the study of the family per se; since domestic labour does not produce surplus value, it did not fit into standard Marxian categories of economic relations. Families have been seen primarily to be areas for the reproduction of labour power which ultimately benefits the capitalists. Marx accepted domestic labour as a "natural" role for women (Sydie,

1987), though he regarded it as the major source of women's oppression. In his view, only as women became members of the paid labour force could they have the kind of political and social influence which would remove gender inequalities in a society and produce truly egalitarian marital relationships.

Feminists differ as to how much they accept the Marxian reliance on economic analysis. Marxist feminists consider that women constitute a class, since they experience a common position of disadvantage in the labour force, serving as a readily available and inexpensive temporary labour supply. They also see class analysis to be appropriate because all women perform unpaid household labour, whether they hold a job outside the home or not. Yet critics point out that women are already differentiated from one another because they identify with their husband's class, and this class placement gives them differential access to a variety of advantages such as better nutrition and health care (Armstrong and Armstrong, 1985).

Feminist perspectives developed in the 1960s on the nature of women's subordination under capitalism culminated in the "domestic labour debate" of the 1970s and 1980s. The core of the debate was whether housework constitutes oppression because its economic contribution to the household is overlooked, or whether the basis of a women's subordination is her tie to the family through her reproductive capacity. In either case, the privatized nature of housework under capitalism is recognized as a substratum for oppression (Armstrong and Armstrong, 1985).

Feminist social historians are examining the circumstances which led to the virtual retirement of women and children from the labour force by the end of the 19th century. Arguments given by working-class men, that it was to lessen their economic exploitation, centred on the idea of the "family wage," an income high enough to support the whole family on what the husband was paid.

Some feminist writers, searching for the bases of patriarchy, have used a critical analysis of Freudian theory as their starting point. Freud is credited with recognizing biological bases for behaviour, but his explanation of how gender roles are acquired through the oedipal complex is seen to be historically limited to the structure of the family under advanced industrial capitalism. While Freud linked healthy sexual-social development to patriarchy, feminist psychoanalysts (Chodorow, 1978) have criticized the concept that a mother has a specialized role in nurturance, since this leads to replicating gender roles; they recommend the benefits of greater direct male participation in a child's emotional life. Yet there would have to be structural changes in society for Chodorow's suggestion to be realized.

Capitalist systems contain a number of other contradictions inhibiting the potential for equalizing the positions of men and women. From a conflict perspective, as long as disparities exist, the stage is set for power imbalances within the family in favour of the husband.

B. Historical Development

The tradition of realism established by Machiavelli and Hobbes conceptualized self-interest and domination as the forces holding a society together. Karl Marx (1818–1883) studied the transition from feudalism to capitalism as two major classes developed, the bourgeoisie and the proletariat; they were seen to be simultaneously in opposition to each other and interdependent. Marx's colleague, Frederick Engels, wrote the first conflict-framework analysis of the family. His book, *The Origins of the Family, Private Property and the State* (1884), traces the relationship between the mode of production and the type of family in a society. Though not without technical error, the broad outlines of his analysis have been generally accepted in Marxist circles. The communal family systems of technologically simple societies seemed to them more egalitarian than the patriarchal families which emerged with settled agriculture. The monogamous family based on private property was seen as the site of women's most severe oppression.

It would be difficult to overestimate the influence of Marx on the conflict perspective; its importance within the discipline of sociology grew during the 1960s and 1970s as it became the platform for attacks against functionalism for failing to analyze ongoing social changes. Randall Collins' (1975) "synthetic conflict" perspective represents a major effort to expand Marxian categories in order to analyze women's positions in the family and society. Collins extends the Marx-Engels notion of the husband as the bourgeoisie and the wife as the proletariat to a more general analysis of economic, sexual, and intergenerational property relations; in his view, it is various combinations of these components which form different types of families.

The women's movement in the 1960s signalled a resurgence of women's collective consciousness about sexual discrimination. Marxism was the starting place for feminist writers such as Mitchell (1974); Firestone (1970) sought answers through a critical analysis of Freudian concepts and ended by rejecting the family and advocating laboratory-based reproduction.

Deserving honourable mention as an attempt to apply the conflict perspective to the micro-level is a body of research gathered on conflict processes (Sprey, 1979). These investigators see families as a lattice-work of competing interests among their members for the scarce resources of money, love, affection, and time. They use laboratory set-tings or intensive interviewing to observe patterns of co-operation and competition. By not considering the contribution of macro-level vari-ables, however, this micro model misses understanding how the larger social structure sets up the preconditions for conflict within the family.

C. Evaluation of the Conflict Framework

Conflict theorists are eager to reveal the value judgments which guide their thinking; following the critical tradition established by Hobbes and Marx, they openly declare themselves in support of the struggles of the poor and oppressed to achieve equality. This framework empha-sizes the potential for change in the social structure; it is therefore in contrast to the structural-functionalists' emphasis on the constraints which the social system places on behaviour.

For functionalists, the needs of society supercede the needs of indi-viduals, and individuals must "fit" into society. Conflict theorists, on the other hand, view individuals as connected with others who share similar social characteristics such as race or sex, and it is these com-mon bases which are mobilized to change the inequities in the social structure.

The debates generated among conflict theorists are not always easy for outsiders to understand, especially when they deal with the "cor-rectness" of various interpretations of Marx's works. Many debates have to do with the degree of emphasis that should be placed on eco-nomic versus ideological factors. Applied to the family, this debate is about the productivity of housework. It is important to remember that this discussion touches on the broader question of why female-headed single-parent households are likely to be impoverished. A radical fem-inist analysis suggests that simply paying a wage for housework will not ultimately produce an egalitarian society (Armstrong and Armstrong, 1985); women will still be cut off from mainstream activities and be dominated by patriarchal structures.

Conflict theorists have argued that experience in the "real" world entails conflict, and that life is much different for males and females and between social classes. Such a viewpoint has been productive of a number of studies including Meg Luxton's ethnographic accounting

(1980) of the significant contribution housewives make to the reproduction of labour power by taking care of the needs of adult family
members. They are thus able to continue to participate in the labour
force. She found that technological changes in housework over three
generations of women tended to devalue the skills and motivation that
once went with the job, but do not diminish its time demands.

Feminist analyses have been productive of new ways of understanding the relationship between the family and women's roles in a society.
Because family life is primarily identified with women, failure to focus
on women's experiences in families is a serious omission. Women have
been over-asked certain research questions, though not always the ones
that lead to a better understanding of their position in society. Questions that deal with who makes the decisions in the family fail to cap-
ture the dynamics of the actual control processes which maintain male
dominance. Men, on the other hand, have been sampled so rarely
on questions of the family that we know litte, for example, about a
father's actual or desired involvement in childcare (Eichler, 1983).

III. SYMBOLIC INTERACTIONISM

A. Definition and Description

Burgess and Locke offer the following definition from the perspective
that the family is a small group:

> The family is a group of persons united by ties of marriage, blood, or
> adoption; constituting a single household; interacting and communicat-
> ing with each other in their respective social roles of husband and wife,
> mother and father, son and daughter, brother and sister; and creating
> and maintaining a common culture (1953, pp.7-8).

Language is the chief avenue for symbolic thought: through ideas
we make a mental representation of the world around us and see the
world from this perspective. Central to symbolic interactionism is the
idea that people continuously interpret and make meaning out of their
experience, their own and others'. Their interpretations are anchored
in actual situations of social interaction. W. I. Thomas noted that for
a person who defines a situation as real, that definition has real consequences (Thomas and Znaniecki, 1918).

Through interaction with others, a person develops a sense of self,
one which reflects the attitudes of others towards oneself. It is through
the primary relationships with "significant others" such as parents and
peers that a child acquires a sense of its competencies and a feeling of

self-worth. A person's "self" is composed of a socialized component called the "me," plus an "I" which represents the more spontaneous behaviour that arises out of biological needs and momentary sensations, etc. (Mead, 1934).

Emerging out of the symbolic interactionist framework is what has come to be called "role theory." A "social actor," that is, an individual in society, is able to take the viewpoint of another, a capacity which symbolic interactionists term "role-taking." This social cognitive ability enables us to anticipate another person's reactions and adjust our own behaviour accordingly. Within the symbolic interactionist framework, the concept of "role" is used to measure many aspects of interrelationships within a family. "Role expectations" guide role performances and are used to evaluate them. For example, the degree of husband-wife consensus on role expectations is an important dimension of relationships. "Role strain" is defined as the sense of discomfort ~~unemployment~~ or tension felt by a person who is experiencing difficulty in fulfilling role expectations; as a concept, it is frequently used in studies of dual-career families.

B. Historical Development

The symbolic interactionist perspective was developed in the United States in the 1920s at the University of Chicago. This more scientific approach to the study of the family superceded an earlier, "reformist" approach which had studied the disorganization of urban, immigrant families. The influential family theorists, Ernest Burgess and Harvey Locke (1945), described the family as having passed from "institution to companionship"; this phrase was meant to indicate that the interior of family life was becoming the most important area for research.

Studies based on this perspective were conducted to determine the factors leading to marital adjustment and marital stability. Although the functionalist perspective held sway from after World War II until the 1960s, quantitative research on the family as a small group had continued since the 1920s. Symbolic interactionism is both an explicit and implicit framework for examining the process of adjustment to divorce and remarriage.

The ideas of William Jones (1890) and George Herbert Mead (1934) played a significant part in the development of Burgess's ideas about the family. While Burgess was interested in developing quantitative measures of the common activities and attitudes that lead to marital adjustment, others have focused on delineating the social processes by means of which marital couples come to define a joint reality. Berger and Luckmann (1966), for example, describe the mutual perspective-taking that takes place in the early years of marriage as a couple in their conversation together subtly shape a new definition of reality.

C. Evaluation of Symbolic Interactionism

This loosely knit framework is so easily applicable that a vast number of researchers can claim to have used it, but few have focused on standardizing concepts and synthesizing research results. For instance, Parsons (1970:80) claims that he relies indirectly on the insights of G. H. Mead, since they so handily parallel those of Freud on whom his case for internalization rests. The term, "role strain," originated with William Goode (1963), who is primarily a structural functionalist, and this term became popular in research. Unfortunately, a welter of variously defined concepts make studies difficult to compare.

To sum up, symbolic interactionism emphasizes the subjective definition of social phenomenon. From this perspective, role-playing is viewed as an interpretive process through which people attempt to integrate their lines of action; in contrast, role definitions in the Parsonian frame of reference serve as social scripts: you are more or less instructed what to do and be. Symbolic interactionists emphasize that individuals take an active part in playing their own roles.

The major criticism of symbolic interactionism is that it analyses social relationships only from a micro-theoretical perspective. It concentrates on what happens within families rather than tracing a connection to the wider society. Because of this oversight, it fails to give explicit consideration to the effects of social class. Elder (1984) argues that some of the early family sociologists had integrated a more structural approach with symbolic interactionism; there was no logical necessity for the exclusion of the macro-level concepts. Meanwhile, the developmental framework to which we now turn claimed to have included factors beyond the family.

IV. THE DEVELOPMENTAL FRAMEWORK: A HYBRID MODEL

A. Definition and Description

The following definition of the family offered by a developmentalist was formulated to reflect the origins of the developmental framework in functionalism and symbolic interactionism:

The family is a semiclosed system of actors occupying interrelated positions defined by the society of which the family system is a part as unique to that system with respect to the role content of the positions and to ideas of kinship relatedness. The definitions of positional role content change over the history of the group (Rodgers, 1973:15).

This framework focuses overall on the tasks family members have to take on as they strive to meet individual and family needs through effective family interaction.

The goals families set for themselves over their life cycle basically correspond to the family functions of nurturance and socialization identified by structural-functionalists. These goals, together with a child's physical maturation, serve to structure the nature of the tasks a family faces at each stage in the family life cycle. The developmental assumptions of the model suggest that a family's effective handling of tasks in the early stages of the family life cycle enhance its ability to cope with tasks belonging to later stages.

The stages themselves are defined by the developing child and the normative expectations that accompany a child's development. Duvall's (1971) widely used model contains eight stages, based largely on the age of the oldest child. Rodgers (1973) proposes a 24-stage model which takes into consideration the ages of the oldest and youngest child. The absolute number of stages is less important than the degree of internal consistency in each stage, according to basic underlying similarities.

Developmentalists justify basing their model on the nuclear family because of its statistical and normative predominance. Even where the family type differs from the "typical" pattern, whether through childlessness, divorce, or death, developmentalists point out that most people still value nuclear family life, whether or not they attain or maintain it.

Ideally, it would be best to study families longitudinally, over the course of the family's total development. In practice, owing to money and time constraints and methodological problems inherent in sampling, most researchers have used cross-sectional data. Each family is placed into the appropriate life-cycle stage, and the effects on them of the various stages are compared according to various measures of family functioning. This procedure is capable of testing for similarities among families within stages, but only longitudinal analysis can determine how earlier stages affect later ones.

B. Historical Development

Several disciplines have contributed to the developmental framework. Among them are psychology and child development, as well as rural sociology and home economics. Originally worked out by home economists to facilitate their work with families, developmentalism was refined and elaborated by sociologists working in the 1930s. The eight-stage model developed by Duvall was produced in the 1950s.

Since the 1960s, a great deal of research attention has been given to the analysis of marital satisfaction over the life cycle; these studies generally document declines in satisfaction with the addition of children to the family, and with enhancement during the child-launching stage. More recently, research on family incomes over the family life cycle shows general increases in the level of income as the family develops; the use of life-cycle stages may help researchers to explore the effects of differences in income over time (Duncan et al., 1986).

C. Evaluation of the Developmental Perspective

A life-cycle approach allows for cross-cultural comparisons. Canadian families have tended to have their children somewhat later than U.S. families, for example, but space them closer together. (Rodgers and Whitney, 1981). In both countries, the portion of the life cycle spent with pre-school children is short-lived, compared to the length of the post-parental period; since Canadian children are launched 3.5 years earlier in the family life cycle, the "empty nest" stage begins even sooner. This concentration of childrearing into a shorter period of time means that more of a couple's married life can be devoted to career development and companionship than in the past. Further detailed research and analyses of these patterns are needed. Results from such studies would prove useful for public policy making. Still another profitable use for the developmental perspective is in historical research. Tamara Hareven (1982) has found that variation in the timing of life-cycle transitions was greater among her late 19th century New England sample than is true for today. A wider range in age at marriage was due to such factors as the need to work to support one's mother and siblings after the death of one's father.

In overall terms, the developmental framework stands as a loose set of prescriptions for adequate family functioning based on the nuclear family model. It tends to be more descriptive than analytical; the normative assumptions of a society are uncritically applied to the required tasks of each stage of family life, although these might vary depending on social class or ethnic background.

However, as more and more people spend a larger proportion of their lives outside a nuclear family context either before or after marriage, the life-cycle framework becomes less and less useful as an explanatory device. Its "lock step" approach does not allow for the possibility of differing sequences for reconstituted families and for other family types such as single-parent households. If it is to remain useful, the life-cycle approach needs to be expanded to include the more complex patterns of life events that contemporary families face.

Several researchers (Nock, 1979; Spanier et al., 1979) present data questioning whether "placing" families in stages of the life cycle is a better predictor of variables in family life than are simple measures like the length of marriage and the presence of children. If these one-dimensional measures were substituted for "stages," families could be analyzed who don't fit into life-cycle stages, e.g., divorced and remarried families. Further studies in this framework will need to show greater flexibility in the way stages are defined and heavier emphasis on studying transitions from one stage to another.

V. EVALUATING CONCEPTUAL FRAMEWORKS

It is premature to ask which conceptual framework is the "right" one. The selection of a conceptual framework is not quite so open-ended that any framework will do. Neither is appropriateness exactly a matter of matching a problem with a framework. Each conceptual framework contains a set of concepts defined to explain family life efficiently within its world view; the framework has its own Gestalt which structures how you ask questions about the family. Most family sociologists espouse a particular framework, some of them passionately. Through graduate school training, a professional comes to emphasize one particular framework and to maintain interest and work in it as a member of specialized professional associations and networks.

There are several criteria which can be used to evaluate conceptual frameworks, however. One important consideration is the amount of writing and research activity that each perspective generates. By these criteria, structural-functionalism is eclipsed by symbolic interactionism and the conflict perspective, especially feminism. Family developmentalism has continued to be applied largely by professionals in the social and health services delivery system.

Research results can be used as a yardstick to determine the amount of support available for propositions derived from the conceptual frameworks. Although studies are not set up as direct tests of the frameworks, the accumulation of findings can render the explanations in the theory more or less plausible. For example, the data that social historians have found in census and birth-registration records in pre-industrial Europe were instrumental in calling into question Parsons' assertions about the relationship between industrialization and the nuclear family. Likewise, the finding that length of marriage and the simple presence of children (not their ages) predict family variables undermines the validity of the normative explanations given for the stage concept.

Theoretical advances do not take place independently of actual social developments within the environment that the theorists themselves share. The process works somewhat like this: social developments produce new behaviours; these behaviours call for new theoretical analyses, and so on.

Consider again the possibilities opened up by increasing technological control over fertility. Assume, for instance, that eventually a fetus could be gestated in a laboratory setting. Would such an innovation finally form a basis for egalitarian gender roles within the family, as Firestone (1972) has argued? Or would capitalism's need of cheap labour predominate, and require women to continue their childbearing role? Answers to such questions depend on our finding out what it is in the life of our society that shapes male and female roles in the family and on correctly appraising its potentialities and constraints. On the other hand, innovations in childbearing might do no more than extend current trends toward later childbearing, so that couples in their forties and fifties could start a family after having had successful careers.

The enterprise of theory-building is in itself a social process and involves social definitions. To assume that women are more naturally associated with childrearing is based, not on an actual biological definition, but on a social definition of the significance of biology. More and more, we live in a socially constructed world which requires our continued intervention through newly thought-out policies, the effects of which also become part of our study. Conceptual frameworks should provide us, not with what we would like to hear, but with a structure for analyzing the realities of family life.

REFERENCES

Adams, Bert. 1971. "Isolation, Function and Beyond: American Kinship in the 1960's." In Carlfred B. Broderick, ed. *A Decade of Family Research and Action*. Minneapolis: National Council on Family Relations.

Armstrong, Pat et al. 1985. *Feminist Marxism or Marxist Feminism: A Debate*. Toronto: Garamond Press.

Bales, Robert F. 1970. *Personality and Interpersonal Behaviour*. New York: Holt Rinehart and Winston.

Berger, P. L. and T. Luckmann. 1966. *The Social Construction of Reality*. New York: Doubleday.

Burgess, Ernest and Harvey Locke. 1963. *The Family from Institution to Companionship*. New York: American Book Co.

Chodorow, Nancy. 1978. *The Reproduction of Mothering*. California: University of California Press.

Collins, Randall. 1975. *Conflict Sociology: Toward an Explanatory Science*. New York: Academic Press.

———. 1987. *Sociology of Marriage and the Family: Gender, Love and Property*. Chicago: Nelson-Hall.

Duncan, Greg J. 1986. "An Overview of Family Economic Mobility." In Arlene Skolnick and Jerome H. Skolnick, eds. *Family in Transition*. 5th edition. Boston: Little, Brown and Co.

Duvall, E. M. 1971. *Family Development*. 4th edition. Philadelphia: Lippincott.

Eichler, Margrit. 1983. *Families in Canada Today: Recent Changes and Their Policy Consequences*. Toronto: Gage.

Engels, Frederick. 1954. *The Origins of the Family, Private Property and the State*. Moscow: Foreign Languages Publishing House, (orig. pub'n 1884).

Elder, Glen. 1984. "Families, Kin and the Life Course: A Sociological Perspective." In Ross D. Parke, ed. *The Family*, Review of Child Development Research, vol. 7. Chicago: University of Chicago Press.

Firestone, Shulamith. 1970. *The Dialectic of Sex*. London: Paladin.

Gouldner, Alvin. 1970. *The Coming Crisis of Western Sociology*. New York: Basic Books.

Goode, Wm. J. 1963. *World Revolution and Family Patterns*. New York: Free Press.

Hareven, Tamara. 1982. "American Families in Transition: Historical Perspectives on Change." In Froma Walsh, ed. *Normal Family Processes*. New York: Guilford Press.

James, William. 1890. *The Principles of Psychology*. Dover Publications.

Laslett, P. and R. Wall, eds. 1972. *Household and Family in Past Time*. Cambridge: Cambridge University Press, pp. 29–34.

LePlay, Frederic. 1935. "La Reforme Sociale." In C. C. Zimmerman and M. E. Frampton, eds. and trans. *Family and Society*. Princeton, New Jersey: Van Nostrand.

Levinger, G. "Task and Social Behaviour in Marriage." *Sociometry* 1964, 27: pp. 443-448.

Luxton, Meg. 1980. *More Than a Labour of Love*. Toronto: Women's Educational Press.

Malinowski, B. 1964. "The Principle of Legitimacy: Parenthood, the Basis of Social Structure." In R. L. Coser, ed. *The Family: Its Structure and Functions*. New York: St. Martin's Press, pp. 3-19.

Mead, George Herbert. 1934. *Mind, Self and Society*. ed. Charles W. Morris, Chicago: University of Chicago Press.

Mitchell, Juliet. 1971. *Women's Estate*. Harmondsworth: Penguin.

Murdock, G. P. 1949. *Social Structure*. New York: Macmillan.

Nock, S. L. 1981. "Family Life Cycle Transitions: Longitudinal Effects on Family Members." *Journal of Marriage and the Family* 43: pp. 703-713.

Parsons, Talcott. 1970. *Social Structure and Personality*. New York: The Free Press.

—— and R. F. Bales. 1956. *Family: Socialization and Interaction Process*. London: Routledge, Kegan & Paul.

Reiss, Ira L. "The Universality of the Family: A Conceptual Analysis." *Journal of Marriage and the Family*, 27, Nov. 1965: pp. 443-453.

Rodgers, Roy H. 1973. *Family Interaction and Transaction*. New Jersey: Prentice-Hall.

—— and Gail Whitney. 1981. "The Family Cycle in Twentieth Century Canada." *Journal of Marriage and the Family*, 43:3 (August) pp. 727-740.

Sennett, R. 1970. *Families Against the City: Middle Class Homes of Industrial Chicago, 1872-1890*. Cambridge, Mass.: Harvard University Press.

Spanier, Graham, et al. 1979. "An Empirical Evaluation of the Family Life Cycle." *Journal of Marriage and the Family*, 41: pp. 15-26.

Sprey, Jetse. 1979. "Conflict Theory and the Study of Marriage and the Family." In Wesley Burr et al. eds. *Contemporary Theories About the Family*. 2nd edition, New York: The Free Press.

Sydie, R. A. 1987. *Natural Women, Cultured Men: A Feminist Perspective on Sociological Theory*. Toronto: Methuen.

Thomas, W. I. 1931. The Unadjusted Girl. Boston: Little, Brown and Co.

Tiryakian, Edward A. 1963. *Sociological Theory, Values and Socio-cultural Change*. New York: Harper and Row.

ANNOTATED BIBLIOGRAPHY

Morgan, D. H. J. *Social Theory and the Family*. 1975. London: Routledge & Kegan Paul. Although somewhat dated, this book provides an excellent background for understanding the issues raised by the functionalist and conflict frameworks, including substantial attention to feminist issues. Morgan examines the historical development of the ideas and problems in the frameworks and offers his reasoned, critical analysis in response.

Armstrong, Pat, Hugh Armstrong, Patricia Connelly, and Angela Miles. 1985. *Feminist Marxism or Marxist Feminism: A Debate*. Toronto: Garamond Press. Not specifically directed as an examination of the family, this book nevertheless sheds great light on the issues in debate. Presented in highly concentrated form, the core arguments in the debate are isolated and used to formulate suggestions for future integration of both types of explanation.

Burr, Wesley, Reuben Hill, F. Ivan Nye and Ira L. Reiss. 1979. *Contemporary Theories About the Family*. Vols. I and II. New York: The Free Press. Written for the serious student, these volumes serve as invaluable reference guides to varied efforts of family sociologists to systematize a wide range of theoretical work. Both volumes reflect a research-based approach to theory-building. Volume I discusses major conceptual frameworks including some, such as systems theory, which are based on ideas originating from clinical practice. Volume II is a compendium of what are termed "substantive theories" dealing with applied areas of study such as mate selection.

Thorne, Barrie and Marilyn Yalom. 1982. *Rethinking the Family: Some Feminist Questions*. New York: Longman. This collection of readings specifically addresses the implications of feminist views for the family. Among the viewpoints represented in the book are those related to changing legal definitions, role conceptions, social class divisions, and social policy issues impacting on the family. Attempts are made to trace out future developments in these areas.

CHAPTER 4

Family Change and Social Policies

MARGRIT EICHLER

INTRODUCTION

Families in Canada have never been static structures, and they have never been all of the same kind.[1] The nuclear family in which father, mother, their own biological children, and nobody else lived happily together has been largely a myth: families were not necessarily happy just because they lived under one roof, and there have always been family disruptions from death and desertion, and from migration through economic necessity.

Yet there are times in which changes are particularly marked, and this is one of them. In this chapter we will first consider briefly some of the most important changes which have been taking place in Canadian families in the past two to three decades. Then the implications of some of these changes will be reviewed for the impact they have on policies affecting families, by examining (a) the models of the family which underlie current policies and (b) the fit of these models with contemporary Canadian reality.

In a slightly different form, this chapter was delivered as a keynote paper at the XXth International CFR Seminar on Social Change and Family Policies, Melbourne, Australia, August, 1984. I would like to thank Lorraine Fairley, who has edited this paper in a substantial manner.

The models that will be identified as underlying present social policies are not officially or consciously elaborated when these policies are created. They are *implicit* rather than explicit models. Yet the assumptions about families built into them become outstripped by rapid change in actual family patterns. Social policies can be forward-oriented or backward-oriented. In the latter case, policies will become increasingly problematic. It is therefore extremely important in a discussion of families and social policies to look at the evolving family in all its aspects, both broadly, in figures that show rates of fertility and longevity, for example, and closer to home, as individual families shape and reshape themselves through individual decisions about child bearing, marriage, divorce, and responsibility for caring for children (not to mention the aged). What are some of the changes in family patterns that are occurring so rapidly in this country?

The most recent data on family makeup and circumstances show a reduction in the number of children born to a mother; longer lives for men and women, but particularly for women, who outlive men by several years; an increase in homes with one parent (usually the mother); many more remarriages; a majority of women, mothers or not, who work for pay outside the home; and a lack of congruence between families and households.

CONTEMPORARY CANADIAN FAMILIES

When looking at trends in families, demographic changes can be observed in Canada similar to those in other industrialized countries.

The Decline in Fertility

One of the most striking changes in families is their decline in fertility. Canadian women have fewer children than ever before. While in 1960 the average number of children per woman was about 3.9, by 1985 it had sunk to less than 1.7.[2] That is, fertility has decreased by more than half in approximately two decades.

This is a common trend in industrialized countries. The twenty countries with the lowest fertility rates in the world in 1982 were, in ascending order, Switzerland, the Federal Republic of Germany, Luxembourg, The Netherlands, Denmark, Sweden, Austria, Belgium, Finland, the German Democratic Republic, Japan, Norway, Singapore, Canada, France, Italy, New Zealand, The United States of America, Great Britain, and Australia (United Nations, 1985:21).

There are many reasons for this decline in fertility. They include better access to methods of birth control and greater longevity, partly as a result of reduced infant mortality. In addition, there seems to be a pattern by which fewer children are born as a country industrializes. As societies move away from agriculture and primary industry, and as mass education becomes available, it costs more to raise children, and they bring less money into the family. The effect of these various trends is that women have fewer children.

Extended Life Expectancy

Life expectancy, by contrast, has risen steadily. For a male born in Canada in 1931, life expectancy at birth was 60 years, and for a female born in that year it was 62.1 years. For a male born in Canada in 1986, life expectancy is estimated to reach 70.2 years, and for a female born in that year 78.3 years.[3] This means that there will be more older people around who will eventually need to be taken care of. However, the need for care differs markedly by sex. Because women marry men who are, on average, two years older than themselves, and because men die earlier than women, most men die while still married, while most women die not married. For instance, in 1984, 62 percent of all men who died that year were married, as compared to 32 percent of the women who died; this means, in other words, that most men have a spouse who looks after them until death, yet women do not. Meantime, there will be fewer younger people to provide the care they need in their extreme old age.

An Increase in Divorce

The divorce rate has increased steadily and dramatically over recent decades, rising from a rate of 39.1 in 1960, which represents 6,980 divorces in that year in Canada, to a rate of 244.4 in 1985, which represents 61,980 divorces. During this period, Canadian divorce law was changed twice. The first unified divorce law entered into force in 1968, and the second major change became effective in 1986, when the waiting period for obtaining a divorce on the basis of marriage breakdown was reduced to one year (from three years). It can be anticipated that in the wake of this change the divorce rate will climb once more. However, at the time of this writing, it is too early to be sure.

Because of the great increase in divorce, there have been many more remarriages. In 1985, 30 percent of all marriages contracted in that year involved at least one previously married partner, compared to 12 percent of all marriages in 1967.[4] The great bulk of that increase is due to divorced rather than widowed persons remarrying; indeed, the proportion of widowed people remarrying has consistently declined.

An Increase in Births to Unmarried Women

Further, there has been a large increase in the percentage of births to unmarried mothers. While in 1960 only 4.3 percent of all children were born to unmarried women, representing 20,413 children, the percentage had risen to 16.7 in 1984, representing 61,265 children.[5]

One consequence of the increase in divorce and births to single women is that the proportion of children living in one-parent households has grown. Approximately 17 percent of all families with children were headed by one parent in 1981,[6] mostly mothers, and three out of seven of them lived below the poverty line.[7] The two factors, having a female head and poverty, are closely connected.[8]

Women's Increased Participation in the Labour Force

It used to be that women dropped out of the labour force when they married. In the 60s, the prevalent pattern was that they worked after marriage until the birth of their first child, taking a job again, perhaps, after the last child entered school.[9]

The participation of married women in the labour force has increased consistently,[10] and today this applies to the majority of Canadian wives and mothers. In 1977, 37 percent of all married women with pre-school children were in the labour force, while, in 1984, the figure was 54 percent. The percentages are higher for mothers with older children (see Table 1). At the same time, the labour force participation of fathers of pre-school children has not declined, as can be seen from Table 2. In other words, fathers have not assumed the child-care tasks mothers are not able to perform during their hours of paid employment.

Effects of these Demographic Changes

Overall, we have noted that fertility has drastically decreased, longevity has increased, the number and proportion of births to unmarried women have increased greatly, and so have divorce and remarriage.

TABLE 1

Labour Force Participation Rates of Women by *Presence of Husband and Children, Annual Averages, Canada, 1977-1984.

		1977	1978	1979	1980	1981	1982	1983	1984
Total number of women in families		45.4	47.4	48.7	50.2	51.7	52.0	53.0	54.2
with husband present	with children aged 0-5	37.3	41.0	42.7	45.0	47.4	48.5	51.5	53.6
	with children under 16	44.8	48.0	49.4	51.8	54.5	55.2	56.8	59.1
no husband present	with children aged 0-5	46.8	45.2	49.6	53.3	51.2	51.6	50.8	50.5
	with children under 16	55.7	56.1	58.3	61.6	61.5	60.9	59.9	61.5

*i.e., for women whose husbands and children are present in the home.
Source: Statistics Canada: Family Characteristics. Cat. 71-533, 1986.

These changes have several consequences of great importance for social policies affecting women. In general, there has been a loosening of the tie between marriage and parenthood. Many men, in particular, do not live with their biological children; (in the case of births to unmarried women, around 90 percent of the women keep their children). As for divorces involving dependent children, only about 15 percent of these children are in the custody of their fathers; about 75 percent are in the custody of their mothers.

As a consequence of these changes in families, our understanding of the concepts relating to families and households needs to be transformed. In the past, and still in many instances today, it is assumed that to be part of a family one must belong to the same household. For adults, this tends to be true. For children, whose parents may have divorced and remarried, this may not be true. After divorce, some non-custodial parents keep close contact with their children, who visit

TABLE 2

Labour Force Participation Rates of Men by *Presence of Wife and Children and Labour Force Status of Wife, Annual Averages, Canada, 1977-1984.

		1977	1978	1979	1980	1981	1982	1983	1984
with wife employed	with children aged 0-5	97.3	93.7	97.8	97.8	98.0	97.5	97.1	97.2
	with children under 16	97.1	93.8	97.4	97.3	97.6	97.0	96.8	97.3
with wife not employed	with children aged 0-5	96.7	91.6	97.1	96.5	96.5	95.5	95.3	95.0
	with children under 16	95.0	90.2	95.2	95.0	94.8	93.9	93.8	93.8
no wife present	with children aged 0-5	90.1	90.4	87.9	83.2	90.9	93.0	81.6	88.2
	with children under 16	87.5	89.2	89.5	90.4	89.4	89.5	87.2	86.7

*i.e., for men whose wives and children are present in the home.
Source: Statistics Canada: Family Characteristics. Cat. 71-533, 1986.

regularly. In such cases, the child belongs to two families which do not share a household: that of the mother and that of the father. To equate family membership with household membership in such cases is, as far as the children are concerned, incorrect.

To best summarize the current situation would be to say that we are now faced with a great diversity of co-existing family types: husband-wife families living with their biological or adopted children; husband-wife families which include the biological children of only one partner; families in which the children of one or two of the adults are living in other households; and solo-parent families. This diversity is multiplied by wage-earning patterns: there are families with one earner, families with two earners, and families with more than two earners.

Given such diversity, it is not surprising that we occasionally find a mismatch between certain social policies and the reality of Canadian families today. The following passage examines those notions about families which underly various types of social policy.

FAMILY MODELS AND SOCIAL POLICIES

As we have seen, Canadian families have changed considerably in recent decades. Canada has never had an *explicit* family policy which consciously tries to foster one particular kind of family. Instead, we have had (and continue to have) a medley of policies which address different issues concerning families. Such a pragmatic approach is not necessarily a bad thing: family policies consciously oriented toward establishing, maintaining, or supporting one particular type of family may be very restrictive. For instance, Ireland has an explicit family policy regarding access to means of birth control: only married couples have legal access to them. This is certainly not in the general interest.

However, in the absence of an explicit family policy in Canada, we need to deduce what model of the family is *implicit* in a particular policy. We do this by asking ourselves: What type of family is included in this policy? What type excluded? What type supported? What type not supported?

By posing these questions to various policies, we arrive at two different models of the family which at the present time underlie the bulk of family-oriented policies in Canada. In the following, I shall outline both of these models, and provide a critique of them. Then I shall present an alternative, theoretical, model of the family for social policies, suggesting that it would be better suited to serve our present-day reality in this country.

But first it is necessary to look at the moral and administrative principles on which many of our current social policies are based.

Moral and Administrative Principles Underlying Many Social Policies

(1) *The Non-interference Principle*: Traditionally, families have been thought of as the building blocks of society. This moral principle makes the family seem both precious and something not to be interfered with, so it has the consequence of requiring families to be self-reliant. If any help is rendered, it should be provided to the family as a whole, in this view; for if the family is a valuable social institution,

it should remain a family. The non-interference principle is inextricable, therefore, from

(2) *The Family-as-Administrative-Unit Principle*: The family is treated as the smallest administrative unit in social policies, according to this principle, not the individual.

Neither of these principles entirely permeates every current policy; nevertheless, both of them can be traced in fiscal, economic, and welfare policies and legislation. They are used to justify *two erroneous concepts of the family* which act as implicit models for much of our social legislation. These are the Patriarchal Model of the Family and the Individual Responsibility Model of the Family. They are "erroneous," because they fail to match reality, thereby putting our social legislation out of whack with the way families actually live.

The Patriarchal Model of the Family

A patriarchal model of the family typically shows the following eight characteristics:

1. The household and family are treated as being identical.
2. As a consequence, a husband is equated with a father, and a wife is equated with a mother.
3. The family is treated as a unit, administratively.
4. The father/husband is seen as responsible for the economic well-being of the family.
5. The wife/mother is seen as responsible for the household and personal care of family members, especially childcare.
6. Conversely, the father/husband is *not* seen as responsible for the household and personal care of family members, especially childcare, and
7. The wife/mother is *not* responsible for the economic well-being of the family.
8. Society may give support to the man who supports his dependents (wife and/or children), but it is not responsible for the economic well-being of the family where there is a husband present, and it is not responsible for the household and personal care of family members, especially childcare, where there is a wife.

This model of the family is premissed on the notion of sex inequality, which expresses itself in a rather strict division of labour between husbands and wives. Since the wife (and mother) is conceived of as the economic dependent of her husband, in this model, her unpaid work in the household, including childcare, is therefore seen as economically valueless. If either spouse ceases to perform his or her prescribed function (e.g., the husband loses his job or deserts the family; or the wife falls ill and is institutionalized), the state is likely to take over the function no longer carried out by one of the spouses. Social welfare policies by which the mother is eligible for welfare only if she does not live with a man are an example of a policy based on the patriarchal model of the family. In such cases, *it is assumed* that the man will take over the function of breadwinner, even if he does not do so. This can create enormous problems for a mother who is dependent on family benefits. Some such examples will be examined in the following critique of this type of family model.

The Individual Responsibility Model of the Family

The individual responsibility model of the family shows several characteristics of the patriarchal model:
1. Household and family are treated as being identical.
2. As a consequence, a husband is equated with a father, and a wife with a mother.
3. The family is treated as the administrative unit.
Nevertheless, it differs from the patriarchal model in significant ways:
4. Both husband and wife are seen as responsible for their own support as well as that of the other.
5. Both father and mother are seen as responsible for the household and personal care of family members, especially children.
6. Society may give support to families, but, in principle, is not responsible for either the economic well-being of the family nor for the personal care of family members, especially childcare, when there is either a husband or wife (or mother or father) present.

Canadian social policies largely reflect this individual responsibility model of the family. All provincial family laws have been amended, from 1978 on, in the direction of assigning equal responsibility for economic well-being and household work and childcare to both husbands and wives. This model, where it is used, has two most interesting consequences: for one, it makes the economic value of unpaid labour in the home somewhat more visible. When both spouses are seen as responsible for their own economic welfare, but the couple truly decide (rather than simply assume) that it is preferable for one of them to stay home, then the replacement value of housework and childcare or what might have been the wages of the stay-at-home spouse become more obvious. The other consequence is implied in characteristics 5 and 6: if a husband/father is responsible for the financial well-being of the family as well as for the housework and care of its members, and if the same applies to a wife/mother, then the state's obligation to take over the role of the absent spouse (that is contained in the patriarchal family model) tends to disappear.

Unfortunately, in discussions of social policy, this tendency is used as an argument that single mothers should go out and earn money. Such a stance fails to understand that, when *one* person is doing the tasks usually performed by *two* people, that is, holding down a paying job and providing care for children, special problems arise and special support is therefore needed. In other words, this model can be used to reduce state support for families in need, since presumably both parents or spouses can fulfill both sets of roles.

The individual responsibility model does not, however, imply that in the case of a husband/wife family both spouses need to hold a paying job; instead, it implies that the contribution of the spouse at home is economically valuable, since otherwise these services would have to be purchased.

Certainly, this model has much to recommend it over the patriarchal model of the family, insofar as it is based on the notion of sex equality rather than female dependence, and is somewhat more in line with current social reality, since the majority of wives are part of the labour force.

Still, some extremely important problems remain. In the following, we will first consider the problems specific to each model, and then look at those they share:

(A) Problems Associated with the Patriarchal Model of the Family as a Basis for Social Policy

The major problems associated with the patriarchal model as a basis for social policy is that it is premissed on notions of female dependency, and thereby helps maintain such dependency. Policies based on these assumptions, and still current in Canada, include social welfare policies which disentitle a woman with children on family benefits when she is judged to be living together with a man. In Ontario in 1980 there were several cases of women in this situation being jailed because they claimed family benefits (see Eichler, 1984). There was no doubt that the benefits were used for their proper purpose, namely to provide the necessities of life for the woman and children. Nor was there any doubt that the men involved had *not* supported the women and children. They were, however, *supposed* to have supported them, under the assumption that it is the husband/father's responsibility to support his wife and her children, and under the assumption that a husband (common-law or legal) equals a father. (This was true in one of the cases, not the other two.) Since that time, the "man in the house" rule has been abolished in Ontario, but a woman is still disentitled from family benefits if she lives together with a man on a full-time basis.

On January 19, 1984, *The Toronto Star* reported on its first page: "Mom's Welfare Fraud Based on 'System'." The story concerned a welfare mother who "defrauded" welfare of more than $37,000 because she was afraid of losing her children. She drew welfare for ten years and received about $270 a month to support herself and her three children. Despite a court order, her former husband never paid child support, which added up to arrears of $19,000. Warrants for his arrest were never executed. The woman had been told that if she had no way of supporting her children she would lose them to the Children's Aid Society. The reason she was judged to have defrauded welfare was that during the period in question she was in fact living together with a man, rather than as a single woman. There is no suggestion that this man was able or willing to support those children, who are not his, and, had she not lived with the man, she would have been entitled to every penny she received.

This is a clear case of a policy premissed on the patriarchal model of the family: the common-law husband is treated as the children's father (which he is not) in terms of support obligations; the family is seen as the administrative unit, not the individual; and the household is equated with the family. Nor did the authorities try very hard to find the ex-husband/father. A few days after the initial story, the newspaper reported that it had managed to do in days what the state had been unable to do in years: that is, locate the missing father who had never paid a cent in child support (Moore and Stefaniuk, 1984).

The judge ordered the woman to repay the money she had received, minus the amount owed her by her husband, over a period of six years. However, she earns only $200 a week as a manual labourer. Supporting three children and herself, how can she repay $18,000 on that salary? The woman argues that: "The system sold us out. . . . You took my children's rights. You didn't protect them. If they were in Children's Aid, you'd be paying $550 a month to support them." (*The Toronto Star*, January 19, 1984, p. 1.) Her analysis is correct.

Other examples of policies derived from a patriarchal model of the family include welfare policies which restrict family benefits to single *mothers* and children (as is still the case in some Canadian provinces, although no longer in most of them — it used to be the case in all), but to which single *fathers* and children are not entitled.

With respect to economic policies, all policies intentionally or unintentionally favouring male over female wage earners conform to a patriarchal model of the family. The distinction between "primary" and "secondary" earner, for instance, expresses an assumption about differential economic responsibilities within families. This becomes even more obvious when looking at policies aimed at "dependents."

For instance, in a recent case brought before the Canadian Human Rights Commission, two Nova Scotia women taking adult vocational training under a Canada Employment and Immigration program

> were not paid the training allowance normally paid to persons supporting dependents because CEIC regulations were interpreted to mean that their husbands were supporting the household. In fact neither man was regularly employed and both women considered that they were supporting their families while taking the training courses. After conciliation, CEIC revised its interpretation of the regulation involved. A family member will be considered to be supporting the household if he or she had the largest income during the last 12 months *and* is fully employed during the training period in question. Because neither complainant's husband meets both of these criteria, the women have been accepted as supporting their families. As part of the settlement, one of the complainants received additional benefits. The other complainant's allowance had already been adjusted while she was still on the course. (Human Rights Commission, 1981:6–7.)

To give one last example from the area of fiscal policy, the marital exemption which allows an income-earning spouse to claim his (or her) non-income-earning spouse as a dependent and thereby receive a reduction in taxes in effect translates into a tax bonus for husbands whose wives are housewives.

Problems with using the patriarchal model as a basis for forming social policy are manifold, but the most important one is that the assumption of female dependency that underlies it is not only outdated, in many instances it would also be unconstitutional, now that Canada has enshrined the principle of sex equality in its Constitution.[12] The whole notion of differential responsibilities for husbands and wives, mothers and fathers is highly restrictive and, where it is strictly applied, continues to generate the dependence of women on a husband/father, thus denying equal opportunity for women and resulting in poverty when, as is usual, the woman outlives the man.

Other types of problems stemming from the use of a patriarchal model of the family come into play in the case of divorce. According to the patriarchal model, the man is responsible for the family's economic well-being. A logical extension is that such responsibility continues beyond the duration of the marriage, for the ex-wives in the form of alimony, for the children in the form of child support. A reasonable judicial stance derived from such a model would be that a full-time housewife and mother would be entitled to continue in those roles after the divorce, and be supported in this by her ex-husband. Yet let us assume that the man remarries, as is usually the case. Does his new wife also have the right to be supported by him? Likely the question will not become an issue until the man and his new wife have a child together. Where, as is likely, the man would not have enough income to support two families totally, we have two competing and incompatible sets of demands on his income. If the support obligation towards his first family is reduced because of his changed circumstances, his first wife and his first set of children are penalized, although nothing in *their* situation has changed. On the other hand, if the support payments to the first family remain the same (and presumably the man's income as well), then the second wife may be forced to get a job so that the first wife can be a housewife. Given that in Canada the likelihood of a marriage ending in divorce is around 40 percent and that most divorced men remarry, this is clearly an important problem.

It should be noted that the current divorce law assumes that ex-spouses will be financially self-supporting as soon as is possible. It therefore conforms to the individual responsibility model, and not any longer to the patriarchal model.

Overall, the patriarchal model of the family is clearly *not* an acceptable basis for social policies, due to its inherent assumptions about female dependency, unevenness of female-male responsibilities and rights, and the increasing number of households in which family and household membership are non-congruent, leading to competing and irreconcilable demands on a man's income, and often to female poverty.

If all this is assumed to be so, how useful is the individual responsibility model of the family as a basis for social policy?

(B) Problems Associated with the Individual Responsibility Model of the Family as a Basis for Social Policy

In Canada, the movement towards the adoption of the individual responsibility model coincides with women's greatly increased participation in the labour force. This partial shift, both where it has

occurred and where it has not, is in itself a very significant development which should be explored in its own right in more detail. However, here the focus will be placed on problems associated with the use
of this model as a basis for social policy.

The first set of problems arises because of the very fact that society
is currently in a transitional stage concerning sex roles, while the second set derives from the continuing monolithic assumptions contained
in this model and shared with the patriarchal model.

As far as the first set of problems is concerned, Canadian society is
slowly moving from an overall patriarchal structure to one based on
the notion of sex equality, though this transition is by no means complete. But it is necessary to point out that, where, for instance, women
have unequal access to economic means, it may be highly unfair to
treat them as if they were equal. For example, to argue that a woman
who has been married for 30 years and who has been a housewife all
that time should be able to support herself after a divorce is patently
unjust, because she is no longer young and has no relevant job experience or training. This set of problems can be resolved by creating
policies which in the long term are based on sex equality but in the
short term recognize and make allowances for historically determined
differences (for an exposition on this issue, see Eichler, 1983:129–134).

The second set of problems is similar to those encountered in the
patriarchal model of the family, and not surprisingly, since they derive
from the same source. Both models have been seen to share three
assumptions, namely that household and family are assumed to be
congruent, that spouses and parents are equated, and that the family
is treated as the smallest unit of administration.

Let us come back to the previous issue of an unmarried woman with
dependent children on family benefits. If the law is adjusted so that
both fathers and mothers become eligible for these benefits, and so
that female as well as male partners become liable for support payments (as is currently the case in Ontario), the law conforms to the
individual responsibility model rather than to the patriarchal model
of the family. However, the problems associated with this policy
remain; they have merely been extended to males as well.

In effect, people on family benefits are prohibited from establishing
a new husband-wife family unless they find a partner willing to assume
financial responsibility, not only for the person on benefits, but also
for her or his children. Given that, under the new family law in
Ontario, a spouse, including a common-law spouse, may acquire a
permanent obligation towards a dependent child simply by virtue of

having treated this child as a dependent at some point in time, whether or not there is a biological relationship, this constitutes a tremendous financial burden on the solvent spouse. Assuming that most welfare agencies hold the ideal of the husband-wife family as preferable to a one-parent household for the children, we then run into a double bind: welfare payments for one-parent households are meant to alleviate their special circumstances, but, because of the way the policies are written, they may actively discourage a move to a husband-wife household.

However, let us consider the alternative. Let us assume that a mother or father would continue to be eligible for benefits even though having, in effect, established a common-law relationship with a person of the other sex, or having married her or him legally. Now let us assume that the new partner has a decent job and income, of the same type as a neighbour who also has two children, but whose spouse would not be eligible for family benefits because their children are the biological children of their marriage. In such a situation, the state would be supporting one type of family and not another in similar circumstances. Potentially, it would contribute to marriage breakups, because it would be financially preferable for a woman to live with a man who was not the father of her children. Clearly, this is not an equitable way to approach the problem either.

If we turn to fiscal policy, the marital exemption is a tax benefit financed out of general tax revenues, and therefore paid for by all taxpayers, including the majority of Canadian wives and husbands in the labour force earning an income and paying tax on it. The benefit is received primarily by a husband with a dependent wife. Presumably, the husband receives household services from his wife. He is subsidized (1) by all single women and men who have a paying job, pay taxes, and do not receive household services from a spouse; (2) by male taxpayers whose wives are not housewives, and who therefore, presumably, have to do a bit more of the housework themselves, and (3) by married women with jobs who remain primarily responsible for household work, in practice if not in law.

On the other hand, mothers with paying jobs can deduct up to $2,000 per year of childcare costs per child under certain circumstances, which constitutes a substantial tax bonus available only to two-earner couples or income-earning one-parent households, but not to one-earner households in which the mother stays home to look after her children. Here is the double bind operating on new grounds, since many people still consider a mother looking after her children on a full-time basis the ideal childcare arrangement; nevertheless, this type of family may receive less public support than the family in which the mother holds a paying job, although they may be in as much need.

Overall, then, while the individual responsibility model is more acceptable than the patriarchal model of the family as a basis for social policy, still, in a situation dealing with diversity in family structures, policies geared toward families of a particular type will inevitably discriminate against families of some other type. This will happen as long as the basic unit of administration remains the family rather than the individual.

Two assumptions lie at the root of the problem: (1) that families have an obligation to support their members economically as well as to provide the physical and emotional care for members in need of it, and (2) the conflicting ideal of equality between the sexes. Within families, some unpaid work is carried out that is crucial, socially necessary, and takes time, which, if devoted to these tasks, cannot be used for earning money: namely, care of dependent children or of dependent adults unable to care for themselves because of illness or handicap. In the patriarchal model of the family, this work was traditionally carried out by women, without pay, and was therefore seen as being economically unimportant, valueless, and unproblematic, since the woman was thought of as a dependent, not an economic contributor. In the individual responsibility model, the need for this work still persists—after all, somebody has to look after the children and the sick. But since the woman is now presumed to be also engaged in economically valuable tasks, i.e., earning money, if she uses her time instead to look after children and/or adults in need of care, it becomes obvious that this task is costing money in the form of salary the woman forgoes. Alternatively, if parents hire someone to look after their children, they will be paying for a service that formerly *seemed* to be available for free, although this was nothing but a side effect of ignoring a woman's socially useful work performed within the home.

If women are supposed to be responsible for their own economic well-being (and potentially for that of others, as well) someone else will have to take over those socially useful tasks that women have traditionally performed (and continue to perform) within the home. Alternatively, unless someone else takes over these tasks, women with children are not free to earn money and therefore to look after their own and potentially others' economic well-being. This is the nature of the hidden sexism in the individual responsibility model of the family, which in concept is non-sexist but which in effect remains sexist by imposing an impossible, in principle unsolvable, task on women (and on men when these same expectations are extended to them).

In other words, if women are to do their share in supporting themselves and the family economically, then the tasks of raising the children and looking after adults in need of care must also be shared between society and the parents in the case of children, and rest solely with society in the case of adults in need of care.

This is hardly a new insight, since the Report of the Royal Commission on the Status of Women in Canada (1970:xii) already stated at its outset that ". . . the care of children is a responsibility to be shared by the mother, the father and society. Unless this shared responsibility is acknowledged and assumed, women cannot be accorded true equality."

The support function of the family must therefore be reconsidered and reformulated. Defining a family's need of support from the state in terms of its structure (whether there is, or is not, a husband in the family, for instance) discriminates against those families that need economic support but don't show the same structural characteristics. And this is linked with the definition of the appropriate unit of administration: where the family is taken as the unit of administration, people in need can be (and are) disentitled from public support on the basis of their family status.

It therefore seems appropriate to develop yet another model of the family, one which would allow for sex equality without creating a paradox. I have called this model "The Social Responsibility Model of the Family."

The Social Responsibility Model of the Family

It is inevitable that, when policies treat people administratively as members of families rather than as individuals, they either openly or inadvertently discriminate against some types of families. This is bound to happen when we are dealing with the mix of families that currently exists in most highly industrialized countries, and certainly in Canada.

The proper response to this problem would be to treat people *administratively* as *individuals*. it may seem a contradiction that, in order to facilitate equal treatment for all types of families, the individual should be used as the basic administrative unit for transfer purposes, and not the family. However, the logic of it is apparent in a review of examples: at present, OAS (Old Age Security) is provided to every individual Canadian over the age of 65, irrespective of marital status. By contrast, GIS (the Guaranteed Income Supplement) is a prop-up payment available to individuals or to couples on the basis of their joint income. As the joint income increases, the GIS payment decreases, until it reaches a threshold beyond which one is not eligible for GIS.

The payment level is determined by marital status. An unmarried person receives a higher payment than one-half of the payment to a married couple, in recognition that it is relatively more expensive to live as a single person than as a couple. However, one of the consequences of this policy is that two unmarried elderly women living together will be collectively entitled to more money than an elderly married couple living together. A policy constructed with a particular family model in mind thus inadvertently ends up discriminating against a married couple.

Returning to the case of a mother who receives family benefits: under the social responsibility model she would be entitled to child support irrespective of whether she were living with a man, legally or otherwise. Moreover, in order that parents who are not living with their biological children would not receive more support than parents who are, equal child support would have to be available to nuclear families. The assumptions attached to the social responsibility model of the family would obviate the anomalies that arise from differences in family situations:

1. Every adult would be considered responsible for his or her own economic well-being. Where this was impossible, the support obligation would shift to the state, not to a family member.
2. For an adult in need of care, whether because of a permanent or temporary illness or handicap (including senility), it would become the responsibility of the state (not of a family member) to pay for the cost of such care.
3. The cost of raising children would be shared by the father, the mother, and the state, irrespective of the marital status of the parents.

These three principles are sufficient as a basis for creating social and economic policies that would avoid the overt sexist bias of the patriarchal model of the family and the paradox inherent in both the patriarchal and individual responsibility models.

By implication, of course, such a model of the family would not assume congruence of household and family membership; it would take, not the family as the smallest administrative unit, but the individual; nor would it assume that a spouse (common-law or legal) necessarily equals a parent and that a non-spouse cannot be a parent. It would furthermore be based on the notion of sex equality and on the notion of societal responsibility for people in need of care, that is, dependent children and handicapped or sick adults.

In what way could such a policy still be called a family policy? In the same way in which family allowances are presently part of a family-oriented policy. The family allowance system in Canada is already premissed on the principles detailed above; it recognizes a societal contribution to be made to the care of children to which the children as individuals are entitled: they keep the right to this benefit no matter who raises them nor in what type of family structure, one-parent, two-parent, guardian, or whatever. As children shift from one adult responsible for them to another, their family benefits follow them.

However, the societal contribution made through family allowances is tiny, and if we were to reformulate our social policies according to the principles stated above, it would necessitate a substantial reorientation in social welfare policies, judicial policies concerning support payments, and economic policies. Some of the social implications of using such a model of the family as a basis for social welfare policies will be considered now, then afterwards, some of the implications they have for economic policies.

Anticipated Consequences of Using the Social Responsibility Model of the Family for Social Welfare Policies

At present, people are entitled to social welfare if they are unable to work and do not live with a spouse who has an income: *or* if they are mothers (parents, in some provinces) and the other parent is unable and/or unwilling to pay for the children's support; *and* if they do not live as part of a couple, whether or not their partner is willing to pay for their support and the children's. If we applied the social responsibility model of the family, on the other hand, people would be entitled to social welfare if they were unable to work, irrespective of whether they were living with a spouse with an income, just as is currently the case in Canada with Unemployment Insurance and Old Age Security, which are paid to the individual regardless of that person's family status. For these two programs, the individual rather than the family is already taken as the administrative unit.

The issue becomes more complicated as we move to the care of dependent children. The cost of raising children involves two distinct components: money needed to pay for the necessities of life—food, shelter, clothing, etc.,—and money needed to pay for the work involved in caring for them. The second component can vary independently from the first, since children are already publicly cared for some of the time when they attend public schools. Since my model suggests that childcare should be a responsibility shared between the parents and the state, one can conceptualize the care function of the state as paying for the cost of care for eight hours a day, five days a week (that is, equivalent to a full-time job) and the care function of the parents as resting with the other 16 hours of the day and night and the two days of the weekend.

Mothers (or fathers, where appropriate) would therefore receive state support which would consist of a care allowance, pro-rated by whatever portion of the eight hours a day, five days a week the state is already paying for the care of the children. If we further assume that such care allowances would be paid to all mothers (or fathers) irrespective of whether they were living with someone who was or was not a parent of the children, and irrespective of whether they had a paying job, we would finally have avoided that double bind which goes with combining the support principle and the assumption that the family is the logical administrative unit. If both parents had paying jobs, moreover, they would be handing over the care allowance *in toto* to a day-care centre or caretaker; if either the mother or the father were at home, that parent would retain the care allowance as a wage replacement.

Welfare mothers would therefore largely disappear as a category, the only difference being that they would receive the difference in the cost of raising children which other people would not receive.

A similar scheme could be instituted for adults in need of care, who would also receive a care allowance to be handed on to whoever provided the care, whether a family member or not. The one drawback to such an approach, and it is a considerable one, is that such a policy would inevitably be expensive.

Anticipated Consequences of Using the Social Responsibility Model of the Family for Economic Policies

If every adult were considered responsible for his or her own economic support, then it would follow that not only must all economic policies strive to attract women and men equally into the labour force but, in addition, they would need to be devised to overcome the barriers some groups of women encounter when trying to enter or re-enter the labour market. Special policies would therefore have to be worked out to facilitate this process. The most serious impediment to equal participation of women and men in the labour market, however, is current levels of unemployment. Still, a case could be made that unemployment is not necessary, and that a full employment policy based on political and institutional commitment, full participation, and decentralization could generate sufficient jobs for all those who want to have a job (see Bellemare in cooperation with Eichler, 1983, for a detailed exposition of this argument).

Such a policy would require, first and foremost, a strong political commitment to achieving full employment in Canada. Concretely, a multiplicity of means could be used (and would need to be) simultaneously to achieve this result. For one, available work could be shared through extending vacation entitlements, allowing employees the option of working at 80 percent of their pay for four years and receiving the fifth year off, also at 80 percent pay, while maintaining all their fringe benefits and seniority. (This option is currently available to members of teachers' federations.) Finally, educational leave could be strongly fostered through employer/government cooperation.

A second avenue consists in the creation of new jobs, particularly in five sectors which are highly labour-intensive and in which expansion would neither constitute a further risk to the environment nor involve the maintenance of outdated methods of production. These five sectors are education, the arts, social services, sports, and pollution-reduction activities.

Third, the labour market would need to be restructured so that it could become more flexible. Among other things, this would involve reducing the distinction between full- and part-time work, vesting all pensions automatically and immediately, creating mechanisms to recognize the experience of workers in *non-related* jobs, and, once again, introducing educational leaves on a large-scale basis.

Fourth, socially useful work performed in the home (i.e., care of people who are unable to look after themselves, such as dependent children and handicapped or sick adults) would need to be recognized as work and treated as such.

In the context of a full employment policy, successfully instituted, care allowances such as those proposed above would become financially feasible. Under such a policy, unemployment costs would be drastically reduced, and, besides, most of those people now receiving benefits would not only no longer receive benefits but pay taxes themselves. Part of the monies could be used to finance the societal contribution to childcare and the care of the aged.

CONCLUSION

Contemporary families in highly industrialized countries share several predominant traits: discrepancies between household and family membership, with resulting inter-household economic obligations, a mix of earning patterns, and a mix of one-parent households and husband-wife families.

There are specific consequences of these patterns for social welfare and economic policies, given that two main principles underlie present policies: namely a non-interference principle and the family-as-administrative-unit principle. These principles are inherent in two *implicit* models of the family inherent in social policies, the patriarchal and the individual responsibility models of the family. While the latter is non-sexist in intention and format, it is nonetheless still premissed on a conception of the family that does not take the family's actual variety into account. Both models present a paradox: the contradiction, given current diversity in family styles, that goes with combining the non-interference principle with taking the family as the smallest administrative unit. This results in discrimination against some types of families.

A third model, the theoretical model of social responsibility, is therefore more appropriate as a basis for contemporary welfare and economic policies. One of the implications for such an approach would be that the difference between economic policy and family policy in issues involving money would disappear. The issue would have to be thought through separately for non-money policies such as those involving zoning (what constitutes a household) or immigration policies (whom one can sponsor to immigrate), to name just two examples.

Another implication would be that *all* families would receive societal support, regardless of their composition or structure. This would take care of the dilemma of whether societal support should go to "working mothers" or to "mothers at home," since support would be tied to the child, and not to whether the mother was part of the labour force. In a time of great variability of family styles, and with no indication that the current process will become any simpler, anything else is unacceptable, since the state should not determine styles of living together in a democratic society.

Further, policies based on the social responsibility model would allow full involvement of fathers as well as mothers in childcare, assuming that any care allowance would be available to either parent.

Most importantly, implementing social policies that start from the notion that care for people in need of care is a social responsibility, rather than a private one, is a precondition for a humane society.

NOTES

1. Cf. Emily Nett, "Canadian Families in Social-Historical Perspective," (1981) 6 *Canadian Journal of Sociology*, pp. 239–260.
2. For trend data and 1960 data, see Margrit Eichler, *Families in Canada Today: Recent Changes and Their Policy Consequences*. Toronto: Gage, 1983, p. 37, t. 2.2. For 1985 data, see Canada: Statistics Canada, *Vital Statistics*, Vol. 1, Births and Deaths 1985, Catalogue 84-204, Ottawa, Minister of Supply and Services, 1986.
3. Canada: Statistics Canada, *Population Projections for Canada and the Provinces*, 1976-2001. Ottawa, Statistics Canada, 1979.
4. For 1967 and trend data, see Eichler, 1983, *op. cit.*, pp. 232–233, t. 7.7. For 1985, see Canada, Statistics Canada, Vital Statistics, Vol. II Marriages and Divorces, Catalogue 84-205, 1986.
5. For 1960 and trend data, see Eichler, 1983, *op. cit.*, p. 206, t. 7.2. Figures for 1987 were calculated for Canada: Statistics Canada, *Vital Statistics*, Vol. I, Births and Deaths, Catalogue 84-204, 1986.
6. Economic Council of Canada, *On the Mend, Twentieth Annual Review* 1983, Ottawa, Minister of Supply and Services, 1983, p. 90.
7. Ibid.
8. Cf. National Council of Welfare, *One in a World of Two's* (A Report by the National Council of Welfare on One-Parent Families in Canada). Ottawa, National Council of Welfare, 1976. For the argument, see Canada: Statistics Canada, *Canada's Lone-Parent Families*, Catalogue 99-933. Ottawa, Minister of Supply and Services, 1984, for the most recent figures.
9. Cf. Sylvia Ostry, *The Female Worker in Canada* (One of a series of labour force studies in the 1961 Census Monograph Programme), Ottawa, Dominion Bureau of Statistics, 1968.
10. See Eichler, 1983, *op. cit.*, p. 170, t. 6.1.

CHAPTER 5

Socialization and Parenting

GEOFFREY TESSON

INTRODUCTION

Like many other terms that are used in a specialized sense, the word "socialization" does not have the same meaning for sociologists that it does in ordinary discourse. Within sociology, "socialization" refers to the process by which we learn the ways of a given society or social group so that we can function within it (Elkin and Handel, 1978). It thus refers to the range of changes that occur from the time a helpless, dependent, young infant begins life and as it progresses through the various stages that lead to full adult membership in society. For sociologists, socialization has a special significance since, not only does its outcome ensure an important element of continuity between generations, it can also be an important source of change. When we raise our children we are, in effect, creating a future society and, while perhaps we have fewer choices than we imagine in how we carry out that task, the choices we do make are critical for determining the character of the society that will follow us.

A distinctly sociological approach to socialization will be followed in this chapter. Much of the literature on children is written from a psychological point of view, yet, while there is a lot of value in this material, it does not give us the whole nor the same picture. What, then, is characteristic of a sociological approach? In the first place, sociologists are concerned, not just with individual relationships, but with *patterns* of relationships. A great deal of popular and some academic literature on children is written from the point of view of what kind of family environment is best for the child. Such a perspective considers the child as a passive recipient of environmental influences, and focuses on how those influences can best be planned for. The sociological approach has a broader focus, and considers each member of the family as part of an interactive system. We have to think of, not only the effect that parents have on their children, but also the effect that children have on their parents. The issue then shifts from the child-centred "What is best for the child?" to the more interactive "What is best for the child or children and parents, considered as a whole?"

Our understanding of children is often hampered by a myopic focus on the individual family, as if it were a self-contained unit insulated from the influence of the surrounding social forces. A sociological perspective attempts to understand how society at large affects the family and especially the parent-child relationship. This means, for example, that it is important to stress such factors as class and income as they affect what occurs within the family; we have to stop treating family issues as if they were the result of personal problems, and see them as societal issues.

CHANGING PATTERNS OF CHILDHOOD

Compared to today's parents, mothers and fathers of families in pre-industrial times appear to have been markedly indifferent toward their offspring. In our society, children hold a very important place within the family, parents often willingly relegating their own needs to second place behind those of their children. Certain earlier practices seem to testify, not only to a lack of affection for children, but often to cruelty toward them. The practice of "swaddling" infants, for example, common at least up until the 16th century (Shorter, 1975), involved wrapping the infant tightly in a bandage which restricted any movement, inhibited circulation, and generally induced a state of stupor in the child (De Mause, 1974:37). Its chief function seems to have been that of obviating the need for constant care of infants who could then be left for hours unattended while their parents went about their daily tasks. Further evidence of indifference is supplied by the practice, most common in France, of putting newborn children out to a wet-nurse. Parents from better-off families would place their infant in the charge of a country woman who would nurse the child until it was weaned. It is clear that some parents took hardly any interest in their offspring until they were returned to them (Shorter, 1975: 175-181).

The death of a child which, for us, comes as a terrible human tragedy, was accepted with apparent equanimity in pre-industrial society. "What kind of people were these," asks Shorter (1975: 173), "who did not even attend the funerals of their deceased infants?"

There is also evidence of considerable physical cruelty directed toward children. The psycho-historian Lloyd De Mause has maintained that the history of childhood shows how much children have been the object of sheer brutality. "The history of childhood," he writes, "is a nightmare from which we have only recently begun to awaken. The further back in history one goes, the lower the level of child care, and the more likely children are to be killed, abandoned, beaten, terrorized and sexually abused" (De Mause, 1974: 1). His account provides a long catalogue of infanticide, neglect, and physical and sexual cruelty toward children. While this portrayal is undoubtedly overdrawn, it is nevertheless reasonable to conclude that physical punishment, often for only minor infractions and sometimes out of sheer spite or frustration, was the norm rather than the exception for most children in the pre-industrial era.

It is necessary, however, to understand the behaviour described here in the context of the nature of society at that time. Thus Shorter (1975) notes that, "Children were brutalized by the daily routines of life as much as by savage outbursts of parental rage" (170); and the English historian, Lawrence Stone (1979), makes the following observation:

> They were in the habit of treating their children occasionally with rough, even extravagant affection in good times, and with casual indifference, and not infrequently with great brutality in drink or in bad times. If they were cruel to their children, it was because they needed to vent their frustrations on somebody, or because they failed to foresee the consequences of their actions, or because that was the way they themselves had been brought up, and they therefore regarded it as the normal and proper method of rearing children (295).

It is tempting to see such treatment of children as De Mause (1974) does, as a form of collective savagery on the part of parents rather than as a response to harsh conditions, and to assume that we ourselves have reached a state of civilization where such treatment is no longer conceivable. However, the growing recognition that a great deal of family violence goes unacknowledged in our own society (Propper, 1984) should curb any feelings of moral superiority (see Chapter 9).

The process of industrialization was accompanied by the growth of what Stone (1979) calls "affective individualism," especially within the context of the family. This process involved four components. First, it meant a decline in authoritarianism in the parental treatment of children, who were allowed an increasing freedom of action. Second, the nuclear family became more detached from the interference of both other relations and the surrounding community. Third, relations between parents and children became more warmly affectionate, as did those between husband and wife. Lastly, children acquired a special status distinct from adults.

These changes were parallelled by a transformation of the economic world from an agrarian system governed largely by feudal traditions to an industrial system regulated by the abstract impersonal mechanisms of the market. Work became increasingly separated from the family, and the family became the locus of more intimate interpersonal relationships. This set the scene for what the historian Christopher Lasch (1977) terms the growing divorce between the private sphere of the family and the public and competitive sphere of the world of work. There remains an important link between the two spheres however, since, as Howard Gadlin (1978) has shown, the shift in parenting patterns from a rigid authoritarianism, aimed at producing conformity to traditional standards, to a focus on the development of the child as a distinct, self-regulating individual is more likely to produce young adults with the mental and personal autonomy needed for functioning within the social anarchy of the labour market.

The other trend that Lasch (1977) has emphasized is the increasing role played by non-family agencies in the socialization of the child. The most important of these is the educational system, which takes over from the family the task of preparing the child for the adult world of work; but health care and social welfare agencies also carry out more and more functions previously the sole responsibility of parents.

One lesson that can be drawn from reviewing these changes is that the nature of interpersonal relations in general, and specifically those between parents and their children, is closely connected with the organization of work in society. This insight was spelled out by David Riesman in the 1950s. His views are quite pertinent to understanding changes we are currently undergoing. Riesman argued that a shift in occupations from production and extraction to the administrative, clerical, and service sectors has led to a changing pattern of personality types from "inner directed" to "other directed." This shift entails a change from a rigid character structure to one which is more responsive to the expectations of others. According to Riesman, this change came about as parents, uncertain what traits to encourage in their children, opted for the development of social flexibility.

ASPECTS OF SOCIALIZATION

As Elkin and Handel (1978) point out, it is somewhat misleading to speak of *the* process of socialization as if it were a single phenomenon. It would be more realistic to think of socialization as involving a number of different processes which are interrelated, but which have to be studied separately if they are to be understood. Indeed, socialization itself may be understood as part of a more general process of development, including everything from physical growth to the most complex patterns of cultural learning. In a review of a broad range of developmental theories, Reese and Overton (1970) discern two contrasting models: those which focus on internal, biologically driven processes, and those which depict development as a learned response to features of the external social environment. This is one way of describing the "nature versus nurture" controversy, which makes it appear as if the relative balance of biological and social factors were an issue to take sides on. Nowadays, most theorists take an interactionist view, seeing both biological and environmental factors as contributing to development, and focusing on patterns of interaction between the two (Featherman and Lerner, 1985; Maccoby, 1984). Physiologically based processes provide the infrastructure on which more variable and environmentally controlled processes are constructed.

"Maturation" refers to biologically programmed changes that are relatively independent of the environment. Physical growth, for example, is largely a maturational process, as is the completion of neurological circuits necessary for such behaviours as walking and speech production. Processes like physical growth require a certain amount of help from the child's environment, such as an adequate diet and a minimum level of physical exercise but, beyond that, the outcomes are largely genetically pre-determined. Other processes, such as the onset of walking, are more environmentally sensitive and can, once the basic muscular and co-ordinating capacity is established, be stimulated through encouragement (Zelazo, et al., 1972). The onset of secondary sex characteristics which occurs during puberty may also be thought of as a maturational process triggered after a certain time-delay by hormonal secretions. However, maturation alone is not responsible for the patterns of sex-typed behaviour that emerge during this period; these are profoundly influenced by the models provided within the whole structured pattern of gender roles within society. Maturation is a necessary condition for socialization, but it is not sufficient for defining the structure of the increasingly complex patterns that characterize adult behaviour. At the most it provides us with a kind of timetable for certain states of readiness.

"Cognitive development" refers to the emergence of patterns of thinking in children. It is best described within the "stage" theory of the Swiss psychologist, Jean Piaget (Piaget and Inhelder, 1969). The stages represent different levels at which thinking processes are organized, focusing in the early years on motor co-ordination (sensory-motor period), in the middle years on the development of symbolic thought (pre-operational concrete and concrete-operational periods) and in adolescence on formal logical structures (formal operational period). These progressive stages in the development of children's thinking tell us that patterns of thought are organized differently at different ages; in other words, we learn something about the internal characteristics of children's minds. They also reveal something about the culture that is the source of the language and symbols with which the mind operates: the stages of a child's intellectual development are not just internal or maturational events; they also reflect an increasing pattern of interaction with the social environment.

Cognition can be considered the foundation on which other more specific skills and developmental patterns become grafted. Social rules, which govern behaviour throughout different relationships and make behaviour within those relationships more predictable, are internalized in the form of cultural norms (Parsons, 1955). But, when social rules are acquired, they possess an important cognitive component, because they have to be assimilated to a more general pattern of social understanding (Schantz, 1983). A study of the development of social understanding in children carried out by the author and his colleagues showed that children operate with a large repertoire of social rules governing such interactions as compliance with authority, asserting their own autonomy, managing communication, and coping with social conflict (Tesson, Lewko, and Bigelow, 1987). From quite a young age, children realize that doing what they are told has to be balanced off against standing up for their rights and opinions, and that there are some people whom one can tell about personal experiences and others who are to be avoided or ignored. The development of social understanding in children appears to take the form of making increasingly discriminating judgments about how to act with different people.

Elliot Turiel makes the distinction between the rules that serve as social conventions in particular situations, such as table manners or the proper way to address a daycare worker, and those functioning as more general moral values, such as not harming other children (Turiel, 1983). Turiel's young subjects were quite aware of the arbitrary nature of social conventions, but considered moral rules, involving more general principles such as fairness or justice, to be more absolute in nature and to transcend any particular social situation. This raises an interesting question as to whether moral rules have a universal quality, or whether they are nothing more than general social conventions.

Lawrence Kohlberg (1969) has studied the development of moral thinking in children, showing a pattern which parallels the cognitive stages found by Piaget. He maintains that children's moral judgments show an increasing tendency to be based on abstract principles of justice which, in the final stage, override social and legal considerations. His research has given rise to considerable controversy about whether his study of highly select groups gives him the right to claim the discovery of universal standards of moral thinking. Critics distinguish both a cultural bias (Simpson, 1974) and a gender bias (Gilligan, 1982) to his views. The fact that Kohlberg's stages were developed from a study involving only American males makes him vulnerable to this charge, particularly when it becomes obvious that groups not included in his sample do not readily satisfy the criteria for attainment of the higher stages.

Another important component of socialization is the development of a conception of the self as an independent and autonomous entity. Mead (1934) has described this as a product of the child's interactions with "significant others." This means that other people, particularly those whose opinion we value, play an important part in shaping the way we see ourselves. The development of an independent sense of self is one of the central aims of socialization, since it represents freedom from both psychological and actual dependence on parents and others that began with the newborn's total dependence on its caretakers. As mature adults, we must be able to think for ourselves, initiate actions, support ourselves economically, and make a broad range of political and legal decisions. The actual growth of independence is associated with an inner feeling of the self as not a follower but an initiator, able to make decisions and take control over one's own life.

Gender identity, the sense we have of ourselves as male or female, is an important part of the self which, like other personality characteristics, has an internal and an external component. On the one hand, gender is experienced as a very personal and private thing, part of the inner sense of self. On the other hand, gender reflects not only current social stereotypes but also the pattern of gender roles within society. Gender roles are undergoing fairly rapid change as more and more women enter the labour market. Since 1980, more than 50 percent of Canadian women have been involved in the labour force (Armstrong and Armstrong, 1983); in the generation since World War II, married women's participation has increased five-fold (Mackie, 1986). While fewer women are part of the labour force than men, even now (Armstrong and Armstrong, 1983), children increasingly have first-hand experience of an alternative role model for women other than the traditional roles of wife and mother.

Finally, it is important not to neglect the socialization of individuals into macro-social structures, the shaping of the individual into the occupational and other economic and legal institutions of adult society. Relatively little work has been done to show how the pattern of early socialization in the family prepares the child for understanding the complex economic, political, and legal concepts associated with industrial societies. A study by Hans Furth (1980) traces the development in children of such notions as where money comes from and how people become political leaders. In particular, Furth studied the emergence of the concept of the separation of role and person which is a key feature of formal social organization. Young children, for example, simply cannot understand that their teachers have lives of their own. As regards socialization into the world of work, Zelizer (1985) has pointed out that it is one of the distinguishing features of the modern family that children are systematically excluded by child labour legislation from gainful employment. A recent study of American teenagers by Greenberger and Steinberg (1986) suggests that when adolescents do work, it contributes little to their development. Not only does it tend to diminish their level of educational performance, it also adds little to family income, most of the money earned being spent on teenage luxuries. While a small number of children who grow up in farming families or in small family businesses may share in their parents' productive activity, the experience of the large majority seems to bear out Lasch's depiction of the family as an essentially private domain insulated from the public sphere of production.

THE LIFE CYCLE AND THE EXPANDING CIRCLE OF RELATIONSHIPS

The process of socialization can be viewed as one in which the child becomes integrated into an ever-expanding network of relationships and structures. Because family patterns can vary considerably (many children now grow up in single-parent families, some have siblings, some do not, and others may live with half-siblings in a reconstituted family after divorce), it should be borne in mind that there is no single construction that can represent the socializing influences affecting all children. Starting with the intimate and emotionally intense relationship of the newborn infant with its mother or other chief caregiver, the growing child experiences more and more new relationships and structures which open up new opportunities for social interaction and impose quite different demands. Each new relationship adds another dimension to the child's social world. Thus, if the mother is the primary caregiver, then the father represents a different kind of challenge, not only because he may act differently toward the child than the mother does, but also because he has to be integrated into an already existing relationship.

Similarly, siblings and peers have to be incorporated into the growing network of relationships, with each in turn adding to the complexity of the child's social world; again, this is not only just because they are different, but also because the demands they place on the child have to be reconciled with the demands already exerted by the previous relationships.

Entry into daycare or school represents a further level of complexity, because the child is now confronted with formal standards of behaviour, especially those related to academic success and failure, whose scope extends beyond face-to-face interaction. Daycare clearly serves to cushion the effects of the transition to school which represents the child's first encounter with the world of formal bureaucracy. Throughout childhood, trying to please one's friends by acquiescing in what they want to do, for example, may lead to antagonizing one's parents, who find this behaviour unacceptable. The more people there are with whom to interact, the more often this kind of conflict has to be resolved. As the child moves into adolescence, it becomes increasingly important, moreover, to be able to understand and function within the systems of the market, the law, and the government. Socialization proceeds at all these levels of development; it is not just limited to the early stages of life.

Problems of adapting to a growing network of relationships are compounded for the increasing number of children whose parents divorce (see Chapter 8). If we take the view that the child's social relationships are grounded in a pattern of secure attachment with its parents (Maccoby, 1980), then if the parental bond is threatened or severed, the child has to start from the ground up again, in addition to coping with the new economic status and changing patterns of friendship that are likely to emerge after divorce. These problems are undoubtedly, as Richardson notes, insufficiently researched. It is especially important that we start looking at them from the child's own perspective: children may be more resilient than we think, but we will not really know unless we take their own accounts of their experiences seriously.

The child's environment is not static, but is constantly changing and imposing new demands. It therefore makes sense to view the process of socialization largely as a response to these changing demands. This is called the "life-course approach" to the study of socialization (Elder, 1984; Featherman and Lerner, 1985). Within this approach, a child's age not only marks the general stages of development such as infancy, childhood, and adolescence (and as they are defined more formally within the psychological stage theories of Piaget (Piaget and Inhelder, 1969) or Kohlberg (1969)) it also connects with the various contexts of the child's social environment. Thus the new patterns of reasoning that emerge in middle childhood can be viewed both as a function of psychological development and also as a response to the school environment. Similarly, as will be discussed further, later, the expanded peer network the child encounters on entering school provides the opportunity for both using and expanding the repertoire of social skills developed within the home environment.

As children grow, not only do they encounter different environments, the nature of those environments is undergoing change itself. As C. Wright Mills (1959) remarked, biography and history intersect in the lives of ordinary people. As we progress through stages of our own lives, we also proceed through a segment of history, within a particular society, economy, and political system. This historical determinism has not been well researched in relation to socialization, but it has been noted by Kanter (1977) that, with the passage of time, parents are subject to changing economic and occupational circumstances which can have an important bearing on their orientation to their children. It is not that high levels of satisfaction and security necessarily make good parents—perhaps children need some exposure to economic insecurity to prepare them for their own future—but that the stress and anxiety resulting from chronic economic uncertainty make it very hard to be the model parents that childcare books recommend. We also live in a culture which maintains a highly privatized conception of family responsibilities, so that there are relatively few sources parents can turn to for help.

One final point is especially important from a sociological view of socialization: it would be useful to have more studies devoted to understanding how changing economic circumstances affect the ways in which parents and children interact. This is not an area that has received a lot of attention, although Glen Elder's (1974) study of children who grew up during the Depression of the 30s provided valuable longitudinal data testifying to children's considerable resilience in the face of economic hardship. However, we do not know how prolonged periods of economic uncertainty affect parenting behaviour. Most children who grew up during the 50s and 60s could be assured that they would be better off than their parents, but there is little evidence to show that this trend can continue (Boyd et al., 1985). Children raised in regions of Canada where the economy is affected by a fluctuating market for resources must feel constant uncertainty about their future. A recent study of young people's attitudes towards the world of work carried out in Sudbury, Ontario, amid a large number of lay-offs in the mining community, showed a very negative orientation to work and, hardly surprisingly, a lack of a discernible work ethic (Pautler and Lewko, 1987).

The foregoing comments stressed the importance of the dynamics of the social environment in which socialization takes place. The following sections will focus on the role played by various crucial agents of socialization. The term "agents" is an important one, because in these roles people are not just individuals but representatives and carriers of external social currents. Because the focus here is on the family, our attention will be limited to the impact on children of their parents, siblings, and peers. This neglects the roles played by other agencies, such as television, the school, and various official bodies (concerned with children's welfare) for which space does not allow an adequate treatment. It is probably worth noting, however, that these influences impinge on a child already shaped in important ways by family factors; if we are to understand their impact, we must bear in mind the effects of interaction with prior influences.

PARENTS AND SOCIALIZATION

Within popular imagery, the family is made up of husband and wife living together in the same household with their biological children. Much of what has been written within the sociology of the family takes this constellation for granted. Yet failure to recognize the diverse forms of family life produces what Eichler (1983) calls the "monolithic bias" of this literature. The reality of family life in Canada is that the popular image is becoming more the exception than the rule.

The divorce rate, which reached 275.5 per 100,000 population in 1983 (see Chapter 8) means that more than 40 percent of all Canadian marriages end in divorce, a figure, as even government statisticians admit, which is probably "only the tip of the family and marriage dissolution iceberg" (McKie et al., 1983). A study by Furstenberg et al. (1983) carried out in the United States, where rates are even higher, revealed that one-third of those born between 1968 and 1969 had experienced family disruption as a result of their parents' divorce. Since three-quarters of divorced men and two-thirds of divorced women remarry (Ambert, 1984), this means that a substantial number of children grow up in reconstituted families. Others remain with single parents: in 1981, 11.3 percent of all families were headed up by a single parent, the large majority of them (82.6 percent) single mothers, although 11 percent of these had never married (Nett, 1986). Even those families which do not experience divorce stand outside the traditional stereotype in which the husband/father is responsible for economic support and the wife/mother is responsible for childcare and other household tasks. The majority of married women now work for pay and, although division of labour within households seems slow to change (Meissner et al., 1975), there are signs that the largest number of men believe they should participate in traditionally female tasks (Eichler, 1983: 83-86). The job of looking after young children also increasingly involves outsiders. A recent national survey showed that more than 50 percent of pre-schoolers were cared for in some shared childcare arrangement (Eichler, 1983: 249).

In speaking of parents and their effects on children, we have to keep in mind this heterogeneous nature of parenthood. The adults who care for a child may not be its biological parents, and a significant number of children have only one caregiver. Social-psychological studies which examine the nature of parent-child interactions often do not take this heterogeneity into account, and therefore readers should be cautious in drawing conclusions from them.

Parents are the most powerful single influence on their children, especially during the early stages of the socialization process. The nature of that influence is two-fold. On the one hand it lies in the detailed regulation of the day-to-day activity of the young child, whether carried out by the parents themselves or by another caregiver. On the other hand, the parents act as agents of transmission of general social characteristics. Because parents occupy a specific location within the social hierarchy, they pass on to their children, often quite unwittingly, the attitudes, social rules, and behaviour patterns that go with it.

Because parents exert such an important influence on their children's lives, and because they hold so much power over them, it is tempting to view their effect on children as absolute. But this would be misleading. Notwithstanding a child's relative powerlessness, children also have an important effect on their parents. Certainly the very fact of having children significantly influences decisions that adults make regarding such things as the jobs or careers they choose, or where they live. The presence of children can also profoundly affect the nature of the husband-wife relationship. Within the social environment of the family, there is increasing evidence that each child elicits a different response from its parents: children are not just neutral or passive parties to the parent-child relationship (Bell and Harper, 1977). A genuinely sociological approach to understanding children views their relationships to adults as two-way interactions, just as in any other social relationship.

Perhaps the most important influence parents have in their children's socialization is their day-to-day treatment of them. Their sensitivity to their children, or the lack of it, has a great deal to do with how the children come to see themselves in relation to others. Following the pioneering work of John Bowlby (1969) on attachment, Mary Ainsworth and her associates have shown that mothers who attempt to understand and are responsive to their baby's crying end up with babies who cry relatively little. On the other hand, mothers who consciously try to manipulate a baby's crying by, for example, letting it cry to teach it not to cry, actually prolong the very behaviour they are trying to change (Bell and Ainsworth, 1972). Ainsworth maintains that a high level of maternal sensitivity and responsiveness to the various signals that the infant emits does not promote an increased dependency of the infant on the mother; on the contrary, it provides a balanced and co-operative relationship, which Ainsworth characterizes as a secure attachment providing a sound foundation for the growing infant's increased independence and confidence (Ainsworth, Bell, and Stayton, 1974).

A similar point, made with respect to parental sensitivity to older children, has been made by Diana Baumrind (1980), who maintains that parents who impose obligations and duties on their children without recognizing their rights and needs—she calls them authoritarian parents—not only do not achieve the kind of conformity they desire, they also impair the child's ultimate social and personality development. There are drawbacks as well to the methods of permissive parents, who do recognize their children's rights and needs but fail to assign them responsibilities and obligations. From Baumrind's point of view, the most effective parent is authoritative in dealing with children. Authoritative parents view their own rights and duties and those of their children as complementary rather than identical. They have high expectations of their children and place high demands on them for maturity, but they are receptive to the children's needs and take account of them in their exercise of control. They also adjust their attempts to control their children's behaviour in response to each child's developing abilities and interests. According to Baumrind (1970), authoritative parenting, unlike authoritarian or permissive techniques, enhances the development of instrumental competence in children, behaviour which is socially responsible and independent. It induces friendliness rather than hostility to peers, co-operation with rather than resistance to adults, an "achievement" rather than a "non-achievement" orientation, dominance rather than submission, and purposiveness rather than aimlessness. There is, of course, a clear cultural bias to this research, in that not everybody may consider "instrumental competence," as Baumrind defines it, to be the primary aim of the socialization of their children. But her research does show the need for parents to take account of their children's point of view when imposing demands on them.

During adolescence, the critical issue is the need for parents to understand and respond to their sons' and daughters' growing autonomy. Adolescence is a time when young people have to prepare for the phasing out of their dependence on their parents as they establish a basis for their own intellectual, social, and economic autonomy. They have to learn to make their own judgments on a range of issues from sexual behaviour to career choice, and so they have to have a sense of themselves as independent decision-makers. The extent to which they can be successful in this process, one which will be described later as significantly influenced by peer friendships, will depend in part on their parents' sensitivity to the changing needs of the adolescent and to the extent that they yield more autonomy as the occasion demands (Youniss and Smollar, 1985). Young people's relationships with their parents must shift from one of unilateral authority to a more mutual sharing of points of view. Parents gain rather than lose influence when they refrain from imposing their will on their children and meet them halfway by recognizing their changing needs and dispositions.

SIBLINGS AND SOCIALIZATION

Brothers and sisters exert a very particular kind of influence on each other. On the one hand, although they are family members, they do not have authority over the other children, as their parents do, unless they are much older than the others. In this respect they are more like peers, in that they are of comparable status. On the other hand, they are unlike peers in that, being members of the same family, their relationship to each other is ascribed, defined by conditions of birth over which they have no control. If a child finds a peer relationship bothersome in some respect, the relationship can be ended or, in a common ecological setting like a classroom or neighbourhood, avoided or distanced with strategies that minimize conflict (Tesson, Lewko, and Bigelow, 1987). It is basic to peer relationships that they are freely entered into. This is not the case for siblings, however. Children may find their relationships with brothers or sisters agreeable or even richly rewarding, but, if they do not, they cannot do much about it. Children do not choose their siblings, neither can they abandon them if they do not like them. Siblings are locked into a relationship with each other which can only be broken by leaving the family.

A second distinctive feature of the sibling relationship is that it is overseen and often significantly controlled by parents. Again, the contrast may be drawn with peers: a relationship with a friend is relatively free of adult interference. Parents may be concerned about their children's choice of friends, but they generally do not intervene. The relationship between siblings is, however, an integral part of the whole system of family relationships. Parents certainly have an interest in how siblings behave toward each other, and may actively police it. The children themselves are often acutely sensitive to differential treatment at the hands of their parents. The siblings relationship cannot be understood in isolation: it has to be viewed as part of a system of relationships.

The relationship between siblings has often been characterized as one of rivalry for the affection and attention of their parents. However, Judy Dunn (1984), who has carried out extensive work on siblings, maintains that there is as much warmth and affection between siblings as there is rivalry. Many first-born children manifest signs of anxiety and sometimes aggression at the birth of a sibling, but even this reaction may be as much a response to the behaviour of the parents as it is to the new child. On the positive side, older brothers and sisters can act as role models for younger children and introduce them to the world of fantasy and play. Based on their clinical work on adult siblings, Bank and Kahn (1982) maintain that, notwithstanding the often quarrelsome nature of children's sibling relationships, they are among the most enduring and supportive relationships that we experience. As people grow older and their parents die, as friends are lost from view and marriages break up, solace can be found in the one relationship which stands the real test of time.

It may be that the source of the tension between siblings, the obligatory nature of the relationship, is also a factor accounting for its endurance. Siblings quarrel a lot, because they cannot escape each other, but it is wrong to see this quarrelling as necessarily bad. A sentimentalized view of children loses sight of their need to practice the art of social conflict: they must learn when they can be assertive and when compliant, when they should stand up for their rights and when they should compromise, when they should control anger and when they should let it out. It is precisely the obligatory nature of the sibling relationship which forces the resolution of issues like these.

One more point should be noted with respect to siblings, which is that, as family size declines, changes will come in the sibling relationship, simply because each child will have fewer siblings, if any. Since even siblings in large families tend to interact predominantly in pairs (Banks and Kahn, 1982), this may not entail a major change. Nevertheless, as Eichler (1983) has pointed out, very little research has been carried out on the effects of changing demographic variables upon patterns within the family.

PEERS AND SOCIALIZATION

Beyond the family, one of the most important socializing influences impinging on children derives from their relations with peers. While "the peer group" is sometimes spoken of as if it represented a homogeneous influence, this is somewhat misleading, since peers can come from a variety of different sources. They may be classmates or other children encountered in the schoolyard, on teams, in clubs, or elsewhere in the neighbourhood. The children of their parents' friends may be a further source of potential friends. In small, close-knit communities, these various groups may overlap, so that children met at school are also neighbours, friends of the family, and team-mates. In more urban societies, they are more likely to be differentiated. Not all peers are friends, however. Oden and her associates (1984) maintain that children define no more than half of the children they know as friends; the others may be partners in various activities or mere acquaintances.

The influence of peers in the socializing process may be both negative and positive. On the negative side, peers can draw the child into a delinquent sub-culture, although for this to happen there has to be an active delinquent sub-culture present within the neighbourhood and some need on the part of the child to identify with it (Cloward and Ohlin, 1960). But even without a delinquent sub-culture, children may have reason to fear each other for, in imitating their parents, they can take on not only the best but also the worst of their friends' behaviour patterns. The often-veiled stereotypes of appearance, social class, ethnicity, and gender which form part of adult culture can, when shorn of any pretence, become blunt weapons in the hands of children bent on seeking status advantage in the schoolyard or the street.

On the positive side, it was noted earlier that the distinguishing feature of children's friendships is that, within the confines of the limits set by the ecological settings of neighbourhood and school, they are relatively freely entered into. Furthermore, they are generally unhampered by adult interference and regulation. It was for these reasons that Piaget (1965) considered children's play relationships as having a life and a logic of their own, independent of adult society, and saw in them an important source of social and intellectual development. This theme has been pursued by a number of contemporary researchers.

William Damon (1983) has pointed to a number of the positive developmental effects of play behaviour in children. Solitary play, while presenting no obvious advantages for social development, does represent a creative and non-literal form of activity which is free from major emotional distress, is pleasurable, and pursued for its own sake. As such it provides an ideal occasion for the exercise of developing skills and the elaboration of mental schemes through the play of the imagination. Social play requires children to integrate their activity with others, and this requires them to acknowledge other points of view. This is thought to be an important step in the development of role-taking, an essential social skill enabling us to see ourselves as others see us and to adjust our behaviour accordingly. In turn, it is associated with the emergence of a stable self-identity (Selman, 1980).

The fact that children are all more or less on an equal footing means that their relationships with each other are much more symmetrical than those they have with adults, especially with their parents. James Youniss (1980) refers to the bilateral pattern of interaction between children as a relationship of reciprocity, in contrast to the asymmetric and unilateral relationships of complementarity they have with adults. He maintains that the reciprocal nature of the relationships between children accounts for their importance in the development of the child's social understanding. Free interchange encourages the notion of the self as an independent agent. Children's relationships with parents are much less conducive to this development, because they ultimately involve compliance with the parents' authority. From a child's standpoint, it is not necessary to understand your parents' point of view, because what they really want is for you to do what they say. Considerations of obedience override those of understanding.

Peers also play an important role in the development of autonomy during adolescence. They share ideas and feelings with each other in a non-threatening way which enables each of them to arrive at a sense of self-identity not simply imposed on them from the outside. They engage in a process of what Youniss and Smollar (1985) call co-construction, developing a feeling for the kind of person they want to be in collaboration and conversation with others going through the same process.

Peers are sometimes viewed as an influence in opposition to parents, drawing the adolescent (especially the male) out of the protective atmosphere of the family in order to develop the independence necessary to survive and function in the competitive world of the market economy (e.g., Parsons, 1951). More recent views (Fasick, 1984; Youniss and Smollar, 1985) suggest that the role of peers is complementary to, rather than in conflict with that of parents. Indeed, Youniss and Smollar suggest that it is through their peer relationships that adolescents come to see their parents in a new light, no longer as external authority figures but more as equals, as persons in their own right who have their own problems and imperfections and with whom confidences and worries can be shared on a more equal footing.

SOCIAL CLASS AND SOCIALIZATION

In important respects, the parents' social location, or class, also defines the ecology of the social environment in which the child grows up. The boy whose mother is a Toronto stockbroker is not only exposed to the attitudes and lifestyle that go with such a situation, he is likely also to live in an upper-middle-class neighbourhood and attend school with children of similar background, and generally to have access to all the cultural facilities of a rich metropolitan centre. The girl whose father works in a paper mill in a small, isolated northern community will absorb many of her parents' ways of thinking and acting, but will also be exposed to a fundamentally different social environment. Parents not only pass personal characteristics on to their children, they also locate them within the broader social structure.

"Social class" is the term that sociologists employ to describe an individual's location within the social hierarchy. It is used in different ways, however, so, to understand the effect of class location on socialization, some clarification is necessary. Within the Marxian tradition, "class" refers to ownership or non-ownership of capital. The relatively small group of people who constitute the economic élite in Canada can be considered a social class in this classical sense. Members of an economic élite can pass their social status on to their offspring through the legal institution of inheritance. Wallace Clement, who has studied the Canadian élite in some detail, argues that inheritance has been a significant factor in maintaining family control over large corporate holdings through successive generations (Clement, 1975). What this means is that, if your father owns a large stake in a major corporation and you inherit it, then you inherit your subsequent social status. Clement also stresses the important role played by private schools in the socialization of the children of the élite.

For most people, however, it is the social and intellectual skills they acquire through the socialization process rather than inherited wealth which determines their subsequent position in society. Studies of social mobility show that their parents' occupational status is the key determinant of children's subsequent educational and occupational status (Boyd et al., 1985). What are not yet completely understood are the mechanisms that achieve this.

Bernstein (1971) has proposed that middle-class children acquire a pattern of language from their parents which is more elaborate and more abstract than working-class language, and that this places them at an advantage within the school system. According to Bernstein, this difference in language use is a reflection of how patterns of relationships differ between middle- and working-class homes. Melvyn Kohn (1977) has focused on the kinds of values parents try to foster in their children, and has shown in a large-scale study that middle-class parents tend to encourage self-direction in their children, whereas working-class parents stress conformity to external authority. Kohn's study is especially important, because he tried to isolate what it is about different occupational experiences that would lead to this effect. What he found was that those parents who had jobs where their work required them to take initiative and which allowed them to form their own judgments were likely to encourage independence in their children, whereas parents who had jobs in which their behaviour was closely regulated favoured obedience and conformity in their children. These findings suggest that different types of parenting behaviour derive from the kinds of social relationships the parents themselves experience in the outside world.

Class background has been shown to affect schooling, particularly through the mechanism of curriculum track placement. Porter, Porter, and Blishen (1982) have shown that social class weighs more heavily than ability in determining whether students are placed in an academic or non-academic setting in high school. The authors suggest that middle-class parents are more active than their working-class counterparts in exerting pressure on the decision-making process and in ensuring that their offspring are given the benefit of the doubt in marginal situations. There is also evidence that children's occupational aspirations are significantly shaped by their parents' occupational status. Gottfredson (1981) has shown that by the time children reach grade 6, they have developed an "adult-like awareness" of social class, and have oriented themselves to their parents' class status and standards for success. While lower-class parents may have higher aspirations for their children than the occupations which they themselves achieved, they still do not put the same pressure for success on their children as parents do who have higher status.

One important qualification has to be made regarding studies of the effects of social class, and that concerns the way in which class is actually measured. Almost invariably it is the husband/father's occupation which is used to define the social class of the family. This is an example of sexist bias in family studies (cf. Eichler, 1983), since it assumes a model of the family where the father is the only breadwinner or, perhaps more importantly, that only the father has meaningful social experience outside of the family; mothers are assumed to experience the world only vicariously through their husbands. This is a dubious assumption, even in the case of women who do not work for pay; it is even more questionable, given that the majority of married women are active in the labour force. Social class is used as a concept because it is thought to encapsulate the particular kind of social experience that parents import into the family from the outside world. In order for it to do that satisfactorily, however, it must include reference to the mother's educational and occupational experience as well as the father's; otherwise, it tells only half the story.

A second point that must be made regarding social class concerns the value judgment that is often made about varying class positions. There is a clear implication in most studies that "middle class" is not only different from "working class"; it is better. Herbert Ginsburg (1972) has criticized a number of studies which depict working-class children's linguistic and intellectual performance as deficient. He maintains that these studies invoke cultural standards which are foreign to the children being evaluated, and fail to recognize positive elements within their modes of thinking and speaking. This is a difficult issue. On the one hand, there are no absolute grounds for making the judgment that middle-class occupations and the culture associated with them should represent the standard by which other positions in society should be evaluated. Yet the failure of children to master these standards entails exclusion from the material advantages associated with middle-class status. It is certainly important to be conscious of the value assumptions that are often embedded in instruments for assessing intellectual and social competence.

THE CHILD'S VIEW OF THE WORLD

Viviana Zelizer (1985) has recently observed that modern society has replaced the former economic and practical value of children by a purely sentimental value. The more thoroughly children are removed and protected from the mainstream of social life, the more we shower them with concern and affection. But just as the idolization of women as objects of beauty and charm has been used to mask a lack of concern with their real interests or needs, so also there is a danger that the sentimentalization of children obscures a lack of genuine interest in their concerns as they see them. Children have very little power compared with adults, but we should not, for that reason, consider their social world as simply derivative of adult society and not worthy of interest in its own right. It is important to investigate what children understand and think about issues of social inequality, economics, or political injustice, not just because it might appear precocious, but because it might both tell us something about our own beliefs and foreshadow the values of the next generation.

REFERENCES

Ainsworth, Mary, D. S., Bell, S. M. and Stayton, D. J. 1974. "Infant-Mother Attachment and Social Development: 'Socialization' as a Product of Reciprocal Responsiveness to Signals." In M. P. M. Richards, ed., *The Integration of a Child into a Social World*. Cambridge: Cambridge University Press, pp. 99-135.

Ambert, Anne-Marie. 1984. "Marriage Dissolution: Structural and Ideological Changes." In Maureen Baker, ed., *The Family: Changing Trends in Canada*. Toronto: McGraw-Hill Ryerson, pp. 85-103.

Armstrong, Pat and Armstrong, Hugh. 1983. *A Working Majority: What Women Must Do for Pay*. Ottawa: Canadian Advisory Council on the Status of Women.

Bank, Stephen and Kahn, Michael. 1982. *The Sibling Bond*. New York: Basic Books.

Baumrind, Diana. 1970. "Socialization and Instrumental Competence in Young Children." *Young Children*, 26, pp. 104-119.

――――. 1980. "New Directions in Socialization Research." *American Psychologist*, 35, pp. 639-652.

Bell, R. Q. and Harper, L. V. 1977. *Child Effects on Adults*. Hillsdale, N.J.: Erlbaum.

Bell, Sylvia M. and Ainsworth, Mary D. S. 1972. "Infant Crying and Maternal Responsiveness." *Child Development*, 43, pp. 1171-1190.

Bernstein, Basil. 1971. *Class, Codes and Control*, vol. 1. London: Routledge & Kegan Paul.

Boyd, Monica, John Goyder, Frank Jones, Hugh McRoberts, Peter Pineo, and John Porter. 1985. *Ascription and Achievement: Studies in Mobility and Status Attainment in Canada*. Ottawa: Carleton University Press.

Clement, Wallace. 1975. *The Canadian Corporate Elite*. Toronto: McClelland and Stewart.

Cloward, Richard A. and Lloyd E. Ohlin. 1960. *Delinquency and Opportunity: A Theory of Delinquent Gangs*. New York: Free Press.

Damon, William. 1977. *The Social World of the Child*. San Francisco: Jossey Bass.

――――. 1983. *Social and Personality Development*. New York: W. W Norton.

De Mause, Lloyd. 1974. "The Evolution of Childhood." In Lloyd De Mause, ed., *The History of Childhood*. New York: The Psychohistory Press, pp. 1-74.

Donaldson, Margaret. 1978. *Children's Minds*. London: Fontana.

Dunn, Judy. 1984. *Sisters and Brothers*. London: Fontana.

Elder, Glen H. 1974. *Children of the Great Depression*. Chicago: University of Chicago Press.

――――. 1984. "Families, Kin and the Life Course: A Sociological Perspective." In Ross D. Parke, ed., *Review of Child Development Research*, vol. 7, *The Family*. Chicago: University of Chicago Press, pp. 80-136.

Elkin, Frederick and Gerald Handel. 1978. *The Child and Society*, 3rd edition. New York: Random House.

Featherman, David L. and Richard M. Lerner. 1985. "Ontogenesis and Sociogenesis: Problematics about Theory and Research about Development and Socialization across the Lifespan." *American Sociological Review* 50, pp. 659–676.

Fasick, Frank A. 1984. "Parents, Peers, Youth Culture and Autonomy in Adolescence." *Adolescence* 19, pp. 143–157.

Furstenberg, Frank F., Nord, Christine W., Peterson, James, L. and Zell, Nicholas. 1983. "The Life-course of Children of Divorce." *American Sociological Review*, 48, pp. 656–667.

Furth, Hans. 1980. *The World of Grown-Ups*. New York: Elsevier.

Gadlin, Howard. 1968. "Child Discipline and the Pursuit of Self: An Historical Interpretation." In H. W. Reese and L. P. Lipsitt, *Advances in Child Development and Behaviour*, vol. 12. New York: Academic Press, pp. 231–265.

Gilligan, Carol. 1982. *In a Different Voice*. Cambridge: Harvard University Press.

Ginsburg, Herbert. 1972. *The Myth of the Deprived Child*. Englewood Cliffs: Prentice-Hall.

Gottfredson, Linda. 1981. "Circumscription and Compromise: A Developmental Theory of Occupational Aspirations." *Journal of Counselling Psychology*, Monograph 28. 6, pp. 545–579.

Greenberger, Ellen and Steinberg, Lawrence. 1986. *When Teenagers Work: The Psychological and Social Costs of Adolescent Employment*. New York: Basic Books.

Kanter, Rosabeth M. 1977. *Work and Family in the United States: A Critical Review and Agenda for Research and Policy*. New York: Russell Sage Foundation.

Kohlberg, Lawrence. 1969. "Stage and Sequence: The Cognitive Developmental Approach to Socialization." In D. A. Gosin, ed., *Handbook of Socialization Theory and Research*. Chicago: Rand McNally, pp. 347–480.

Kohn, Melvin. 1977. *Class and Conformity*. Chicago: University of Chicago Press.

Lasch, Christopher. 1977. *Haven in a Heartless World*. New York: Basic Books.

Maccoby, Eleanor E. 1980. *Social Development*. New York: Harcourt Brace Jovanovich.

——— . 1984. *Socialization and Developmental Change*. Child Development, 55, pp. 317–328.

Mackie, Marlene. 1986. "Gender Relations." In R. Hagedorn, ed., *Sociology*, 3rd edition. Toronto: Holt Rinehart and Winston, pp. 99–131.

McKie, D. C., Prentice, B., and Reed, P. 1983. *Divorce: Law and the Family in Canada*. Ottawa: Statistics Canada.

McRoberts, Hugh, A. 1985. "Mobility and Attainment in Canada: The Effects of Origin." In Monica Boyd, John Goyder, Frank Jones, Hugh McRoberts, Peter Pineo and John Porter, *Ascription and Achievement: Studies in Mobility and Status Attainment in Canada*. Ottawa: Carleton University Press, pp. 67-100.

Mead, George, H. 1934. *Mind, Self and Society*. Chicago: University of Chicago Press.

Meissner, Martin, Humphreys, Elizabeth W., Meis, Scott, M., and Scheu, William J. 1975. "No Exit for Wives: Sexual Division of Labour and the Cumulation of Household Demands." *Canadian Review of Sociology and Anthropology*, 12, pp. 424-439.

Mills, C. Wright. 1959. *The Sociological Imagination*. New York: Oxford University Press.

Nett, Emily, E. 1986. "The Family." In Robert Hagedorn, ed., Sociology, 3rd edition. Toronto: Holt Rinehart and Winston. pp. 343-379.

Oden, Sherri, Herzberger, Sharon, D., Mangione, Peter L., Wheeler, Valerie, A. 1984. "Children's Peer Relationships: An Examination of Social Process." In John C. Masters and Kerry Yarkin-Levin, eds., *Boundary Areas in Social and Developmental Psychology*. New York: Academic Press, pp. 131-160.

Parsons, Talcott. 1951. *The Social System*. Glencoe, III: The Free Press.

Paulter, Katherine J. and Lewko, John H. 1987. "Children's and Adolescents' Views of the World in Times of Economic Uncertainty." In John H. Lewko, eds., *How Children and Adolescents View the World of Work*, New Directions for Child Development, (William Damon, Editor-in-Chief), No. 35. San Francisco: Jossey Bass, pp. 21-31.

Piaget, Jean. 1965. *The Moral Judgment of the Child*. New York: Free Press.

Piaget Jean and Barbel Inhelder. 1969. *The Psychology of the Child*. New York: Basic Books.

Porter, John, Marion Porter, and Bernard Blishen. 1982. *Stations and Callings*. Agincourt: Methuen.

Propper, Alice. 1984. "The Invisible Reality: Patterns and Power in Family Violence." In M. Baker, ed., *The Family: Changing Trends in Canada*. Toronto: McGraw-Hill Ryerson, pp. 104-128.

Reese, Hayne W. and Willis F. Overton. 1970. "Models of Development and Theories of Development." In L. R. Goulet and P. B. Baltes, eds., *Life-Span Developmental Psychology: Research and Theory*. New York: Academic Press. pp. 115-145.

Riesman, David. 1950. *The Lonely Crowd*. New Haven, Conn.: Yale University Press.

Schantz, Carolyn. 1983. "Social Cognition." In J. Flavell and E. Markham, eds., *Cognitive Development*, vol. 4 of P. H. Mussen, ed. *Handbook of Child Psychology*. New York: Wiley, pp. 495-555.

Selman, Robert. 1980. *The Growth of Interpersonal Understanding*. New York: Academic Press.

Shorter, Edward. 1975. *The Making of the Modern Family*. New York: Basic Books.

Simpson, Elizabeth L. 1974. "Moral Development Research: A Case Study of Scientific Cultural Bias." *Human Development*, 17, pp. 81-106.

Stone, Lawrence. 1979. *The Family, Sex and Marriage in England 1500-1800*. Harmondsworth, U.K.: Penguin.

Tesson, Geoffrey, John Lewko, and Brian Bigelow. 1987. "The Social Rules that Children Use in their Interpersonal Relations." In J. Meacham, ed., *Interpersonal Relations: Family, Peers and Friends*. New York: Karger, pp. 36-58.

Turiel, Elliot. 1983. *The Development of Social Knowledge*. Cambridge: Cambridge University Press.

Wrong, Dennis. 1961. "The Oversocialized Conception of Man in Contemporary Sociology." *American Sociological Review*, 26, pp. 183-193.

Youniss, James. 1980. *Parents and Peers in Social Development*. Chicago: University of Chicago Press.

Youniss, James and Smollar, Jacqueline. 1985. *Adolescent Relations with Mothers, Fathers and Friends*. Chicago: University of Chicago Press.

Zelazo, P. R., Zelazo, N. A., and Kolb, S. 1972. "Walking in the Newborn." *Science*, 176, pp. 314-315.

Zelizer, Viviana. 1985. *Pricing the Priceless Child: The Changing Social Value of Children*. New York: Basic Books.

CHAPTER 6

The Conflicting Demands of "Work" and "Home"

PAT ARMSTRONG AND HUGH ARMSTRONG

INTRODUCTION

For a number of reasons, it is no simple task to analyze conflicts between "work" and "home." First, work and home are not separate, independent areas easily divided into private and public spheres. To a large extent, income from the market sets the conditions and possibilities for the household, while household practices have an impact on the market. Women, for example, may be pushed to seek paid work because of falling male wages, and women's employment may in turn mean that more restaurant meals are bought. Tensions and pleasures from paid work often go home with the worker, while family considerations frequently influence the job. Second, the maintenance of personal relationships and the provision of personal services in the home involve both paid and unpaid work; at the same time, some paid jobs are done at home and some unpaid work is performed in the market. Babysitting may be done at home with or without wages; the sick may be cared for in the hospital by both paid and volunteer workers. Third, each kind of work can itself create conflict, or may conflict with other kinds of work and with personal relationships. Parenting, for instance, can be both a joyful experience and a painful one, capable of disrupting marriages and interfering with paid employment. Fourth, the implications of each kind of work are frequently different for women and men as well as for people from various ages, classes, and ethnic or racial groups. Finally, family structures and work of all kinds are changing rapidly.

To bring some order to the analysis of these changing and complex relationships, this article organizes the examination of conflicts around the various kinds of work women and men perform. In addition to investigating the conflicts related to the work itself, it also considers the impact of different work arrangements on three other major areas of domestic conflict—sex, money, and kids.

Our research has made us increasingly aware of such conflicts. Along with theorists who represented a range of perspectives, we began a number of years ago to document and explain the simultaneous change and lack of change in women's work; the dramatic rise in female labour force participation and the continuing ghetto-ization of women in and out of the home. Although some theorists understood these patterns in terms of choices women made or ideas they held, while others emphasized the limits on women's choice or pointed to developments in economic structures, all looked to the links between "home" and "work," between "family" and "job" (see Armstrong and Armstrong, 1978: chapters 5 and 6). The common approach was not surprising, given women's family responsibilities and ideas about women's ties to the home. The complex and overlapping nature of the two spheres became increasingly obvious, and so did the variation in the forms of women's labour. The conflicts built into the structures also became apparent, although researchers disagreed about the emphasis to be placed on these conflicts, and on women's part in mediating the tensions that arise.

In spite of the attention given conflicts generated by changes in women's work in recent years, we are still a long way from a comprehensive picture (see Armstrong and Armstrong, 1986; Eichler, 1986; Eichler and Lapointe, 1985). Like researchers such as Connelly and MacDonald, and Luxton, Livingstone, and Seccombe, we are now using a case study to further examine the relationships amongst different forms of work and family life. For the moment, however, we are in many areas able to discuss only the potential for conflict, rather than document its existence.

The research is even more limited in the case of men. While investigations of women's work have usually begun with the assumption that their domestic responsibilities influence their paid employment and that their paid work interferes with their family life, research on men has most often begun with the assumption that work and home are separate and largely unrelated. Consequently, our discussion of conflicts created for and by men is necessarily more restricted than it is for women. In many areas, the effects of changing conditions remain to be explored.

WOMEN'S WORK

Housework

Although domestic technology has made some household chores faster and easier to do, and although many goods and services previously produced within the household are now available for sale in the market, there is still work to be done in the home. Meals need to be planned, food purchased, stored, prepared, and served. Dishes need to be washed. Clothes need to be bought, cleaned, repaired, and put away. Houses need to be vacuumed, bathrooms and kitchens washed, cleaning organized. Bills need to be paid, budgets juggled, snow shovelled, lawns mowed, and appliances maintained.

The precise tasks, the standards kept, and the amount of time required vary with social class, family structure, age, ethnicity, race, and, as the next sections indicate, with the number and ages of children as well as with the demands of other kinds of work. Small, old, or ill-repaired homes often require more time to clean than those with modern surfaces and adequate storage and living space. Apartments relieve occupants of outdoor and repair work, although the way that proprietors maintain them varies widely. High costs and limited space mean that many households must forego those appliances that actually do save labour. For example, as of May 1986, just over a third of households had dishwashers, and about a quarter still had to do without their own clothes washers and dryers (calculated from Statistics Canada, 1986a). Meals in restaurants or fast food outlets, cleaning, repair, and laundry services are all more expensive than doing the work yourself. Such services are beyond the reach of the one in every two Canadian households that is female-headed and the one in three households headed by someone under the age of 25 and living below the poverty line (National Council of Welfare, 1986). They are unavailable as well to the many other families that escape poverty but survive on tight budgets. Tight budgets not only mean that fewer appliances and services can be purchased; they also mean that more time must be spent planning and shopping for bargains.

In spite of these wide variations, there are two clear and common patterns in this domestic labour. Research from coast to coast demonstrates that housework is mainly women's work, and that it takes an enormous amount of time. A Vancouver study (Meissner et al., 1975:431) concluded that "most married women do the regular, necessary, and most time-consuming work in the household every day." Meg Luxton (1980) found that, on average, housewives in Flin Flon, Manitoba spent just over 33 hours a week preparing food and cleaning house. Each laundry load consumed another 55 minutes before all the clothes were put away, and the preparation of lunches for school and work added an additional two and a half hours to a woman's working week. Research in Halifax (Clark and Harvey, 1976) revealed very similar patterns in terms of both the distribution of labour and work time. A more recent survey conducted across Canada reported that very little has changed. In 1981, women not in the labour force devoted an average of 33 hours week to housework, shopping, and household maintenance (Statistics Canada, 1985b:19).

Of course, in the 1980s only a minority of women devote themselves exclusively to caring for houses and husbands. In large numbers, women have been moving into paid jobs. This has not, however, meant the complete disappearance of the full-time housewife. In 1983, more than half of the women with or without husbands but without children under 16 years of age were not in the labour force (Statistics Canada, 1985a:49). It can be assumed that almost all of these women work full-time doing housework. Yet it cannot be assumed that all of them stay out of the market by choice. Many are older women with little formal education or employment experience and with limited employment opportunities. Others live in areas of the country where there are few jobs available for women.

When women work full-time in the home, the potential for some conflict is reduced. The division of labour is often clearly established, beyond debate. The woman does the housework. If a man is present, his major contribution is usually the provision of the household's money income, although he may be retired or unemployed and may occasionally help with some domestic chores.

Moreover, there is likely to be little dispute about whose job has priority, given that male earnings are so obviously crucial to household survival. British research on married couples led Janet Finch (1983:2) to conclude that the relationship between a wife's and a husband's job is two-way: "His work both structures her life and elicits her contributions to it." Depending on the nature of the husband's job, the wife's efforts may reap "positive economic benefits" and provide "a very real outlet for her creative energies" (Finch, 1983:152).

In addition, a woman working full-time in the home may have more time and energy to deal with the tensions brought home by her husband. A study of immigrant families in Canada (Ng and Ramirez, 1981:45) reported that a wife's duty "is to safeguard and preserve his earning power as well as possible, and to keep the family together. In this regard, the woman becomes the 'buffer' between the outside world and the home."

While the potential for conflict may be reduced in some areas, it may be increased in others. Finch (1983:152) qualified her conclusions, pointing out that the benefits acquired by a woman through contributing to her husband's job "can only be gained within the overall context of dependency." When women are dependent on male earnings, conflicts may arise over a husband's lack of success in employment or over a wife's spending patterns. The Ng and Ramirez study of immigrant women found that disagreements over money were not infrequent, and were settled either by the husband's veto or by the husband assuming responsibility for purchasing. But such procedures did not necessarily end the conflict. As one women explained, "He feels superior and treats me like a dummy sometimes" (Ng and Ramirez, 1981:43). Such struggles over spending, women's housecleaning standards, male employment and power may be exacerbated by the constraints created by relying on a single income or by a woman's lack of choice in full-time housework.

Conflicts may also arise out of housework itself. Male and female standards may not be the same. Women may resent husbands who consume in minutes, and with few signs of appreciation, food that took all day to prepare. Men may wonder what women do all day on "their" pay because many household jobs, such as planning meals or washing drapes, are largely invisible, and because many chores, such as shopping or searching for inexpensive recipes, may look like leisure activities. A study of a Canadian working-class community (Lorimer and Phillips, 1971:36) found that women were expected to do the housework and raise the children and that, while husbands varied somewhat in their standards, a woman's failure to carry out either of these responsibilities was considered very serious.

Isolated and dependent, performing work that is either invisible or that quickly disappears, demanding to be done again, many women rebel, give up, or mask their strains with drugs. As Ng and Ramirez (1981:39) have pointed out, it is not surprising that "many immigrant women suffer depression and severe anxiety." Other Canadian research (see Cooperstock and Lennard, 1987; Harding, 1987) has demonstrated how tranquillizers are used extensively to quiet the conflicts created by the occupation "housewife." The work itself is frequently a source of tension. A recent poll indicated that vacuuming was the chore disliked most by a third of Canadian housewives, followed by ironing, scrubbing floors, and cleaning bathrooms (reported in the Montreal *Gazette*, Dec. 10, 1986). However inegalitarian and unrealistically nostalgic their vision, the growing demands from groups such as REAL Women for protection of women's full-time work in the home and for recognition of their contribution suggests that, in addition to the conflicts created by dependency, there are also pressures created by the nature and evaluation of housework, pressures which do not come simply from feminists.

The economic dependency resulting from full-time housework may also influence sexual relationships. Women without access to many other resources may use sex to gain power or goods. As a woman interviewed in Luxton's (1980:64) Flin Flon study explained, "If I want something, I just get all sexy and loving, and after I tell him what I want." Penny Kome's (1982:48) research on housework produced similar responses. One woman "said she'd performed sexual favours for her husband in order to get her household allowance." When sex is a primary means of access to power, aging can be a particular threat in a culture that links youth to sexual attractiveness. Full-time housewives may be threatened as well by the contacts men make at work, not only with young women but with men and women of all ages who share more of their husband's daily experiences than do wives who see them only on weekends and after a tiring day on the job. Full-time housework may create at least as many conflicts as it resolves, especially during times of falling wages and rising female labour force participation.

Care for Others

The care of the children, the sick, and the elderly also involves work which, in spite of the expansion of childcare centers and medical services, is still mainly done in the home. Children need to be washed, clothed, fed, cuddled, disciplined, chauffeured, trained, helped with homework, and accompanied to school plays. Elderly people do not need help with their homework, but they often do need to be entertained. When the young or the old are sick, the labour required for their care expands and intensifies.

As with housework, the precise tasks, the standards, and the amount of time required vary with social class, age, ethnicity, and race. Young children need constant supervision, while older ones need more concentrated periods of assistance. Houses with yards to play in, toys to play with, and cupboards for storing dangerous materials make supervision easier. Some women can afford paid substitutes to help with the work. Many others are always on call. Some have a large network of friends and kin to share the burdens, while others, especially recent immigrants, have few people close to them to draw on for support.

But here, too, there are common patterns. The caring work is mainly women's work, and this labour also takes enormous amounts of time and energy. Time-budget studies done in Halifax (Clark and Harvey, 1976), Vancouver (Meissner et al., 1975), and across Canada (in Statistics Canada, 1985b:19) estimated that women working full-time in the home devoted an average of 1.3 hours a day exclusively to child-care. But such figures ignore the fact that with each child there is more food to prepare, more dishes to wash, more mess to clean up. They also fail to count the supervision that goes along with watching television and shopping and the times children are delivered to and watched at hockey games and ballet lessons. According to one American study (Myrdal and Klein, 1956:35), in terms of time spent working in the home "one child adds 18 more hours to this total, two children add 28, three or more children mean 39 additional hours to this total per week."

Estimates of the time spent caring for the sick or the elderly are more difficult to find. That this is women's work, however, is clearly established in the literature. Recent research conducted for the Canadian Advisory Council on the Status of Women (Heller, 1986:11) found that three-quarters of the 165 women interviewed across Canada had "sole responsibility for family health care at home," and that many of those who got help received it from other women.

When children are young, it is women who drop out of the labour force to look after them. Indeed, it is mothers of young children who constitute the majority of full-time homemakers. In recent years, many more mothers of young children have been remaining in the labour force after the birth of a child. Yet, in 1985, almost half of the mothers who had a pre-school child and whose husbands were employed did not have paid jobs. Fewer than half of those with a child under three years of age did paid work. Only a third of the mothers who had a child under three but who did not have an employed husband had a job in the labour market (calculated from Statistics Canada, 1985a).

Many of these women stay at home because they want to raise their children, and because they believe mothers provide the best care. A poll conducted in 1982 indicated that nearly 90 percent of Canadians thought married women should take paid work, but only 38 percent thought women should be employed when their children are young (Boyd, 1984:12). It cannot be assumed, however, that all of the women who stay home do so by choice. Good childcare is scarce and expensive. According to a 1984 estimate, spaces in licensed daycare centres or in licensed family homes could accommodate only nine percent of the children whose parents are employed or in school for at least 20 hours per week (Status of Women Canada, 1986:51). Such care can "virtually double the cost of raising a child" (Status of Women Canada, 1986:15). For those many women who are paid very low wages in the market or who cannot find care of decent quality or at the required hours, staying home is the only option.

When women stay home, three problems may be resolved. First, someone is there to care for the children all the time. Second, the issue of who has responsibility for them is largely settled. Third, the work of childcare is unlikely to interfere with men's paid employment.

This strategy does not resolve all the conflicts related to childcare, however. Disputes still frequently erupt over questions of methods and standards. Fathers away all day doing exhausting labour may demand children who are seen but not heard, while mothers may have become accustomed to the racket. Flin Flon mothers interviewed by Luxton (180:92) explained how they have to mediate conflicts between fathers and children over acceptable behaviour and keep children quiet while fathers who have come off shift-work sleep. Mothers home with the children all day may become more attuned to modern practices and more tolerant of a range of behaviour. Toronto immigrant women studied by Gannagé (1986:72) described conflicts over childrearing practices that were related to old-country patriarchal standards. One woman "often struggled with her husband to persuade him to relax the rules concerning the right of their nine-year-old daughter to play with boys."

In addition, disagreements may arise over money. When women withdraw from the labour force in order to raise children, expenses go up as income goes down, and tensions may rise. Husbands and wives may disagree, as well, about the expenditures necessary for childrearing. Mothers, more responsible for the work and more aware of the benefits to be derived from new equipment and services, may meet resistance from fathers who pay the bills. Moreover, when budgets are tight, husbands and wives are less able to afford the leisure activities or merely the time by themselves that can help relieve tensions. For the one woman in ten who parents alone, full-time motherhood usually means poverty, with all its accompanying strains and conflicts.

Children can also create problems for sexual relationships. Mothers may be too exhausted or tense for sex. Fearing the children will interrupt or hear, they may refuse to participate.

The nature of the work itself frequently provides a basis for conflict. Like housework, childcare is isolated. Studies of both immigrant women (Gannagé, 1986; Ng and Ramirez, 1981) and Canadian-born women (Kome, 1982; Luxton, 1980) reveal that not having an adult to talk to and being constantly on call are major sources of tension for full-time mothers. It means that frustrations build up during the day. It also means that women want an adult conversation from husbands who have often spent their day in discussion and merely want a quiet night at home.

Although the polls indicate that a majority of Canadians believe that mother care is the best care, women are given the responsibility but not the authority to look after children. Experts tell women how to raise their children, and blame mothers for failures (see Strong-Boag, 1982: Reiger, 1985). Consequently, mothers are often caught between different kinds of advice, and worry about whether or not they are doing it right. Whatever their practices, it is difficult to be successful, because women have only limited control over their children, given the influence of peers, media, schools, and experts, and since children are active in their own socialization. These tensions are not eliminated by full-time mothering. Such tensions may be felt in particular by those mothers who do not mother full-time by choice.

Moreover, the care of children and the care of houses often conflict. More women stay home to look after children than do so to clean house but, because they are home, they are also expected to maintain high standards of household cleanliness. As a woman involved in Kome's (1982:27) housework study explained, she stays home in order to be a good mother but, "I even snap at the kids sometimes when they make a mess where I've just cleaned."

And, finally, childrearing is itself a contradictory activity. Mothers are supposed to dedicate themselves to eliminating their children's need for them. This may be a particular problem for women who devote themselves full-time to childrearing. All mothers face the struggle of raising children who are trying to raise themselves, but full-time mothers have the additional problem of working for their own early retirement from their main job. Of course, when the offspring become independent, or are perceived from the perspective of one generation or another to have become independent, they do not necessarily leave home. Indeed, in recent years, high unemployment rates and extended schooling have meant that offspring are staying home longer and are returning more frequently to live with their parents. Adult children living at home may create new conflicts over independence, and may create more financial tensions as well. Full-time motherhood can resolve some issues, but it does not eliminate all bases for conflict and can create new ideas for dispute.

Similarly, though women who stay home and tend the sick and elderly can deal with many of the problems related to the allocation of time and responsibility, areas of conflict remain. Substitute care is even more expensive and difficult to find for these dependents than it is for children. Few people feel competent or are willing to look after the severely disabled or bedridden. You cannot simply call in the 17-year-old next door. Moreover, children can be packed up and taken along on shopping expeditions and other outings, but it is much more difficult to do so with the sick or the elderly, whose care is more isolating, demanding, and constant than is childcare. And this work is less likely than childcare to be a matter of choice. Whether it comes from caring for children or the elderly, the tension resulting from this unremitting labour can erupt in child abuse, "granny bashing," and broken marriages.

One way many women who are not in the labour force escape the strains of domestic labour is by taking on volunteer work. More flexible than paid employment, volunteer work often provides both social contacts and a sense of social worth. Nevertheless, it introduces competing demands in terms of time, energy, and responsibility, and thus can conflict with women's other work.

Homework

Faced with falling wages, rising prices, high unemployment, and perhaps lone parenting, many women find they cannot afford to devote all of their time to housework and to caring for children and the elderly. One strategy women use in order to cope with the competing demands for income and care is to earn money at home.

Homework has provided income for generations of immigrant women who buy their own machines and sew clothes for the garment industry (see Johnson and Johnson, 1982). Many others babysit or work as typists at home. Such women constitute the majority of homeworkers. For many of these women, this kind of work is the only option, because the wages available in other jobs make alternative care too expensive, and because many have only a limited facility in English or French. What is often referred to as the underground economy is not exclusively populated by immigrant women, however. Home childcare is often provided by women born in Canada. Home typing services abound, and many women now do word processing in their "electronic cottages." *The Financial Post* (1982:20) estimated that in 1981 "more than one million Canadians, mostly women, threw home parties to sell personal care or home items." *Chatelaine* magazine (October, 1982:44) reported that women working at home offer services "ranging from bookkeeping to beauty counselling," and offered tips for women on "Making Money in Your Home."

For some women, homework provides not only significant income but also challenging, flexible employment and social contacts. However, for most women, it provides only a small income and a great deal of stress. Housework is never done; paid work is never done. There is constant pressure to produce, and no clearly defined time away from either job. And the stress is reinforced by isolation.

Demands from husbands and children frequently conflict with those of paid work. At home because the children are there, women often have little time to spend with them. They may have to restrict children's play areas and activities in order to accommodate their other work. Home, too, because they need to keep house, women often find their house a mess precisely because they do their other work there. As one woman put it in describing her cousin's homework, "She would try to do everything. She would jump up from the machine, feed the baby, quick sew a zipper, stir the pot on the stove, rush back to her machine, rush back to change the baby and keep on sewing. She would eat her own sandwich while she kept sewing" (Johnson and Johnson, 1982:80). Such a pace is bound to have an impact not only on women's relationships with their children but also on those with their husbands as well. For women who parent alone, there is the additional pressure of inadequate income, even greater isolation, and perhaps the fear of discovery by welfare officers. Homework may help relieve financial stress and provide care services, but it may also significantly raise the level of stress in the home.

Like women who leave paid employment entirely, women who do homework find their options for the future limited, especially in times of high unemployment. They drop behind other women in terms of employment experiences and skills that are rewarded in the market. As a result, when children grow up or the elderly die, homework may still be their only means of earning an income.

Part-time Paid Work

Yet another strategy women use in order to juggle their many responsibilities is part-time employment. More than a quarter of the women with paid jobs work fewer than 30 hours a week at them, in hospitals, schools, offices, banks, stores, and factories. Many more work for only part of the year. In 1985, over a third of the women with husbands and with pre-school children were employed part-time. The proportion was smaller for women whose children were young but who did not have a husband at home. Only one in five of them took part-time work (Statistics Canada, 1985b:55).

For some women, part-time work allows them to earn needed income, to retain skills, and to gain social contacts. At the same time, women can assume major responsibility for homes, children, the sick, and the elderly. The greater flexibility and shorter hours often associated with part-time employment may remove some of the pressures created by homework and by inadequate income, while still ensuring both that someone is there for the children and that mother gets out of the house.

But many women who work part-time do not do so by choice. Some would prefer to care for family and home full-time, but economic pressures push them to take on paid employment. Others want or need to work full-time in the market, but the scarcity of either good affordable alternative care or full-time jobs makes such employment impossible. In 1985, 44 percent of the married women who worked part-time in the labour force took these jobs because they could not find full-time work or because personal and family responsibilities prevented them from working full-time. This was the case for over half of the widowed, separated, or divorced women employed part-time (calculated from Statistics Canada, 1985a:Table 83). Lack of choice can itself create conflicts for both the women and their families.

It is not only lack of choice that can create problems for women employed part-time, however. While part-time work does provide some income, it usually offers only low wages for limited hours, and seldom offers sick benefits, maternity leave, pensions, or unemployment insurance protection. For women with husbands, this means that their job is secondary, that they remain dependent, and that they retain the major responsibility for domestic work in spite of their additional labour. When someone needs to stay home with children, give up their job so a vacation can be arranged or so a move can be made to new employment opportunities, it is the woman's job that is sacrificed. For women without husbands, part-time employment almost invariably means living on a very low income, yet such employment may jeopardize support payments from husbands or the state. In both kinds of households, wages from part-time work may not be sufficient to relieve the financial strain, or to allow for leisure activities, labour-saving devices, or paid substitutes.

Part-time work does not necessarily solve childcare and housework problems either. Hours of work do not always coincide with the hours children need care. Few part-time jobs begin after 9 a.m., end before school finishes for the day, or provide time to go home to make lunch. Few match the school summer holidays, Christmas, Easter, and mid-term breaks or teachers' professional days off. Many part-time jobs, such as those in hospitals, schools, and restaurants, require that workers be "on call." This lack of predictability makes substitute care particularly difficult to arrange and severely disrupts housework patterns.

By working on shifts, weekends, and at night, women can do their paid work while their husbands are home, and thus avoid childcare costs and care by strangers. A woman interviewed in Johnson's (1986:18) study of working families explained that her "husband works evenings, from 5 p.m. until 1:30 or 2 a.m. My work hours are from 7 a.m. until 4 p.m. We avoid childcare expenses and it gives the kids enough time to spend with both parents." However, such schedules mean that parents have little or no time alone. Sexual relationships are difficult to maintain. Fatigue created by odd hours and dual demands may also mean that tensions mount between parents and children as well as between parents. Disputes over housework and childcare may develop when hours are unpredictable, when husbands and wives are home at different times, and when chores are sometimes alternated rather than shared. In most cases, women's responsibility for domestic labour is ensured by their more limited hours in paid work, but their actual work hours are increased by their assumption of a second job.

As White (1983:12) concluded in her study of part-time work, it "represents not so much the free choice of an ideal solution as a necessary compromise between conflicting pressures and a response to working conditions." For those women who are married to men with decent incomes and who can find challenging work at reasonable wages, part-time work may resolve a number of conflicts. For the many who are pushed into unpredictable hours at low wages and who need more income, part-time work may create more problems than it solves. For most women, part-time work limits their future employment possibilities and provides little protection for their old age.

Full-time Paid Work

For an increasing number of women, the only option is full-time participation in the labour force. Just over a third of all married women were employed full-time by 1985 (calculated from Statistics Canada, 1985a:Tables 61 and 80). Of course, some women have acquired challenging careers that make paid work a real choice. Others prefer any market job to the isolation of domestic work. But most have little alternative to full-time employment, whatever the additional benefits they find in such work. Study after study has demonstrated the economic pressures that push married women into the labour market (see, for example, Armstrong and Armstrong, 1983; Connelly and MacDonald, 1983; Luxton, 1981). According to a Statistics Canada report (Pryor, 1984:14), a wife's income was "the significant factor" preventing family income from declining in the 1970s. By the 1979–81 period, "increases in wives' income were no longer able to offset the declines in husbands' average income." For many households, adequate standards of living can no longer be maintained, even with the combined wages of men working full-time and women part-time. Women's need for income is even greater when they parent alone. These women have a one-in-two chance of living in poverty.

The restrictive conditions of maternity leave also encourage women to stay in the market, and help account for the significant increase in the labour force participation of mothers of young children. Except for the Northwest Territories and the Yukon, all jurisdictions in Canada provide some job protection for women employed full-time who get pregnant (Canadian Advisory Council on the Status of Women, 1984:9–12). Most provinces allow women 17 weeks' maternity leave, although a few have provision for 18 weeks and some permit a six-week extension. If women meet the often rigid requirements, they have a legal right to a job after their maternity leave is over. This short period, however, merely provides time for recovery from childbirth. It does not allow time to care for the baby. Even if women can afford to give up their earnings for a couple of years, many will need income in the near future. When unemployment is high and jobs are difficult to find, fewer women can risk dropping out of the labour force in order to stay home with the baby. Instead they handle the tensions of a double workload.

The pressures of working in the labour force are reflected in current fertility trends, although of course these are not the only factors influencing the changing patterns. "Canadians now have fewer children, later in their lives and more may choose to forego parenthood altogether" (Romanuic, 1984:8). Better access to birth control has made these trends possible. But it is rising labour force participation, along with the virtual absence of support services and of accommodation in employment conditions, that have often made them necessary. Women frequently delay parenting until they have established themselves sufficiently in their paid work to risk some time away from their job. A growing number now feel they cannot take the risk at all. When women do bear children, they also carry the major responsibility for childrearing and the major consequences in terms of their paid employment. They may have to take jobs which allow them to accommodate children's demands or refuse promotions that would interfere with their childcare responsibilities.

Finding alternative care creates problems for many women who are employed full-time in the market. Scarce and expensive, daycare also provides very restricted hours of service. Even if women have matching hours, traffic or weather can delay them, and women worry about picking their children up on time. Daycare centres provide no care when children are sick, and there are few services available for older children. When, during an interview conducted for the study later published as *A Working Majority* (1983), we asked a woman what she did when her children were sick, she replied, "Panic."

Women unable to find space in childcare centres must rely on relatives, neighbours, or some other form of unlicensed care. Such care is often unreliable. Babysitters frequently quit, and the turnover not only leaves a gap in childcare but also produces anxiety about the consequences for the children of constantly changing caretakers. Even when the same person is regularly available, women still worry about the quality of care. Are the children safe, are they fed and cleaned, do they spend all day in front of the television, what ideas are they learning? Many women feel guilty about leaving their children, and cringe when the children call the sitter "Mommy" by mistake. Most are unhappy about missing major parts of their children's development. With full-time hours as currently defined, "by the time you got home, did dinner, it would be the kids' bedtime. There'd be no time to play with them" (Johnson, 1986:5).

While research attention has focused on the problems of care related to young children, the issues are not resolved when children enter school. Indeed, school hours and schedules make care even more difficult to arrange. Moreover, as children grow up, the problems change rather than disappear. Women worry about what their adolescent children are doing alone at home and who they are doing it with (see Armstrong and Armstrong, 1983:204; Richards, 1985:286). A cook and mother of two explained, "All I have to say is that a working mother, when she has to work and leave her kids at home, it's pretty hard whether she's married or single. It's very hard. A mother that works and raises a family has to be pretty strong, very strong" (Armstrong and Armstrong, 1983:203).

Few full-time jobs are structured in ways that accommodate parenting. Research undertaken by the Social Planning Council of Metropolitan Toronto found that only a small minority of employers offer flexible work hours, parental leave, work-at-home projects, workplace childcare or job-sharing schemes which would help people do their parenting work while holding on to their labour force jobs (Johnson, 1986). When such arrangements are possible, they "are primarily associated with women in the work force rather than with men" (Rogers, 1986:6). When women do opt for such arrangements, if often means "sacrificing benefits, job security, or chances for advancement" (Johnson, 1986:20).

It is not only childcare that remains women's primary responsibility even when they take on full-time labour force jobs. Vancouver research found that, when women in childless households entered the labour force, their husbands averaged an extra six minutes of regular housework a week. If the couple had children, husbands contributed an additional hour a week (Meissner et al., 1975). Toronto research conducted in 1980 revealed very similar patterns of increasing female labour time and little change in male hours of work (Michelson, 1985). When Halifax women enter the labour force, "the wife does most of the adapting; she reduces her household work and leisure hours quite significantly" (Clark and Harvey, 1976:64). In Maritime fishing communities, "most of the young husbands, 'helped' by 'starting supper,' drying dishes, and hanging out clothes," but it was women who shouldered most of the burden by working faster and harder when they were home (Connelly and MacDonald, 1983:65). A study done across Canada in 1981 indicated that men did half as much domestic work as their employed wives. Moreover, men with wives in the labour force did *less* work in the home than men whose wives did not work for pay (Statistics Canada, 1985b:19). Another cross-Canada study concluded that almost three-quarters of the women employed full-time in the labour force assume the major responsibility for family health care (Heller, 1986:12). Even when women have highly paid careers or when, like their partners, they are graduate students, it is women who adjust their work to fit household responsibilities (McFarlane, 1975; Hitchman, 1976). In the small proportion of households that can afford to hire services or to purchase prepared goods, it is still mainly women who do the work of hiring and purchasing. And in the many lone-parent households headed by women, there is no question of who takes the responsibility.

In assuming the responsibility, women ensure that the work gets done, but they do not necessarily eliminate conflicts over domestic chores. Toronto research has indicated housework to be the major source of dispute in households, more important than issues related to sex, money, or relatives (cited in Kome, 1982:19). Similarly, an American study "found that 'who does what' consistently topped the couple's list of issues leading to conflict and disagreement" (cited in Phillips, 1987:32). The fatigue and the time pressures created by doing two jobs push women to demand help and leave them with less patience or energy to deal with other tensions developing in the home.

Moreover, women feel guilty about not maintaining their houses as they or others think they should be maintained. As one mother explained to us, "When you're gone nine hours a day, it's not easy to come home to keep a house up to standards. . . . If you keep up one, you fall down on the other. You have to be a pretty super lady to keep both of them going" (Armstrong and Armstrong, 1983:202).

Tired and tense, women may find they have little interest in sex. There is a story told of a sex counsellor who recommended a large dose of male housework in a home where the woman frequently claimed she was too tired for sex. After following the advice, the couple found they had a new problem. Now the husband was too tired for sex. With two jobs, sexual relationships may also suffer from hours that do not coincide, leaving little time for a couple to be alone.

When women take on full-time work, there may be a question of whose job has priority in terms of time off for sick children, vacations, moves for promotion, or staying late at the office. The problem is particularly acute in the minority of households where both have careers that require travel or moves. In most households, however, women's jobs are secondary, because women earn less than men. On average, women's full-time wages are about 36 percent lower than men's. "Wives who were employed full-time in 1980 contributed an average of 40 percent of family income" (Status of Women Canada, 1986:13). Women are also less likely than men to be eligible for fringe benefits such as pension and sick leave. Consequently, wives' jobs are more dispensable than those of men, and women remain more dependent on marriage economically than men do. Women's full-time employment may increase their power and independence, but their lower wages usually mean that male preferences more often prevail. Indeed, power struggles may increase as women take on more work but do not gain equal say.

Women's full-time employment can help ease financial strains and may mean that women and men share more similar work experiences. Yet it may also mean that couples have little leisure time together and that they spend much more time with others on the job. Although full-time employment gets women out of the house and extends their contacts and resources, it also creates a double day, often increasing pressures in many areas without providing the compensation of equal power or pay.

The potential for conflict between full-time employment and domestic responsibilities is so great that many women are forced to choose between holding a job and creating a family. One American study found in a sample of 1975 female graduates from Harvard Business School, that, by the time they reached their mid-thirties, 40 percent were not married and three-quarters had not had a child (cited in Schwartz, 1987:D-5). Without support systems and without wives to carry the domestic workload, many women find that the only way to have a career is not to have a family.

Unemployment

Not having paid employment can also create problems for women. In 1985, one in ten women counted as part of the labour force had no paid work. Women's official unemployment rate was higher than men's, even though women's unemployment is less likely to be counted.

Research on the specific impact of female unemployment is not extensive, perhaps because female unemployment is not considered a matter of concern. Yet the available evidence has indicated that the economic consequences of unemployment are often more severe for women than for men (Burke, 1985). Women are less likely than men to receive unemployment insurance. When they do qualify, their benefits are usually lower than men's (Armstrong, 1988). When women lose their paid jobs, their chances of finding comparable employment are also lower than those of men. The financial need of unemployed women without husbands is obvious, but it cannot be assumed that marriage saves unemployed women from economic hardship. According to a Statistics Canada study (Nakamura et al., 1979:54), "the families of unemployed wives are more needy than either the families of wives not in the labour force or of currently working wives, particularly for wives in the older age groups." Moreover, the highest female unemployment rates are found amongst women whose husbands are also unemployed. Unemployment, then, means financial strain for women and their families.

A wide range of other strains increases with unemployment (see Kirsh, 1983). Grayson (1987:272) found in his study of unemployment following a plant shutdown that women's stress levels rose. Many reported sleeplessness. Depression was not uncommon. One man reported that his wife's "whole life revolved around her job, to the detriment of our marriage" after the plant closure.

Male unemployment also has a significant impact on women. Family incomes fall more dramatically when male income disappears, given men's higher wages and fringe benefits. Leisure activities and many services have to be abandoned (Johnson and Abramovitch, 1986). It is usually women who have to make the food dollar stretch and who have to handle the rising tensions. In Grayson's (1987:272) study, the wife of an unemployed worker explained, "I'm trying to talk quietly, sort of acting as mediator and trying to make things very pleasant." In some cases, a woman's efforts are not enough, and a man's tensions erupt into violence (Grayson, 1987:272). Both male and female unemployment create conflicts for women at home.

MEN'S WORK

Labour Force Work

From an early age, men know they will be expected to work full-time in the labour force. More years spent in school, earlier retirement, longer vacations and shorter work weeks, along with higher levels of unemployment, have meant that men's time spent in paid work has been gradually declining. Nevertheless, in 1986 about nine out of ten males between the ages of 25 and 64 were in the labour force. Over 97 percent of employed males in this age group had full-time jobs, averaging 42 hours of paid work a week. Moreover, one in 25 of the married men held more than one labour force job (calculated from Statistics Canada, 1986b: Tables 55, 78, 80 and 86).

Not only are men much more likely than women to work full-time in the market, they are also much less likely to have their employment patterns altered by family demands. On the basis of a survey conducted for Statistics Canada, Burch (1985:26) concluded that the "exigencies of marriage, pregnancy and childcare had a major impact on the continuity of work for a large majority of women, but almost no impact on men."

This does not mean, however, that men's paid work and family life do not influence each other. Few men have much choice about taking full-time employment, and few have the opportunity to stay home with their children. Men are not usually granted leaves when their children are born. Legislation in Saskatchewan and Manitoba allows fathers to take six weeks' unpaid leave, while Quebec permits men two days. The other provinces and the territories have no provision for paternity leave. However, fathers who are employed under the jurisdiction of the Canada Labour Code and who have custody of a newborn child can take up to 24 weeks off and still keep their jobs (Status of Women Canada, 1986:22-23). Other arrangements with employers are possible but, in an Ontario sample, only 5 percent of workplaces entitled male employees to paternity or adoption leave (Johnson, 1986:iii). Furthermore, men's paid work is more likely than women's to involve travel, reducing their time with children and wives. And more men hold two or more paid jobs, further reducing their time awake at home.

The lack of other benefits provisions and the structure of most labour force jobs also serve to limit male involvement in childcare. As the Status of Women Canada's Task Force on Childcare (1986:19) pointed out, "Very few workers have access to extended child care leave that is unpaid, none to paid extended leave, and very few have the right to paid or unpaid leave for the purpose of caring for sick family members or dealing with other family emergencies." Given men's higher wages and current levels of unemployment, few households can afford to lose male wages or take the risk of men dropping out of the market while they provide care. Interviewed by Gannagé (1986:59), a union organizer asked, "Why on earth would they have a husband stay home and lose twice as much money as she would staying home?"

Fathers' participation in the care of children and others is not, how-ever, just a matter of time or of the calculation of economic benefit. Many men, and women, still firmly believe that such care is women's responsibility (Boyd, 1984:49). In addition, few men have had the opportunity to develop the confidence and skills required for this line of work. As is the case with women who work full-time in the market, men have little time or energy left for housework. But, while a poll taken in 1981 indicated that over 70 percent of the males surveyed thought men should be expected to share in the general housework, the research cited above indicates that only a small proportion trans-late these thoughts into action. Of the women polled in the same year, just over a third said that their husbands helped "fairly regularly." On the other hand, almost half the husbands thought they did (Boy, 1984: 39–41). The potential for conflict here is obvious.

With little choice about providing the bulk of the household income, men may feel they have the right to make major decisions and may resent challenges to their authority. Many feel resentful about supporting women and children, especially when the contributions of those defined as dependents are largely invisible. As Luxton (1980:66) has pointed out, women and children's dependency on men leaves men little choice about taking paid work or about staying in jobs they dislike. In *Hearts of Men: American Dreams and the Flight From Commitment*, Barbara Ehrenreich (1983:13) argued that there has been "a male revolt — though hardly organized and seldom conscious of its goals — against the breadwinner ethic." At the same time, many men feel their authority threatened and their breadwinner status undermined when their wives enter the labour force, and when male wages fail to keep up with household needs. Seventy percent of the men polled in 1982 thought that "the dominant role of the husband in the Canadian family" was declining, and more men thought this was bad than thought it was good (in Boyd, 1984:33–34). Although many women, too, disapproved of the decline in husbands' importance, it is clear that such trends can be a source of conflict. Younger and better educated men and women were more likely than others to support these developments, however, suggesting that problems arising from these issues are at least not likely to increase in the future.

For both women and men, tensions from paid work spill over into the home. Women we interviewed for a hospital case study told us they yell more at their husbands and children after a bad day on the job. A lone parent described how she marched the two miles home from the hospital in order to work off her job frustrations before she faced her young children. She developed this strategy because she remembered how her father's anger about his job invaded their family life. The strains on men may be even more visible and more likely to result in violence. Women interviewed by Luxton (1980:68–69) attributed their husbands' irritability and violent attacks to the rage generated by, but not expressed at, their jobs. Economically dependent on men, women often pressure their husbands to be responsible employees. Consequently, men frequently "see their wives as constantly nagging, forcing them to work when they hate it" (Luxton, 1980:66). Much has been written in recent years about male abuse of women and children (see, for example, Cole, 1982; Guberman and Wolfe, 1985; MacLeod, 1980), but much more investigation needs to be done on the link between conditions on the job and relations at home (see Chapter 9).

The tensions created by men's labour force work vary with the nature of their jobs. They also vary with the nature of women's work. But few male jobs have only a positive impact on family life.

Unemployment

When men lose their paid employment, there are serious consequences for both the men and their families. Although male unemployment declined somewhat in the mid 1980s, an average of 441,000 men 25 years of age and over were unemployed in 1986. On average, the head of the household — usually a man — was unemployed in 371,000 families during that year (Statistics Canada, 1986b:Tables 56 and 99). For most men, paid work provides not only a source of income but also a basis for identity, social contacts, and marital power. All of these are threatened by unemployment. Unemployed Toronto men interviewed by Johnson and Abramovitch (1986:1 and 12) complained of boredom, depression, idleness, and loss of self-esteem. Many felt their health deteriorated. Grayson's study of former SKF employees indicated that stress levels and irritability increased when jobs disappeared. Moods changed; some became quiet and withdrawn. Men in both studies frequently cut off social contacts, because they could not afford to participate in the same way as others, and because such contacts became painful.

These developments influence relationships with partners and with children. In Johnson and Abramovitch's (1986:31) study, almost a third of the men felt that their unemployment had created problems in their marriage. The wife of an unemployed man interviewed by Grayson (1987:272) explained that "a lot of guys have come to the end of the line, especially the marriages." Fights over finances, housework, children, job searches, and decision-making increase. There is little money for leisure activities and, although men at least have the time, they often have little interest in them. Wives may become frustrated with their husbands' withdrawal and with their failure to take over responsibility for domestic chores while their wives do paid work. Husbands in turn feel unprepared for household tasks and may resist taking the responsibility because such work further threatens their already low self-esteem. Loss of the major income and often of benefits as well increases financial strain (Johnson and Abramovitch, 1986). Sexual relationships, too, may suffer. As one woman interviewed for our hospital study explained, there is no sex when your husband is unemployed.

Unemployment does offer men the possibility of spending more time with their children. Half the men in Johnson and Abramovitch's (1986:12) study felt this was one of the few positive consequences of losing their jobs. But lack of training and of choice about doing the work, combined with the other effects of unemployment, meant that men unemployed for long periods began to "describe their children in negative terms" (Johnson and Abramovitch, 1986:13). Their father's depression and the family's strained finances begin to show up in the children's school work, and in children's more negative evaluations of their fathers. Frustrated with conditions at home, some children begin to challenge their father's authority just when he is guarding it most. Moreover, fathers are around more to challenge and be challenged. Although male unemployment may bring some families closer together, it increases tensions in most households.

For many men, retirement creates similar strains, particularly when income declines dramatically. Old age means poverty and ill health for many more women than men and produces other problems as well (see Cohen, 1984), but most elderly women still have their domestic work to do. When men retire, they often have little to keep them occupied. If retirement is followed by a move to an apartment, as it frequently is, men lose the few maintenance jobs they did around the house. If men do become involved in domestic chores after years of avoidance, the result is frequently new conflicts. Women who have managed the household alone resent interference after all these years, especially if the man wants to change the routine or requires training to do the work. Job-related social contacts disappear and men may have to rely on their wives' connections to relieve the isolation. Retired men show high symptom rates for fainting, inertia, nervous breakdowns, heart palpitations, and dizziness (Oakley, 1974:232), developments which may put further pressures on marital relationships. When men retire from paid employment before their younger wives, additional strains are created by the reversal of dependency. Retirement can mean a well-deserved rest and leisure to take up new pursuits, but it may also mean increasing tension in the home.

Part-time Employment

Only 8 percent of employed males worked part-time in 1986, and most of them were either young or old. Over two-thirds of the men employed part-time were under 25 years of age, and another 7 percent were over 65 (calculated from Statistics Canada, 1986b:Table 80). Men do not, like many women, work part-time in order to accommodate family responsibilities. Almost half of those employed part-time are going to school. However, a third of them took part-time jobs because they could not find full-time work. For these men, part-time work provides some income and social contacts. But the insecurity, low prestige, and meagre wages associated with part-time jobs mean that the families of these men often face the same strains as those of men without any paid work.

Housework

Very few men work full-time keeping house (Burch, 1985:26). The need for income, men's generally higher wages, and a value system which denigrates housework, especially when it is done by a man (Eichler, 1977), prevent men from devoting themselves primarily to housework. Although the number of househusbands may be growing slightly, Australian research (Brewer, 1983:7) indicates that this practice "is confined to professional couples drawing good salaries. In keeping with the majority of decisions about dual working in low income families the need to guarantee economic sufficiency is paramount."

CONCLUSION

Does the potential for conflict described here mean that such strains are inevitable, whatever the work women and men do? Obviously, not all tensions can be eliminated, but they could be reduced and more equitably distributed by different conditions of work and different support systems. Shorter hours of paid work for women and men would give them more equal opportunities to care for children and the elderly and to do their domestic work. Parental leave would also help. Good, accessible child and adolescent care facilities would reduce strains, not only for adults but for children as well. Better pensions and homecare for the elderly would allow them more independence.

Equal pay for work of equal value, in addition to better access to all jobs and training, would reduce dependence on male wages. Improved, more secure conditions of paid employment would mean fewer tensions at home. Such proposals entail the recognition that most families now depend on two incomes, that necessary labour is done in the home as well as in the market, that home and work are interpenetrating spheres, and that women cannot now participate in either sphere on a basis equal to that of men.

REFERENCES

Armstrong, Pat. 1983. "Unemployment: A Women's Issue." In Lorne Tepperman and James Curtis, eds. *Readings in Sociology: An Introduction*. Toronto: McGraw-Hill Ryerson.

Armstrong, Pat and Hugh Armstrong. 1983. *A Working Majority: What Women Must Do For Pay*. Ottawa: Supply and Services Canada for the Canadian Advisory Council on the Status of Women.

———. 1986 "Beyond Numbers: Problems with Quantitative Data." In Greta Hofmann Nemaroff, ed. *Women and Men*. Markham: Fitzhenry and Whiteside, pp. 54–79.

Boyd, Monica. 1984. *Canadian Attitudes Toward Women: Thirty Years of Change*. Ottawa: Supply and Services for Labour Canada.

Brewer, Graeme. 1983. "The Impact of Work on Family Functioning: A Review of the Literature." Occasional Paper Number 3. Melbourne: Institute of Family Studies.

Burch, Thomas K. 1985. *Family History Survey: Preliminary Findings*. Housing, Family and Social Statistics Canada. Ottawa: Supply and Services Canada (Cat. no. 99-955).

Burke, R. 1985. "Comparison of Men and Women Following a Plant Shutdown." *Psychological Reports* 57: pp. 59–66.

Canadian Advisory Council on the Status of Women. 1985. "Juggling a Family and a Job." Ottawa: Canadian Advisory Council on the Status of Women.

Chatelaine. 1982. "Making Money in Your Home." (October).

Clark, Susan and Andrew S. Harvey. 1976. "The Sexual Division of Labour: The Use of Time." *Atlantis* 2(1, Fall): pp. 46–65.

Cohen, Leah. 1984. *Small Expectations: Society's Betrayal of Older Women*. Toronto: McClelland and Stewart.

Cole, Susan G. 1982. "Home Sweet Home?" In Maureen Fitzgerald, Connie Guberman and Margie Wolfe, eds. *Still Ain't Satisfied*. Toronto: Women's Press, pp. 55–67.

Connelly, M. Patricia and Martha MacDonald. 1983. "Women's Work: Domestic and Wage Labour in a Nova Scotia Community." *Studies in Political Economy* 10 (Winter): pp. 45–72.

Cooperstock, Ruth and Henry L. Lennard. 1987. "Role Strains and Tranquillizer Use." In David Coburn, Carl D'Arcy, George M. Torrance, and Peter New, eds. *Health and Canadian Society: Sociological Perspectives*. 2nd edition. Markham: Fitzhenry and Whiteside, pp. 314–332.

Ehrenreich, Barbara. 1983. *Hearts of Men: American Dreams and the Flight from Commitment*. New York: Anchor Books.

Eichler, Margrit. 1977. "The Prestige of the Occupation Housewife." In Patricia Marchak, ed. *The Working Sexes*. Vancouver: The Institute of Industrial Relations, pp. 151–175.

—— . 1985. "And the Work Never Ends: Feminist Contributions." *The Canadian Review of Sociology and Anthropology* 22 (5, December): pp. 619–644.

Eichler, Margrit and Jeanne Lapointe. 1985. *On the Treatment of the Sexes in Research*. Ottawa: Supply and Services for the Social Sciences and Humanities Research Council of Canada.

Finch, Janet. 1983. *Married to the Job: Wives' Incorporation in Men's Work*. London: George Allen & Unwin.

Grayson, J. Paul. 1987. "The Closure of a Factory and Its Impact on Health." In David Coburn, Carl D'Arcy, George Torrance and Peter New, eds. *Health and Canadian Society: Sociological Perspectives*, 2nd edition. Markham: Fitzhenry and Whiteside, pp. 262–279.

Guberman, Connie and Margie Wolfe, eds. 1985. *No Safe Place: Violence Against Women and Children*. Toronto: Women's Press.

Harding, Jim. 1987. "The Pharmaceutical Industry as a Public-Health Hazard and as an Institution of Social Control." In David Coburn, Carl D'Arcy, George M. Torrance and Peter New, eds. *Health and Canadian Society: Sociological Perspectives*. 2nd edition. Markham: Fitzhenry and Whiteside, pp. 545–564.

Heller, Anita Fochs. 1986. *Health and Home: Women as Health Guardians*. Ottawa: Canadian Advisory Council on the Status of Women.

Hitchman, Gladys Symons. 1976. "The Effects of Graduate Education on the Sexual Division of Labour in the Canadian Family." Paper presented at the Western Association of Sociology and Anthropology Annual Meetings.

Johnson, Laura C. 1986. *Working Families: Workplace Supports for Families*. Toronto: Social Planning Council of Metropolitan Toronto.

Johnson, Laura C. and Rona Abramovitch. 1986. "Between Jobs: Paternal Unemployment and Family Life." Toronto: Social Planning Council of Metropolitan Toronto.

Johnson, Laura C. with Robert E. Johnson. 1982. *The Seam Allowance: Industrial Home Sewing in Canada*. Toronto: Women's Press.

Kirsh, Sharon. 1983. *Unemployment: Its Impact on Body and Soul*. Toronto: Canadian Mental Health Association.

Kohl, Helen. 1982. "Enterprise Begins at Home: A Million Canadian Women Throw Sales Parties For Fun and Profit." *The Financial Post* (Oct. 15): pp. 20–28.

Kome, Penney. 1982. *Somebody Has To Do It: Whose Work is Housework?* Toronto: McClelland and Stewart.

Lorimer, James and Myfanwy Phillips. 1971. *Working People: Life in a Downtown City Neighbourhood*. Toronto: James Lewis & Samuel.

Luxton, Meg. 1980. *More Than a Labour of Love: Three Generations of Women's Work in the Home*. Toronto: Women's Press.

——. 1981 "Taking on the Double Day." *Atlantis* 7(1, Fall): pp. 15–16.

MacLeod, Linda. 1980. *Wife Battering in Canada: The Vicious Circle*. Ottawa: Supply and Services Canada for the Canadian Advisory Council on the Status of Women.

McFarlane, Bruce. 1975. "Married Life and Adaptations to a Professional Role: Married Women Dentists in Canada." In Parvez S. Wakil, ed. *Marriage, Family and Society*. Toronto: Butterworths, pp. 359–66.

Meissner, Martin, Elizabeth W. Humphreys, Scott M. Meis and William J. Scheu. 1975. "No Exit For Wives: Sexual Division of Labour and the Culmination of Household Demands." *The Canadian Review of Sociology and Anthropology* 12(4, Part 1, November): pp. 424–39.

Michelson, William. 1985. "Divergent Convergence: The Daily Routines of Employed Spouses as a Public Affairs Agenda." *Public Affairs Report* 26 (4): pp. 1–10.

Myrdal, Alva and Viola Klein. 1956. *Women's Two Roles*. London: Routledge & Kegan Paul.

Nakamura, Alice, Masao Nakamura and Dallas Cullen in collaboration with Dwight Grant and Harriet Orcutt. 1979. *Employment and Earnings of Married Females*. Ottawa: Statistics Canada.

National Council of Welfare. 1986. "Progress Against Poverty." Ottawa: Mimeo.

Ng, Roxana and Judith Raminez. 1981. "Immigrant Housewives in Canada." Toronto: Booklet.

Oakley, Ann. 1974. *The Sociology of Housework*. New York: Pantheon.

Phillips, Catherine. 1987. "Encouraging the Reluctant Father." *Chatelaine* (January).

Pryor, Edward. 1984. *Canadian Husband-Wife Families: Labour Force Participation and Income Trends 1971–81*. Economic Characteristics Division 42. Statistics Canada. Ottawa: Supply and Services Canada (Cat. no. 8-3100-543).

Reiger, Kerreen. 1984. *The Disenchantment of the Home: Modernizing the Australian Family 1880–1940*. Melbourne: Oxford University Press.

Richards, Lyn. 1985. *Having Families: Marriage, Parenthood and Social Pressures in Australia*. Ringwood, Victoria: Penguin.

Rogers, Judy. 1986. "Attitudes Towards Alternative Work Arrangements— A Qualitative Assessment Among Employers in Metropolitan Toronto." Toronto: Social Planning Council of Metropolitan Toronto.

Romanuic, A. 1984. *Fertility in Canada: From Baby-boom to Baby-bust*. Demography Division, Statistics Canada. Ottawa: Supply and Services (Cat. no. 91-524E).

Schwartz, Susan. 1987. "Women Let Down By the Corporate Life." *The Gazette*. Montreal (January 19): D-5.

Statistics Canada. 1985a. *The Labour Force*. Ottawa: Supply and Services Canada (Cat. no. 71-001) December.

——. 1985b *Women in Canada. A Statistical Report*. Ottawa: Supply and Services Canada (Cat. no. 89-503E).

——. 1986a *Household Facilities and Equipment, 1986*. Ottawa: Supply and Services Canada (Cat. no. 64-202).

——. 1986b *The Labour Force*. Ottawa: Supply and Services Canada (Cat. no. 71-001) December.

Status of Women Canada. 1986. *Report of the Task Force on Child Care*. Ottawa: Supply and Services Canada.

Strong-Boag, Veronica. 1982. "Intruders in the Nursery: Childcare Professionals Reshape the Years One to Five, 1920–1940." In Joy Parr, ed. *Childhood and Family in Canadian History*. Toronto: McClelland and Stewart, pp. 160–178.

White, Julie. 1983. *Women and Part-Time Work*. Ottawa: Supply and Services Canada for the Canadian Advisory Council on the Status of Women.

CHAPTER 7

Changing Perspectives on Divorce

JOHN F. PETERS

INTRODUCTION

No one wants a divorce. For those who go through it, it can be a traumatic experience. Yet, although emotional scars mark each marital
separation, most individuals survive the personal and social stress of
such a breakup. Some even emerge with a sense of renewal.

How does the sociologist look at the subject of divorce? In what way
is the severance between two married people a social phenomenon? In
the first place, marriage is a social institution established under a specific legal system, and with particular social expectations varying
somewhat by sub-culture, age, and sex. Similarly, divorce is a social-
legal act whose procedures have consequences for finances, domicile,
and child care and custody. These broader dimensions, including the
historical antecedents for our present divorce practices, are addressed
in this chapter from the sociological perspective of structural functionalism. Divorce is seen as part of the social institution of the family.

At the same time there are questions more microscopic in dimension. How does an individual actually come to decide there is no alternative but to divorce? What is the process undergone in leaving
marriage and once again becoming single? The symbolic interactionist
perspective is a useful tool for examining these questions.

This chapter will deal first with divorce in Canada before the mon-
umental legal changes that took place with the passage of the Divorce

Act of 1968. The consequences of these changes will be discussed, and the Divorce Act passed in June, 1986 that eventually resulted; the significance of quantitative changes in divorce will be reviewed, using Canadian statistics. The chapter will also look at the post-separation period. (The topic of children and divorce is found in Chapter 8.) It concludes with the subject of remarriage.

Early History

There are very few countries, apart from Ireland, that do not permit divorce. However, every society or sub-culture, even including the conservative Old Order Mennonites of Canada, has some means of arranging for the dissolution of a marriage. There is no society where the ceremonial vow of "until death do us part" is kept by all of its members.

So far as the history of divorce in Canada is concerned, there was no written law in Indian tribes or among the Inuit prior to the arrival of Europeans in North America; the literature on native peoples has little, if anything, to say about marriage dissolution. However, these people did have families, an effective kin structure, and parent-child bonding. Their means of food gathering and hunting had an effect upon human interaction and on reciprocal exchange between spouses. When "marriage" was terminated by death or voluntary choice, and the couple had had children, relatives usually cared for the offspring. Individuals and families adjusted as necessary.

The arrival of European explorers and traders created some disorganization in the native family structure. Some Europeans remained permanently with their Indian wives. Others left after siring several children; their intent had never been to remain in the marriage or in the Indian community until their death. Many of the English returned to England and established their "Canadian" families there. In an attempt to stabilize relations between Europeans and native women, the Hudson's Bay Company instituted a seven-year period of celibacy for its employees, and forbade company employees to let their Indian offspring accompany them to the old country. Nor did the British community appreciate its menfolk sending money to support their families in the frontier regions of Canada.

During the 100-year period between 1867 and 1968, the only effective ground for divorce in Canada was adultery. (There was one exception; Nova Scotia included the ground of cruelty.) Yet further explanation is necessary. Canadian divorce law came out of English common law. Up until 1925 a husband could be relatively successful in getting a divorce on the grounds of his wife's adultery. However, a wife desiring a divorce had to show her unfaithful husband to be guilty also of some other aggravation without "reasonable excuse." This double standard came out of the Victorian belief that a husband's extramarital affairs were a natural occurrence. It also showed the married wife to have few legal rights, that she was not much more than property. Within a few years after this double standard was changed in 1925, the proportion of wives among petitioners for divorce climbed from 47 to 59 percent, remaining fairly constant at about two-thirds of all petitions over the past two decades.

It is worth noting one further characteristic of early Canadian divorce law. While a man could peitition for a divorce from wherever he lived, a woman had to go to the province of her husband's domicile in order to file for divorce. This requirement was repealed in 1930, with the proviso that the wife must prove the husband to be guilty of adultery, as well as of wilfully deserting her. Pike (1975, 118) states that such "political fossil(s)" were not abandoned before 1968 because "of a powerful combination of religious opposition, ethnic particularism, and calculated political inertia which effectively blocked repeated attempts at the federal level." These laws clearly show a double standard reflecting a social system which set many more substantial barriers to divorce for women than for men.

The history of early Canadian law also shows a lack of geographical accessibility to the divorce courts. Though a number of provinces had them, it was not until 1930 that the largest province, Ontario, gained authority to establish its own divorce court. Prince Edward Island did not have its own court until 1945; Quebec and Newfoundland did not acquire this right until as recently as 1968. There was a strange meshing of political, religious, and social factors within provinces and between the federal and provincial governments that interfered with provincial authority and jurisdiction. The only recourse for individuals seeking divorce in these provinces was to apply to the federal government in Ottawa. Obviously, this was a strong deterrent to pursuing a legal divorce, particularly for the poor.

As stated earlier, the grounds of adultery was the only means of getting a divorce until 1968. Most other countries had already moved beyond "adultery only" grounds; England did, as early as 1937. But Canadians remained entrenched in a legal apparatus of divorce that was not consistent with the realities of the post-World War II era.

Under such constraints, some couples sought other solutions; the act of adultery was sometimes fabricated to placate the courts (Pike, 1975: 120). Some couples with financial means sought a "migratory" divorce by meeting residence requirements in Mexico or the United States. The number of unrecorded separations was probably large. The 1941 census of Canada reports 80,137 persons who were legally separated, compared to 14,032 persons who were classified as being divorced.

Pike regards the vesting of parliamentary divorce upon the Superior Court of Quebec as having been achieved with remarkable ease. There was virtually no provocation or opposition by political or religious groups. He states that this "is in itself a telling commentary on the substantial extent to which a process of secularization of social values and norms had occurred in the province during the 1950s and 1960s" (1975:124).

The long-awaited legislation was passed when the Liberal government of Lester B. Pearson was fairly sure that the opposition parties or major interest groups would not disapprove.

THE DIVORCE ACT, 1968

The Divorce Act, 1968, was a significant piece of legislation which granted divorce for marital offence or marriage breakdown. The latter category was devised in an effort to recognize the concept of "no-fault" divorce. The legal grounds for marriage breakdown were (a) addiction to drugs or alcohol, (b) desertion by the petitioner for not less than five years, and (c) separation for not less than three years. Grounds for marital offence in the Act were (a) adultery, (b) physical cruelty, and (c) mental cruelty.

As was expected, the number of divorces granted in Canada escalated: from 11,343 to 26,093 in 1969. Every province could now process its own divorce applications. Undoubtedly there was a backlog of divorce petitioners from the old system, but, in general, the number of divorces continued to rise until 1983. No province or territory was exempt from a marked increase. Quebec's divorce rate jumped by almost 500 percent with the new legislation.

In less than ten years, divorce was a household word: most Canadians had a relative, friend, or acquaintance divorcing or divorced. Though the stigma of divorce remained, especially for women, it was not as pervasive as in earlier decades. And remarriage was increasingly seen as an option for non-Roman Catholics.

The annual statistics gathered by Statistics Canada permit careful analysis of the period when this Divorce Act was law, between 1968 and 1985. (After 1971, data on more variables within divorce became available, such as the grounds for divorce, the sex of the petitioner, and the number of children involved in each case.)

In 1985 61,980 divorces were granted in Canada, or 244 divorces per 100,000 population. Countries such as Sweden, the U.S.S.R., and the United States exceed Canada's rate. Since divorces are dependent upon the number of people married, a measurement using this variable is also useful. Sweden's number of divorces per 1,000 marriages is 556, far in excess of Canada's figure of 337. But Swedish people are not as prone to marry, compared to Canadians, so the figure represents an even higher proportion of the adult population.

It is also helpful to investigate the grounds used for divorce. A large proportion of Canadians divorcing have used the grounds of three years' separation, between 29 and 33 percent of them doing so in the 15-year period before 1986. This is a type of no-fault divorce, in that the courts do not place guilt or blame upon either of the partners. McKie, Prentice, and Reed (1983) show that these grounds are fairly easily processed, in most cases taking three or four minutes of court time. However, the partners must have lived apart for the three-year period, a stipulation some people found too stringent in the 70s and early 80s. The couple could make attempts to reconcile the marriage, but living together could never exceed 90 days without jeopardizing the three-year separation ruling.

The next most commonly used grounds for divorce was adultery. It was used by between 28½ and 31 percent of all petitioners annually. In such cases the petitioner did not have to wait the three-year period before filing for divorce.

Mental cruelty was initially used as grounds by only 15 percent of the petitioners during the period under analysis; but by 1985 it was being used by at least 22 percent of all applicants. Physical cruelty as grounds for divorce was used by between 13 and 15 percent of all petitioners annually. While judges asked for only limited evidence of adultery, grounds of physical or mental cruelty required substantial evidence, such as statements from professionals (a medical doctor or psychiatrist) or photographs (in cases involving physical cruelty). Applications for divorce on grounds of physical and mental cruelty take longer to process in the courts, as a consequence.

At this point an understanding of court procedure is in order. Though a divorce may be processed without a lawyer, the vast majority of petitioners seek the advice and direction of a solicitor. The fees for such services generally begin at about $1,200. Most lawyers refuse to handle a divorce for both the petitioner and the defendant, even if the couple comes to a mutual decision to divorce. Lawyers want to protect themselves from some later accusation of not having represented one of the clients adequately.

After the lawyer makes sure the alleged grounds used by the petitioner are consistent with the law, the petition is filed in the court and the defendant is "served." The defendant is informed by the court that his or her partner has filed for divorce, and is given 20–30 days to challenge the petition if both are in the same province, or 90 days if one of them is in another province. A court hearing is scheduled, which often has to be set for 3–8 months into the future because of the backlog of divorce petitions, a frequent problem in Canadian divorce courts. If the judge has been satisfied with the case, a divorce *nisi* is issued and the couple has another 90 days to wait before the divorce absolute is issued. The 90-day waiting period was passed by law to safeguard the institution of marriage, allowing either one of the couple to withdraw the divorce petition. Its institution may have been well intentioned, but it had the effect of prolonging a relationship which had long since died.

The median age of the divorced has declined over time. In 1969 the median age for women was 37.3 years, while in 1985 it was 34.1 years. The median age was 40.6 for men in 1969, but dropped to 36.7 years by 1985.

The trend toward a lower age at divorce is significant. Table 1 shows that the proportion of men and women divorcing under age 25 is declining, and that the proportion of those aged 50 and over has declined only minimally. The increasing average age at marriage

TABLE 1

Divorces by Age of Wife and Husband
Under Age 20, 20–24 and 50 and over at
Time of Divorce in Percent, 1972, 1979, and 1985

Year	Wife				Husband		
	under 20	20–24	50 +		under 20	20–24	50 +
1972	.6	13.0	11.0		.0	5.6	16.8
1979	.5	12.8	9.4		.0	5.5	13.6
1985	.2	8.0	9.1		.0	3.2	13.7

Marriages and Divorces, Vital Statistics, Vol. II, 1975, 1979, and 1985, Ottawa, Ministry of Supply and Services.

would have affected the younger-age cohort. Older people with a more conservative view of divorce are less likely to divorce, but with time, the acceptance of more liberal views, and increased association with divorced people, they are more likely to consider divorce as a possibility for themselves.

Age at marriage is inversely related to the divorce rate. The McKie, et al. (1983:79) research shows that, though men and women aged 20 and under make up 5.9 and 26.3 percent respectively of all those marrying, they represent about twice that proportion amongst those divorcing (12.7 and 42.4 respectively).

The median duration of marriage for those seeking divorce has also declined from 12.1 years in 1972 to 10.9 years in 1985. A fuller treatment of this subject is found in McKie et al., 1983.

Table 2 indicates the number of dependent children of those divorcing. Couples with no children made up 44 percent of the divorced in 1972, while in 1985 the percentage was 48.5 percent. The proportion of those with one child remained much the same; of those with four or more children declined. Two factors contribute to this change. In the first place, families now have fewer children and, second, the average age of the divorced is declining.

Previous marital status at the time of divorce and remarriage is another significant variable. In 1972 divorcing husbands who had previously been divorced represented 5.4 percent of all those divorcing. Divorcing wives who had previously been divorced represented 5.3 percent. By 1985 husbands previously divorced made up 10.8 percent of

TABLE 2

Divorces by Number of Dependent Children
in Percent, 1972, 1979, and 1985

Number of Children	1972	1979	1985
0	44.2	45.9	48.5
1	21.9	23.1	22.1
2	18.4	20.6	21.9
3	9.2	7.2	6.0
4	3.9	2.2	1.2
5+	2.4	1.0	.3
	100.0	100.0	100.0

Marriages and Divorces, Vital Statistics, Vol. II, 1975, 1979, and 1985, Ottawa, Ministry of Supply and Services.

those divorcing, and wives previously divorced made up 10.6 percent. Their actual numbers had increased 3.8 times. This trend shows an increasing acceptance of remarriage for divorced persons, a topic to be discussed later in this chapter.

DIVORCE BY REGION

Each of the variables related to divorce discussed above could be further analyzed by geographical region. Distinctions of religion, ethnicity, family or kin association, age and sex distribution, rural or urban community, and economic opportunity directly affect the divorce rate. Table 3 shows the divorce rate by province.

Many people associate a low divorce rate with the province of Quebec. After all, is not the Roman Catholic church a restraining force upon divorce? Quebec did have a comparatively low divorce rate up until 1973. But by the next year its divorce rate was comparable to the national rate, and it has remained close to it ever since.

Though it is sometimes assumed that Ontario holds the highest divorce rate, it is the two most westerly provinces which consistently

TABLE 3

Divorces Granted and Rate per 100,000 Population,
by Province, 1985

Province	Number	Rate per 100,000 Population
Canada	61,980	244.4
Newfoundland	561	96.6
P.E.I.	213	167.6
Nova Scotia	2,337	256.4
NewBrunswick	1,360	189.1
Quebec	15,814	240.3
Ontario	20,854	230.0
Manitoba	2,314	216.3
Saskatchewan	1,927	189.0
Alberta	8,102	344.9
British Columbia	8,330	288.0
Yukon and Northwest Territories	168	228.0

Marriages and Divorces, Vital Statistics, Vol. II, 1985, Ottawa, Ministry of Supply and Services, Table 10, p. 16.

have the highest number of divorces granted. It is possible that this could be accounted for because these provinces do not historically provide the extended family attachment nor the long-standing community roots found in eastern Canada.

On the other hand, divorce rates in eastern Canada are comparatively low, markedly so in the provinces of Newfoundland, Prince Edward Island, and New Brunswick. Careful study might well show these provinces to have a substantial community ethos, larger families, a tighter kinship network, and a more conservative religious practice when compared to British Columbia and Alberta. However, all provinces show a gradual increase, confirming that societies are not stagnant, but ever changing, as dynamic social forces play against one another.

ANNULMENT

Apart from the death of one of the partners, there are three ways in which a marriage can be dissolved in Canada. A couple may be divorced, the most frequent choice; they may choose to separate but not divorce, for religious or personal reasons; or the marriage can be annulled. There is no legal status for separation, though a lawyer can help draw up a separation agreement. A separation agreement dealing with finances and child custody has been used as a legal interim arrangement until a divorce could be processed. Given that the three-year period of separation was chosen as a grounds for divorce by at least 30 percent of all divorce petitioners between 1968 and 1985, one can readily see the necessity of a separation agreement. A similar percentage might opt for a separation agreement with no immediate intention of pursuing a legal divorce.

The third way of dissolving a marriage, by annulment, differs from other forms of marriage dissolution in that the focus is upon what happened before the marriage. Annulment declares that the marriage is null and void, that it never really existed in the first place. One reason for the annulment may be that the marriage was never consummated through sexual intercourse. But other reasons, those of misrepresentation, are more frequent in contemporary society: if one partner had already been married; if a woman were pregnant by another man than her husband; if one partner had a venereal disease; if income was falsely represented; or if a character defect was discovered in a partner. Another common ground for annulment is that one of the partners had been incapable of understanding marriage prior to the union.

The Roman Catholic Church originated the practice of annulment, underscoring marriage as a sacrament. A marriage following an annulment would not be considered a remarriage. Canada has no legal category of annulment, though a few other countries do. Many Roman Catholic dioceses have a tribunal for making judgments upon these matters; other dioceses do not process annulments. Such geographical variations in access to annulment recall accessibility to divorce by province before 1968. Sociologically speaking, it appears that reasons for annulment today do not differ much from reasons for divorce, but are processed in the church's own way.

The annulled marriage is a problem on several counts. The non-Roman Catholic community considers persons with an annulled marriage still married but separated. And marriage or remarriage is not possible, legally, after annulment. Children born prior to the annulment are legitimate in the eyes of the Roman Catholic church. The church recommends that a person whose marriage was annulled seek a legal divorce, thereby clarifying his or her marital status within the community, and thus allowing the possibility of future marriage.

THE DIVORCE ACT, 1985

Within a few years after the 1968 Divorce Act became law, there were strong voices asking for further changes in the divorce law. The Canadian Bar Association (1973) and the Federal Advisory Council on the Status of Women (1976) suggested that the court processing the case should assess the interests of the children concerned. It was also recommended that a divorcing couple and not the courts should determine the status of the marriage relationship; "fault" was not to prejudice legal proceedings and legal resolutions. And a one-year (or even six months') period of separation was deemed appropriate grounds for divorce. Supposedly, it would simplify court proceedings and reduce emotional tension for those involved. By 1975 the Law Reform Commission presented recommendations which were even more radical, asking that divorce be granted without any designated period of waiting. Given this pressure for change in the Divorce Act, it seems strange that legislation was not altered until 1986.*

In the early 80s Parliament was more concerned with other issues, both domestic and international, and so proposals for change in the

---

*Although the legislation for it was not passed until June, 1968, the name of the Act is the Divorce Act 1985.

divorce laws were not made law until June of 1986. Just as the 1968 laws were a giant step from traditional to more modern attitudes, the new law better represents an urban society concerned with individual and human rights. For the first year in which the law prevailed, lawyers and judges tested the ramifications of the simplified "no-fault" code.

The Divorce Act 1985 simplifies divorce procedures. Divorce is now granted on one of three grounds. The first is that of mental or physical cruelty. These grounds which, as previously, must be adequately substantiated, can resolve marital tension through divorce in a matter of months, should this be necessary.

The grounds of mental cruelty had been used increasingly through the period 1969-85. This factor shows a changing view of marriage, to one focused upon the rights of the individual. The grounds of mental cruelty might continue to be used under the new law, but many petitioners have found it easier to use the grounds of one-year separation discussed below.

Divorce may also be obtained on grounds of adultery. (These grounds were used a good deal after the Act of 1968.)

The most significant change in the law is that a married couple may now obtain a divorce after living separately for one year. In this ruling, the law seeks to reduce the stress of marital differences and their duration. It seeks to honour the intent of the applicants, without the courts legislating morality. This is a specific instance of human rights taking precedent over a religious code of ethics. Moreover, the institution of marriage is respected: a full 12 months of separation is required. A few critics of the Divorce Law would have liked grounds similar to Sweden's, where a couple can file for divorce by mutual consent and receive the divorce in 25 days. At the present time in this country, such a law would be viewed as a threat to the institution of marriage, making divorce "too easy."

A high regard for marriage is further seen in the new law, by which lawyers and judges are required to ascertain that recourse to reconciliation has been made, and that the couple are aware of counselling agencies. Under the new Act, once custody and property rights are agreed upon, and where both parties consent to the divorce, the process is simple, and can be administered in a matter of days. Using the grounds of a one-year separation, an applicant may file before the 12-month period and theoretically obtain the divorce on the first anniversary of the separation.

As already stated, there could have been a more radical divorce law.

A couple cannot now simply terminate their relationship by mutual consent; a twelve months' separation (and not six months') is meant to allow time for serious thought about terminating a relationship.

The new law endorses two principles of the present age: individualism and equality. No woman is to be an "alimony drone," eternally financially dependent upon her ex-spouse. Most provinces have instituted a clear 50 percent division of property in divorce settlements. Further support for unemployable or under-employed spouses may be negotiated, but only for a limited period of time. Such a practice is intended to cut dependency between the one-time married pair.

Though the law was established with good intentions, it can be seen that, under the California law it resembles (Weitzman 1985), three groups of women are destined to be at a great disadvantage. Mothers with young children are generally not able to enter the work force full-time, or train for employment. Older housewives from traditional marriages will find it equally difficult to retrain or enter the labour force; in a competitive labour market, they are barely considered employable. The third group are women in transition. These women have been homemakers most of their lives, and may have been employed part-time or have done volunteer work, arranging these activities around caring for their husbands and children. If at this later stage in life they wish to be self-sufficient and maintain a middle-class style of life, they will likely find it necessary to spend some years in professional training (Weitzman, 1985:184–192).

Weitzman claims that the law and practice of the courts mark a major transformation in the family. The traditional legal view of marriage as a partnership is altered by rewarding individual achievement over family partnership (1986:374). "It suggests that a woman who chooses to be a housewife or a mother risks a great penalty, because if she is later divorced she will pay heavily for that choice" (1986:371). Placing one's first priority on the family, even with working part- or full-time, means losing out financially in the divorce settlement.

Most provinces require a 50-50 settlement of all assets accumulated through the marriage. In a marriage where the husband has been the major earner, and the wife has contributed minimally in direct earnings, she may intially gain in the settlement. But after a few years, when her living is dependent upon her own earnings, she may find herself financially short-changed because of her long absence from the work world.

The equal division of property achieved in Canadian divorce legislation in the last decade is seen as a major gain by feminists. Yet an increasing number of fathers feel that women are favoured in the courts in matters of child custody. Unfortunately, this issue is much more complex than property settlement (see Chapter 8).

The Divorce Act 1985 is a social and legal response to changing trends in Canadian society. It shows a secularized interpretation of marriage and divorce, conscious of individual and human rights. The new legislation is being applied to a social environment quite different from that of the 60s and 70s: the number of civil weddings has increased, and church weddings often have less religious significance; overall, couples are marrying at a later age; the number of people who cohabit before marriage has increased; most women want to keep their own identity independent of their husband's; birth control is widely accepted; and couples wait longer after marriage to have their first child.

The actual changes in marriage and divorce practice brought about by the new law were evident at once. Court processing is simplified. Divorces can be obtained in less time, so the average age at divorce is bound to decline. The grounds of alcoholic addiction or five-year desertion as found in the now-dated Act of 1968 will be almost totally subsumed under the grounds of one-year separation; the proportion of persons using the grounds of one-year separation will continue to be the largest by far. No more than before will the real reasons for a divorce be obvious, because petitioners most often opt for what will most efficiently achieve the goal of divorce.

CAUSES FOR THE TERMINATION OF MARRIAGE

The reasons for separation or divorce are numerous and complex. In dealing with individual persons or families, social workers and counsellors address a multiplicity of family problems and tensions. In a sense each case is unique: the particular feelings, fears, and perceptions of reality aroused in a case are real to each individual.

Though cases vary in their particulars, family researchers have found several basic variables directly related to marriage dissolution. In the first place, marriage at an early age (under 20) is related to a high possibility of divorce: about 8 percent of all brides annually are under 20 years of age, yet 34 percent of all women who divorce were married before they were 20 years of age. Young brides clearly make up a high proportion of those divorcing. Second, a brief courtship period varies inversely with marriage permanence. Third, alcoholism and drug addiction also contribute to divorce.

Fourth, economic deprivation or a lack of economic stability directly relates to marriage dissolution. A major change in lifestyle, like unemployment for the primary wage earner, may bring stress which affects the relationship. Other major changes, such as the death of a child or the permanent disability of a child or spouse may create stress leading to separation or divorce.

Fifth, the lack of marriage homogamy also contributes to marital stress. Difference in social status, values, age, race, or education may cause unanticipated social difficulties. Finally, those who have not had an earlier divorce experience rate better in marriage than those who have gone through the legal divorce process. This will be further discussed under the topic of remarriage. Looking at the other side of the coin, individuals who have come out of a happy, stable family are more likely to have a long-lasting marriage.

In contemporary society, marriage is viewed as an institution providing a degree of happiness and complementing one's personal interests and pursuits. When the happiness looked for in marriage is not found, alternatives are sought. There is no capitalist or socialist modern society without a high divorce rate; in general, traditional or peasant societies show less frequent dissolution.

In the pre-World War II era, couples who were unhappy often stayed together because of religious convictions or because of the fear of social censure. (This description still fits some couples today). Some chose to remain married, because divorce would radically reduce the income available for themselves and their children. Though family size has been greatly reduced and the majority of wedded women are now employed, women still generally experience a lower income and less economic support after divorce than do men. However, it could be judged from the figures for divorce which escalated after 1968, that, for generations, divorce was not chosen as a solution to marital unhappiness simply because *it was not possible* for most people.

Social scientists have coined the concept "emotional divorce" for a marriage where a couple live in the same residence but have no real bond. The Cuber and Harroff (1965) research makes reference to "passive congenial" and the "conflict-habituated" relationships which in many ways typify the emotionally divorced model. Neighbours and acquaintances may not even be aware of this form of co-existence. Emotional divorce may be more common than publicly perceived; marriages may stay intact for the reasons given above, for the sake of the children, or because the couple's prime interest is other than the family or the marriage.

Traditional marriage had different expectations, compared to modern marriage. Actual physical survival was a key concern for husband and wife in early French Canada and Upper Canada, during the pioneer days of the West, and through the Depression. Possibly one dimension of love often not verbalized was that of sustaining one another by supplying food and shelter. Children also contributed economically to family survival. The couple may not have demonstrated much affection for one another, but they did sustain themselves and their offspring with a lot of hard work. What only their families knew was how many couples in an earlier stage of our history lived in a state of "emotional divorce."

For many families, the character of their relationships has changed. It is not unheard of for young families to move away from next of kin intentionally, so as to avoid frequent social contact. Young married couples often establish close ties with fellow employees or with university classmates, as a substitute for extended-family relationships. Furthermore, married people may engage in career or leisure activity independent of their partners. The urban environment has also given people a higher degree of anonymity not commonly associated with rural or small-town communities, although for many couples this is as much a preservative for marriage as small-town scrutiny.

The state has also become more enmeshed with the welfare of the family. We have compulsory schooling until age 16, pensions after 65, and, more recently, state intervention in child and wife abuse, and, to a lesser degree, its involvement in the process of divorce. (See Chapter 9 for a further discussion of this topic.)

In the wide arena of societal change and a rising divorce rate, the women's movement deserves special mention. Women have become more independent and have greater self-esteem. They are less likely to look upon a husband for financial support or to marriage as a source of social approval; their participation in the labour market has grown significantly (Wilson, 1983). The effect of this development has had a profound impact upon the family. Many women who have been in a traditional marriage for years have changed their expectations. Some husbands accustomed to a traditional marriage have become bewildered or defensive; others see a more rewarding relationship possible with their wives, and are relieved not to have to be the sole breadwinner and family authority.

From a structural functionalist perspective, society is in a process of change because of the dynamic balance between various social institutions. Changes in the economy, e.g., an increase in the employment of women, force a new balance in the family system. New values found in the secular urban community, such as a fresh appreciation of human rights, create a readjustment of the family organization. A more comfortable life style and better health conditions have added at least ten years to the life span and, with the technology that provided relatively safe contraceptives, have effected a new equilibrium in the family.

But family change, and, more specifically, separation and divorce can also be looked at from the perspective of symbolic interaction. This more narrowly focussed analysis concentrates on the interaction of husband and wife, parent and child, and the interpretation of words, symbols, and behaviour. Marriage may mean one thing to one partner (companionship and emotional support) and something else to the other partner (sexual license). Bernard (1981) distinguishes between "his" marriage and "her" marriage. Similarly, divorce may be seen as potential freedom and growth for one partner, and rejection and solitariness for the other. Over time, one's perception of the institution of marriage, kin relationships, and parental and marital roles changes, affecting self-identity and social self-image throughout the period of separation, divorce, remarriage, or changing parental relationships, and with self-image continually being reformulated through these rather traumatic experiences.

THE FAMILY AND THE COURTS

Family law is divided between the jurisdiction of the federal and the provincial courts. The federal courts have jurisdiction in divorce, annulment, adoption, and the partition of matrimonial property. The provincial courts share jurisdiction in custody, access, and maintenance, while having sole jurisdiction in matters relating to juvenile delinquency and child neglect. This creates confusion and often unnecessary adversarial tension between two adults seeking a divorce, since a single case of divorce can include various combinations of all these problems.

In the city of Edmonton, Alberta, it was hoped to resolve this disarray of jurisdictions by creating a Unified Family Court. Established in 1971, it has been relatively successful. The two courts and family counsellors have easy access to one another under one roof. British Columbia, New Brunswick, Newfoundland, Saskatchewan, and Ontario have followed suit. All subscribe to a philosophy of seeking to reduce litigation, and on the grounds of humanity and cost present the option of out-of-court mediation. Such a format allows the divorcing couples to decide their own destiny, rather than have it determined by the laws of the land.

THE SEPARATING PROCESS

Gershenfeld has taken the period leading to the divorce and found it to have seven fairly common and relevant stages (1981). The first is disillusionment, when the couple's mutual attraction has declined. Expectations for the relationship are not being met. In the "erosion" stage that follows, hostility and verbal assaults are roused by discussions relating to children, house maintenance, and expenditures.

The third stage in the detachment process is mental separation. Boredom pervades the relationship. The couple carry out their activities separately, and purposely avoid one another. When one or both of them come to the point where life in this marriage is not feasible, steps are taken toward separation. It may be months before the other partner or friends know of this decision. However, the process of dissolution begins with such actions as consulting a lawyer, checking the joint bank account, actively seeking information about legal procedures and rights, and possibly seeking out members of the opposite sex for companionship.

The fourth stage is the worst. The couple having come to actual physical separation, stress is at its maximum. This period is filled with indecision, loneliness, and thoughts of abandonment.

Gershenfeld calls the fifth stage one of mourning, in realization that no perfect world of marriage, law, community, and justice is to be found. The feelings of the separated person may fluctuate between such extremes as vengeance and fond memories of past birthdays and family vacations. A sixth stage, of second adolescence, may bring a desperate search for a new identity and freedom. In the final stage of exploration and hard work, some resolution is found. These stages vary in intensity and duration according to the individual. Some problems are resolved quickly, others endure. Support groups, friends and professional counsellors may be helpful. Yet some of these behaviours may be carried into a subsequent remarriage, especially if there is insufficient time between.

AFTER THE SEPARATION

Some good research has been done on adjustment after separation. Raschke shows that personal stress for the separated is lower for those who are socially involved (1977:131). She found social activity to be minimal in the early stages of separation, to increase considerably, then to decline again. Men were more active socially than women.

I have identified seven style styles of social participation or focal concerns of the separated person. The first is that of the *isolate*, who withdraws from society. The second is the attempt of the *sex seeker* to fill the void and recover from past rejection with new sexual partners. In the third style, the *career-oriented*, a major focus is to become established in appropriate employment or education that can ultimately contribute to economic independence. Not surprisingly, this is most frequently a concern of separated women.

In the next style, of *family focus*, the parent who gains the custody of the child or children rebuilds from the hurt of the past, in a new one-parent-child relationship that becomes close and meaningful. Its counterpart is the ambivalent parental role of the non-custodial parent (who is most often the male in Canadian society), and whose position is confusing and frustrating, legally, socially, and personally.

The sixth style is that of the *companion seeker* who feels the loss of an intimate and seeks a partner with some degree of permanence. This search is made with care and caution. The last style is one of *resolution*, exemplified by divorced people who have developed a good individual and social self-image and have goals they seek to attain.

The seven styles have a degree of fluidity and merging, as individuals move from one style to another or, in pursuing a career and caring for a family, experience two or three styles simultaneously.

Morton Hunt found three major modes of sexual activity following marital separation, in research done among a middle-class, formerly married population (1966). Of the three types, the smaller group are the *abstainers* who never or rarely become involved in post-marital affairs. Either they are uninterested, view such activity as meaningless, are afraid of failure, or have deep religious values opposed to it. This type is similar in some ways to the isolate style mentioned above. On the other hand, the *users*, forming the largest of the three groups, sees sex as a part of a process of redefinition of self and affirmation of masculinity or femininity. Sexual activity is viewed neither as promiscuity nor as a basis for a permanent love relationship. This style puts its exponents at risk of pregnancy, erosion of the capacity to love, and negative parental role modelling (1966:134). The *addict* sees the sexual partner as a convenience, in liaisons that are casual and fleeting. Addicts may possess low self-esteem and a deep-rooted neurosis that could have contributed to the breakdown of their previous marriage.

REMARRIAGE

Just as divorce is increasingly being accepted, so is remarriage. As of 1985, approximately 18 percent of Canadians marrying (66,798) had been divorced, a marked increase from four and a half percent in 1968. The proportion of remarriages will continue to rise, not only because of the larger number of divorced persons, but also because there is less social stigma attached to separated and divorced people, nowadays. The fact that many who dissolved their union seek remarriage shows that marriage as an institution is not on its way out.

Provinces differ in their remarriage rates, showing a direct relation to the proportion of their residents who divorce. A small number who divorce will not remarry, because they feel it is against biblical teaching. Divorced men are more likely to remarry than divorced women. The younger the age at divorce the greater the likelihood of remarriage. At least half of the divorced brides marry a bridegroom who was also divorced. There are social factors, however, which create considerable caution on the part of some of the divorced who might otherwise remarry. Some women who have achieved autonomy following divorce hesitate to enter a possibly subservient relationship. Men who have developed a prestigious and lucrative career are hesitant over what they might lose, if a second marriage were dissolved. At the same time, social norms increasingly permit the alternative of sexual liaisons and temporary cohabitation.

There are several significant contrasts between those who are marrying for the first time and the remarrying divorced. The obvious is that the divorced have already had a marriage experience. Many carry emotional scars from the earlier marriage. Some have children; the presence of children in the divorcée's new marriage is the most important consideration. The single parent not only seeks a companion and lover (and possibly economic security) but also another parent for the children. Custodial parents often vacillate between whether the new mate should be to their liking, or to the liking of each of the children as well.

There are several other personal and social considerations to be made in remarriage. Compared to people marrying for the first time, divorced persons remarrying generally have larger financial assets and property, as well as debt payments and loans to honour. They will have established a whole range of social relationships during the time of their marriage; some of these will persist after divorce, others disintegrate. They will have greater independence from their parents, compared to people marrying for the first time, and greater experience of life, though this may have produced some inflexible values. And patterns of behaviour unchanged since the first marriage, an inability to handle crises or hostility toward the opposite sex, perhaps, will affect the prospects for a remarriage.

The spread in age between remarrying partners is generally much greater than the average 2.2-year age difference between men and women marrying for the first time, and personal values, economic status, and ethnic identity are less likely to be similar. (To a student of the family, such divergent characteristics signal possible odds against marriage permanence.) The couple is more likely to have a civil rather than a religious wedding; the period of engagement will likely have been briefer, and the wedding ceremony less elaborate with fewer guests.

Some would argue that a remarriage following marriage failure and divorce is unlikely to succeed. However, many people who remarry put great effort into sustaining the marriage. The fact that they remarry is evidence that they are not against the institution of marriage, but rather that their first was not a good match. In addition, they are older and presumably have learned something about life, relationships, and adjustment in their first marriages. On a purely statistical basis, more second marriages end in divorce than do first marriages, but the rate does not exceed 50 percent. Here another comparison must be made between the first-married and the divorced, remarried population. The life experiences of these two groups can be quite different. The remarried population have in all likelihood encountered adverse economic, psychological, and social situations. And if they had children, their divorce and remarriage brought additional challenges and responsibility.

CONCLUSION

This chapter has shown historical and contemporary variables which bring social change and affect the legal system. Structural factors found in the institutions of government, economics, religion, and the historical family, were seen to have a mutual interplay. It is obvious that the influence of institutional religion on marriage has greatly declined, while economics and personal ethics play an increasing role.

Separation has been shown to be a process, with an evolving and changing attitude toward such elements as the community, the law, religion, one's partner, one's self, the children, and careers.

The Divorce Act 1985 was a negotiated law conceived in compromise and democratically processed, addressing specific needs within the Canadian society. The adversarial process of the divorce courts was denounced, and individuals were to determine their own marital destiny, rather than the arbiters of the law. However, despite the proposal made by the Law Reform Commission as early as 1975, marriage dissolution is not granted on demand. Individuals must submit to a one-year waiting period. And marriage breakdown is still evident within the grounds of adultery and physical and mental cruelty. It is possible that, after a decade or more, new laws will grant a true no-fault divorce in which divorce is granted upon demand.

About four decades ago the popular and insightful anthropologist Margaret Mead recommended two stages for marriage (1949). A first contract undertaken by a couple would involve a temporary mutuality, a second, made only after the first proved successful, would allow for child bearing and childrearing. Such a family form could become more than an academic's wishful thinking.

The changing status of women continues to have an impact on family living, family mutuality, and childrearing practices. Women's rights will become more clearly defined as well as more acceptable socially, to the extent that economic conditions encourage their participation in the labour force.

Economic conditions will affect the duration of marital unions. Technology and international trading conditions may induce greater unemployment and more part-time work, especially among the unskilled and semi-skilled. Such conditions are often hard on marriage, and necessitate major family reorganization.

Whatever the social and economic conditions they find themselves in, individuals will continue to seek self-fulfillment and happiness, as singles, marrieds, parents, divorcées, and remarrieds. Our economic, educational, political, and family systems will play an important role in shaping these personal goals within and outside family boundaries.

REFERENCES

Ambert, Anne-Marie. 1980. *Divorce in Canada*. Toronto: Academic Press.

Ambert, Anne-Marie, and Maureen Baker. 1984. "Marriage Dissolution: Structural and Ideological Changes." In M. Baker, ed. *The Family*. Toronto; McGraw-Hill Ryerson.

Baker, Maureen, ed. 1984. *The Family, Changing Trends in Canada*. Toronto: Gage.

Bernard, Jessie. 1981. "The Good Provider Role: Its Rise and Fall." *American Psychologist*, vol. 36, 1, pp. 1–12.

Cuber, John F. and Peggy Harroff. 1965. *The Significant Americans*. Baltimore: Penguin.

Eichler, M. 1983. *Families in Canada Today*. Toronto: Gage.

Farber, Bernard. 1964. *Family Organization and Interaction*. San Francisco: Chandler.

Gershenfeld, M. 1981. Lecture, Philadelphia.

Kircheisen, F. M. 1929. *Napoleon I, Emperor of the French*, (F. Collins transl.). London: Hutchinson and Co.

Lasch, C. 1978. *The Culture of Narcissism*. New York: Norton.

Larocque, Paul. 1968. The Evolution of the Canadian Divorce Law, Thesis, Dept. of Political Science, Queen's University, Kingston, Ont.

Levinger, George. 1976. "A Social Psychological Perspective on Marital Dissolution," *Journal of Social Issues*, vol. 32, No. 1, pp. 21–47.

Luxton, M. 1980. *More Than a Labour of Love: Three Generations of Women's Work in The Home*. Toronto: The Women's Press.

McKie, D. C., B. Prentice, and P. Reed. 1983. *Divorce: Law and the Family in Canada*. Ottawa, Ministry of Supply and Services.

Mead, Margaret. 1949. *Male and Female*. New York: William Morrow and Co.

Pike, Robert. 1975. "Legal Access and the Incidence of Divorce in Canada; A Socio-Historical Analysis," *Canadian Review of Sociology and Anthropology*, vol. 12, No. 2.

Proceedings of the Special Joint Committee of the Senate and House of Commons on Divorce, 1967, pp. 1515–1516.

Riddell, W. R. 1924. "The Criminal Law in Reference to Marriage in Upper Canada," Ontario Historical Society Papers and Records, vol. 21, pp. 233–235.

Scanzoni, J. 1983. *Shaping Tomorrow's Family*. Beverly Hills: Sage.

———. 1972. *Sexual Bargaining: Power Politics in American Marriage*. Chicago: University of Chicago Press.

Smelser, J. and E. H. Erikson, eds. 1980. *Themes of Love and Work in Adulthood*. Cambridge, Mass.: Harvard University Press.

Statistics Canada, *Marriages and Divorces Vol. II*, 1985. 1986. Ottawa: Supply and Services.

Statistics Canada, *Family Expenditure in Canada*. 1984. Ottawa: Supply and Services.

Studies on Divorce. 1975. Ottawa, Information Canada.

United Nations Demographic Year Book. 1983.

Weitzman, L. J. 1985. *The Divorce Revolution*. New York: Free Press.

Wilson, S. J. 1982. *Women, the Family and The Economy*. Toronto: McGraw-Hill Ryerson.

CHAPTER 8

Children of Divorce

C. JAMES RICHARDSON

INTRODUCTION

One day, three-year-old Jacob asked his father: "When will I get *my* other Daddy?" He was thinking about his half-brother and half-sister who have two "Daddies." Jacob is a child born into a remarriage family. His half-brother and half-sister live their lives in two remarriage families and have a half-brother (himself) in their mother's house and a recently born half-sister in their father's house. Like many children of joint custody, they alternate weeks in each home. So Jacob, who is very much attached to them, must experience their sudden disappearance and equally sudden reappearance into his life. He often finds this distressing but is also intrigued, confused and, perhaps, frightened by the fact that there is a baby and a father of his brother and sister whom he has never seen and a whole set of family events which he hears about but is not a part of. Evidently, he is resigned to this multiplication of fathers and siblings happening to him, one day.

Or consider the case of Andrew who is now in his early teens. His parents divorced when he was about age seven. As with many children of divorce, he found himself living in a female-headed, single-parent family. Visits with his father became more and more infrequent and sporadic until, to all intents and purposes, he had no father at all. When, a couple of years later, his mother remarried, he became very attached and close to his stepfather. Recently, that marriage went the way of many remarriages and also ended in divorce. Much against his mother's wishes, Andrew wants to continue to see and spend time with his "new" father, and the feeling is mutual. Yet it is unclear whether the stepfather has any legal right to demand that contact be maintained with this child of an earlier marriage.

The topic of this chapter is Children of Divorce. Most of it will focus on the children's experience and the impact on them of living through their parents' marriage breakdown. This is because, no matter how amicable the separation, divorce is almost always a disruptive and traumatic experience for everyone, but particularly for children as they find themselves caught up in their parents' personal and social disorganization and eventual reorganization. This is a series of life changes not of their devising, over which they have little control and from which, usually, they have very little to gain. Yet these changes strike at the very core of their world.

Divorce and the family patterns that develop from it send shock waves throughout the whole family system, and have consequences which go beyond the immediate family and the adjustment period following separation. The breakdown of marriage brings about a change in family structure and a reorganization and restructuring of family ties and kinship relations. Aside from the emotional trauma which seems, inevitably, to accompany even the most amicable of separations, divorce also shatters taken-for-granted notions of what is meant by family and how, as a small group, a family relates to other families and other parts of the community. These are changes and effects that we are only beginning to understand or, for that matter, even envision very fully.

THE SCOPE OF THE PROBLEM

As the divorce rate continues to remain high in most western societies, more and more children will go through the breakup of their parents' marriage. While divorce rates in Canada have levelled off and even abated, at least temporarily, about 70,000 divorces occur annually. About half (48 percent) of these involve dependent children, which means that, each year, around 55,000 children are affected by their parents' divorce.[1] To these figures must be added the number of separations and desertions which occur under provincial jurisdiction and are not, therefore, picked up in the federal divorce statistics.[2] As McVey and Robinson point out, reliance on divorce statistics alone seriously underestimates the actual rate of marital dissolution in Canadian society. Their conservative estimate is that this rate is about double what the divorce statistics tell us. Probably the number of children affected annually in Canada by marriage breakdown is much closer to 100,000.[3]

Admittedly, this figure pales in comparison to the estimated two million children per year who go through the divorce experience in the United States. National studies of the life course of children suggest that from one-third to two-fifths of American children will spend at least part of their lives not living continuously with both biological parents.[4] Glick, an American demographer, estimates that by 1990 this figure will be closer to 50 percent.[5]

Children have always been at risk of family dissolution and of spending part of their lives in a single-parent family. Indeed, demographers tell us that the rate of family dissolution hasn't changed much over this century: only the causes have changed. What resulted in earlier decades from the early death of one parent is now caused by the breakdown of the parents' marriage.[6] At the same time, death and divorce, while bringing about a similar change in family structure, are not likely to be viewed the same way by children nor to have the same kinds of consequences. Loss of a parent through death is obviously painful, but it is at least something over which we have no control. However, from the child's point of view, marital breakdown, the possible loss of one parent, and the end of "normal" family life seem avoidable and unnecessary. Moreover, where one parent ceases to play a part in the child's life, the sense of loss will no doubt be intensified by feelings of resentment, abandonment, and bitterness. Family dissolution because of divorce may, then, be more devastating for children than dissolution because of death.

There are a variety of reasons why the divorce rate is likely to remain high, and there seems little we can or should do about that. Indeed, reform of divorce legislation and procedures is a belated response to divorce having become a rather "normal" process, one which, in the long run, is often the rational decision for people to make. Yet, while it is recognized that divorce may have positive consequences, there remains considerable concern about its psychological, social, and economic consequences for children and with finding ways to minimize these possible effects.

One focus of this chapter, then, is to look briefly at what is known about children and divorce and to consider some of the realities of the separation and divorce process. But because separation and divorce are essentially legal processes, a second task must be to examine the legal context in which marriage breakdown occurs, and to consider some of the alternatives to the traditional adversary process which it is hoped will improve the situation of children following the breakup of their parents' marriage. Finally, because so many divorced people remarry, it will be useful to look briefly at some issues related to children in remarriage families.

PROBLEMS IN STUDYING CHILDREN IN DIVORCE

More than anyone else, small children live their lives in the circumscribed world of the family. Intuitively, therefore, we expect changes in family patterns or structure to have a momentous impact on children and children's lives. Marriage breakdown obviously begins a process of major restructuring of the family and a bewildering array of alternatives. There is, first of all, the transition from living in a nuclear family with two parents to living in a single-parent family, often with a substantial reduction in standard of living. For some children there will also be a sense of abandonment when one parent — usually the father — becomes absent. Others must learn to cope with the tension and awkwardness of now having a "weekend" father. A minority will go through the as yet little-known experience of alternating between two homes and two diverging lifestyles as a result of a joint custody arrangement. And for many children there is the likelihood that they will acquire one or more stepparents as their parents make the shift from divorce back into marriage.

In recent years there has been a tendency to romanticize divorce as a creative, rehabilitative, and liberating process. It may often be all of these things. But, along the way, it may also be highly stressful and disruptive for at least some, if not all, family members. That the actual divorce hearing is, for most people, not the protracted and highly emotional "Kramer vs Kramer" situation but a rather ritualistic formality taking less than 15 minutes, often hides the amount of prior anguish, hostility, fighting and negotiation which preceded it; the divorce hearing is often the tail end of a long and highly disruptive uncoupling process.

But, just as there are many types of marriage, so there are many types of divorce. Some couples, on their own or with the help of professionals, may end their marriage rather amicably and continue to cooperate in matters affecting their children. Others will continue to be hostile to one another long after the divorce is granted, and may use the children to wound and attack one another.[7] Moreover, the breakdown of a marriage in an impoverished family will have quite different economic consequences and entail quite different stresses than in families better able to handle legal costs and setting up new households.

There is also the question of whether, when we talk about the effects of divorce on children, we are concerned with such short-term effects as regression, return to bed-wetting, discipline problems, truancy, and juvenile delinquency, or with long-term effects on their later adult personality and interpersonal behaviour and skills such as, for example, an inability to form close relationships, lower self-esteem, or the greater likelihood that they, too, will become divorced.

RESEARCH INTO THE EFFECTS OF DIVORCE ON CHILDREN

Understandably, given the complexity of the problems facing children and the variety of ways couples go about ending a marriage, researchers have put considerable effort into assessing the impact on children of divorce and separation. With some simplification, we can say that this research falls into several related categories or areas of inquiry. First, a sizeable body of research has sought, but quite unsuccessfully, to demonstrate that divorce is a direct cause of a number of emotional, cognitive, and behavioural problems in children. These include such things as retarded emotional development, poor school performance, delinquency, and discipline problems.[8] A second and closely related body of research is what has come to be called the "father absent" literature. That is, since most separated or divorced families are headed by females, there has been considerable effort devoted to determining the consequences for children of growing up without a father or alternative male figure.[9]

Another body of research has been concerned with the more easily measured and obvious economic consequences that follow from marriage breakdown, and the impact these have on the subsequent life chances of children.[10] Finally, much of the more recent research has attempted to describe children's experience and their feelings about divorce, and to assess the various factors associated with this important change in a child's life.[11]

Despite our intuitive sense that the breakup of the parents' marriage should have momentous and easily observable consequences for children, it turns out to be extremely difficult to generalize about the aftermath of divorce and separation. Rather, those doing research in this area have been unable to demonstrate conclusively that children suffer *measurable* short-term or long-term detrimental effects directly attributable to either the process of divorce or to living in a single-parent family afterwards. Why should this be the case? One reason for this inconclusiveness is that the situation of divorcing people is so varied. But there are more substantive methodological problems that have also led to uncertain and often contradictory findings.

An important question that must first be asked is: who is doing the research? After reviewing the literature on divorce outcomes, Anne Marie Ambert, a York University sociologist, concludes that there are really two major branches of literature on divorce, the sociological and the psychiatric. She suggests that the findings from sociological research are, on the whole, more positive and paint a less gloomy picture than those generated from clinical research. The reason for the difference is that, by definition, people seen by clinicians have specific problems of one kind or another. In contrast, sociologists will usually have studied a more representative cross-section of divorcing or separating families. A case in point is the ten-year study by Judith Wallerstein and Joan Kelly, *Surviving the Breakup*, which will be discussed later in this chapter. As important as this study is, it cannot be said for sure that what they have found applies equally to all divorces, because the authors of this study obtained their respondents by promising counselling over a five-year period. It is likely, then, that the parents and children they studied would be skewed toward the distressed end of the divorce population.[12]

Whatever the source of the research, the major problem in determining the effects of divorce on children is that it is extraordinarily difficult to sort out what is an effect of divorce per se and what is the result of other factors. In particular, we can expect that prior to actual separation there will usually have been considerable marital discord. Although it seems that children are sometimes not aware of this, or of the magnitude of the conflict between their parents, there nevertheless remains the question of whether it is the experience of having lived in an unhappy family or the breakup of their parents' marriage which is the crucial factor.

Ann Goetting concludes, after reviewing the literature, that it is the former: family discord is a more important determinant of various kinds of negative effects in children than the change in marital structure.[13] She cites a number of studies suggesting that the most detrimental situation for a child is an unhappy intact home. On most measures, children from divorced homes fall somewhere between those from unhappy intact homes and those from happy intact homes. This suggests that, overall, divorce may have positive, not negative, effects.

There is, as well, the question of the values held by those doing the research; while social scientists may not be deliberately biased in their work, their views about what *ought* to be inevitably shape the kinds of questions they ask. For example, in the 1950s and 1960s divorce was most often viewed as disastrous, a singular event which undermined and destroyed the family. Children of divorce were usually depicted as "products of broken homes," victims to be pitied. By the early 1970s the focus shifted to a conception of divorce as a "creative process," a process not of disorganization but of reorganization. Divorce, it was argued, should be thought of less as a problem than as a solution to other kinds of problems. Traditional marriage and the nuclear family were seen as hampering self-actualization and self-fulfillment and as serving to maintain sexual inequality and exploitation of women. Researchers have not exactly come full circle in the 1980s, but they have begun to look more closely at the economic, social, and emotional costs of marriage breakdown, and to view the conventional nuclear family more positively.[14] In short, since the questions we have asked about family and marriage breakdown have not been consistent, we should hardly expect that the findings would somehow add up to a cumulative body of knowledge.

Another complicating factor in understanding what the impact of divorce is, exactly, is the psychological state of the divorcing parents. Kelly, in her recent research, has found that on a variety of measures, divorced couples fall mid-way between a normal population and a population of people who have been admitted to a psychiatric hospital.[15] Follow-up measures, taken two years later, show, on average, a movement back to normal. The question is, of course, which is cause and which is effect? Does the experience of divorce make people more psychotic, or are people who are relatively psychotic more likely to become divorced? Whichever is true, it is apparent that, for a time, children must cope not only with a changed family structure but also with being parented by people who may be on the borderline of becoming psychotic. We cannot, then, conclude that divorce, itself, is a crucial factor in creating problems for children.

As well, there is a tendency to exaggerate the importance of the intact nuclear family and to assume that any disruption of that pattern will be detrimental to children. This is especially evident in the large body of research which has concentrated on the impact of father absence on children. This focus is understandable because, in the majority of divorces and separations, children are, in fact, living with their mothers and in many instances rarely see their fathers. One American study found that a majority of children of divorce had had no contact whatsoever with their father in the past year. Only one child in six (16 percent) had seen his or her father once a week. Another 17 percent saw their fathers at least once a month, while 15 percent saw him at least once a year. The remaining 52 percent had had no contact in the past year and, of these, 36 percent (of the total sample) had no contact in the last five years.[16]

As with other research in this area, the results of father-absence research are inconclusive. While some studies have found negative effects for children where the father is absent, many have not; and some have even reported positive effects for children of having their father absent from the family. What is apparent is that father absence is related to poverty and, in turn, poverty is related to a variety of behavioural and psychological problems.

Besides the factor of poverty, we should, perhaps, not be too surprised that father absence, in and of itself, has not turned out to be all that significant. Underlying research into children and divorce is the assumption that in all intact families, fathers are actively involved in parenting and play a significant role in children's lives. In at least some families this may not be the case. Christopher Lasch, for example, contends that the modern family, though patriarchal, is to all intents and purposes *father-absent*. He suggests that the father is, in effect, a "tired night visitor," an observation supported by one study which found that the average father spends only 12 minutes per day interacting with his children.[17] The amount of time spent with children may not be the most important factor and, while not actively engaged in parenting, the father may still be extremely important to children. But these kinds of observations do suggest that we should not exaggerate the quality of life children experience in intact families or assume that the dissolution of some kinds of families is necessarily a bad thing for children. Indeed, as some research suggests, if fathers maintain contact with their children at all, they become, of necessity, more involved in parenting after separation than before.[18]

CHILDREN'S EXPERIENCE OF MARITAL BREAKDOWN

The inconclusive nature of research on divorce outcomes and father absence should not be taken to mean that the breakup of the parents' marriage does not have emotional impact on children. Indeed, as more and more studies have been done which rely on the accounts of children themselves, we are learning that parents may often seriously underestimate or be unaware of how extremely difficult a time it is for children and what feelings of anger, bitterness, confusion, and guilt are engendered. Much of this, particularly guilt, may be inexplicable to adults. For example, a psychologist recently recounted how a five-year-old boy she counselled is convinced that had he not had a fight with his parents about eating his spaghetti, his parents would not have separated. He blames himself for the fact that his father no longer lives with him.[19]

Research that has drawn directly on the experiences of children close to the time of the marriage breakup provides a rather consistent picture. A British study, by Ann Mitchell, highlights the degree of confusion, surprise, and disbelief most children feel when their parents split up. While many of the children had been aware of arguments between their parents and sometimes violence, most of them had felt their family life to be basically happy. Nor did they see the conflict as a sufficient reason for their parents to end the marriage.[20]

Echoing this is Wallerstein and Kelly's account of the latency children in their sample:[21]

> Despite detailed and often very personal knowledge of the serious causes underlying the divorce decision including repeated scenes of violence between the parents, most of these children were unable to see (initially) any justification for the parental decision to divorce.[22]

As the authors relate, despite having watched their father torture their mother by holding her down on the floor and sticking bobby pins in her nose, the children in the family described initially opposed the mother's decision to divorce. Similar findings emerge from a unique and recent British study. The researchers advertised for volunteers who had been under 18 when their parents had separated. Those who responded ranged in present age from age six to age 57. Their mainly retrospective accounts again show that many of the children had experienced their parents' separation with disbelief, and hoped for a reconciliation. Few felt that the level of marital disagreement warranted an end to the marriage.[23]

Most studies of children in divorce have been able to take only one measure, and have had to rely mainly on parents' and children's memories of feelings at the time of the separation. That is, there have been few longitudinal studies designed to follow children from the point of separation to several years after. The much-cited exception is the ambitious study by Judith Wallerstein and Joan Kelly, *Surviving the Breakup*. The authors studied 60 California families (with 131 children) from the point of separation through a five-year follow-up. In addition, one of the authors (Wallerstein) is carrying out a ten-year follow-up study of these same families.

Surviving the Breakup is a rich and complex study, not easy to summarize in a few paragraphs. However, in general, it shows that for all of the children the breakup of their parents' marriage was a highly stressful and disruptive experience, and that the effects of the divorce persist long after the actual separation. At the time of the separation, the breakup of the family evoked in these children "shock, intense fears and grieving." While all lived in Marin County, California, notorious for its high rate of marital instability, the ordinariness of marriage breakdown was irrelevant to their level of distress and fear about what the future would hold. Nor did it seem to matter what level of conflict had preceded the parents' decision to separate.

The research suggests also that divorce has different kinds of impact and evokes different responses in children of different ages. Pre-school children were often very confused about the meaning of the separation, and blamed themselves. Their response was to regress in terms of toilet training and speech. Older children generally understood what was happening but manifested their concerns through anger and depression. At the 18-month follow-up, things had not improved very much, and some children were found to be actually worse off than when initially interviewed. Even at the five-year point, some 37 percent of the children were still "moderately to severely depressed." This finding, and the fact that many of the children had not come to terms with their parents' divorce, lead the authors to conclude that divorce is a process which takes place over a much more extended period than had previously been assumed.

The findings from the Wallerstein and Kelly study present a rather bleak picture of the effects of divorce on children. However, we should be cautious about generalizing their findings as being necessarily true of all children of divorce. As noted earlier, the respondents in this study were ones who had been seen as in need of counselling and came from families perhaps more distressed than the normal population of divorcing families. Also, the children were interviewed on a fairly intensive basis, as well as being counselled. It may be that any group of children when subjected to this close scrutiny by trained counsellors would eventually be seen as manifesting many of these same symptoms. As the authors acknowledge, by the five-year follow-up, many other factors besides the divorce of their parents had also been at work. Finally, the children of the study were not compared with a group of children from intact families.

It is well to note, too, that even among these unhappy children the authors report how, with the passage of time, while anger and hostility still lingered, the "turbulent responses" at the time of the separation had largely abated. And, in interpreting their findings, there is the question of whether "the glass is half-full or half-empty": while over one-third of the children still showed signs of depression and anger, two-thirds did not. Nor could the authors find evidence of other effects which have been associated with divorce. For example, school performance did not seem to be affected by the experience of marital breakup.

Despite these qualifications, *Surviving the Breakup* is an important study. Its real contribution is made, not in showing that children are upset and distressed when their parents separate—we would expect that—but in its ability to identify what helps or hinders children to adjust to their new situation. Two key factors emerge as helpful: 1) easy access and an ongoing relationship with a non-custodial parent, and 2) a post-divorce mother-father relationship in which conflict is kept to a minimum. As will be discussed shortly, these two findings bolster the case for joint custody and shared parenting and the need for separation and divorce counselling and mediation.

Similar conclusions emerge from the other widely cited American study by Mavis Hetherington and her colleagues at the University of Virginia. These researchers carried out a two-year longitudinal study of 96 pre-school children, half of whom were from divorced families. Their focus was on the effect of disruption and disorganization in the parents' lives and its impact on children's behaviour, development, and relationship with their parents. At one year after divorce, they found that:

> Children in divorced families were more dependent, disobedient, aggressive, whining, demanding and unaffectionate than children in intact families.[24]

As in the Wallerstein and Kelly study, support and encouragement between the divorced parents contributed to an earlier adjustment of the children. This study also points to the fact that younger children do better when the custodial parent is able to establish or re-establish an orderly and supportive household routine. Yet, as the authors conclude, there is no way to avoid the problems associated with divorce and separation entirely: these invariably involve disruption and disorganization. While most people do begin to cope with many of their problems, the course of adjustment is more painful and difficult than most people had expected. The authors suggest that this points to the need for more support systems and post-divorce counselling, if we want the worst effects of divorce to be mitigated or eliminated. The evidently disruptive transition from married status to divorced status has led to an attempt to understand the uncoupling process more fully.

THE UNCOUPLING PROCESS

A variety of authors have likened the stages of divorce to the stages of dying as described by Kübler-Ross: 1) Denial 2) Anger 3) Bargaining 4) Depression and 5) Acceptance.[25] In sociological terms, divorce, like the transition from "patient-who-will-get-well" to "terminal patient" is a status passage, a change in status with rather predictable stages to go through. As Ambert describes it, "divorce is a normal process with specific tasks to be mastered, recognizable stress to be dealt with and satisfaction and goals to be sought for."[26] The notion of divorce as a process akin to dying is of course only an analogy, but it is a useful one in that the Kübler-Ross model stresses that not only the patient but also other family members must, if they are to be supportive of the dying person, go through the various stages to acceptance. So it is with the divorce process. Members of the families of the divorcing couple must also come to terms with and accept the end of the marriage, and see that perhaps no one is really at fault or that both are equally to blame for the breakup. There is little benefit to the divorcing couple if other family members are acting as "cheerleaders," encouraging their side to take positions which end up in an intractable dispute.

To say that divorce is a process with recognizable stages and problems is not of great help to people going through the experience. It is small comfort to know that one's irrational and disruptive behaviour is quite normal and to be expected. People who experience marriage breakdown invariably feel themselves unique, though friends and relatives may see them as acting pretty much like others they have watched go through the same experience, including, perhaps, themselves. Few men, for example, admitting that they have separated, will take much comfort in being told to make sure to get enough to eat and not to drink too much. Yet, for most separating or divorcing men, this is probably sound and realistic advice. The point is that, in the first year or so, children will likely find that their parents are not quite the same people they were before. Even if they are not behaving in very irrational ways, they will be mastering new and reviving old roles which have little to do with parenting.

Spanier and Casto suggest that there are two distinct but overlapping adjustments divorcing and separating couples must make. The first is the adjustment to the dissolution of the marriage. These include the practical aspects of the legal process, informing people in one's social world about the change and dealing with the new emotions which surface.[27] Second, people must adjust to the process of setting up a new lifestyle. Women who seemed to have no other role in life but mothering may now be coping with the unfamiliar role of becoming a breadwinner and of acting economically independent. Others may be going through the anxiety of returning to college or university, a difficult enough transition for most adults, whatever their marital situation. Both parents may also be re-entering the dating and marriage market, returning to and developing, however awkwardly, uncomfortably, and self-consciously, sides of themselves which the children will never have seen and which they themselves never expected to use again in their lives.

Probably, most of these transitions, these new roles, are not so much child-centred as just the opposite. Indeed, as those who do marriage and separation counselling will attest, for a time, at least, most divorcing people are exceptionally self-centred and unable to be very sympathetic to others, including, at times, their own children. In general, as Hetherington's study shows, while people do adjust to their new status, the first year is usually chaotic, disruptive, and stressful for some members of the family.[28] And, as Robert Weiss notes, this first year is a period of intense ambivalence. "Individuals who have shared in the decision to separate may alternate between deep depression accompanied by lessened self-esteem and euphoria accompanied by heightened self confidence and in each state feel that the other state was a temporary mood."[29]

At the same time, there is, inevitably, guilt and concern about what the breakup will mean and do to the children. Over the past two years, I have been studying the impact of divorce mediation on divorcing and separating couples. Members of the research team have found that, for these people, the paramount concern is that the children not be caught up in the conflict. Most, for example, did not want their children to go to court or to talk with the mediator. Many who sought the help of a mediator or counsellor did so, not so much to resolve a dispute, as reassurance that what they had decided would be in the best interests of their children.[30] It is for this reason, as most studies of children in divorce show, that parents are extremely reluctant to tell their children much about what is happening. In any event, considerable inconsistency should be expected in the first year or so. At times, one or both parents will feel a more self-conscious and guilt-tinged concern about parenting; at other times, as they try out new or rusty roles, they feel distant from their children.

ECONOMIC CONSEQUENCES OF MARRIAGE BREAKDOWN

After the divorce there are now two households sharing the same family income. It seems inevitable that, under the best of circumstances, there will be a lowering of the standard of living for everyone. But the best of circumstances seldom seem to occur, and the situation is much more unequal that one might initially imagine. In what is, perhaps, the most intensive and ambitious study to date, Lenore Weitzman finds that, in the United States, when income is compared to *needs*, divorced men experience on average a 42 percent *increase* in their standard of living in the first year after divorce, while divorced women (and their children) experience a 73 percent *decline*. As she points out:

> These apparently simple statistics have far-reaching social and economic consequences. For most women and children, divorce means precipitous downward mobility—both economically and socially. The reduction in income brings residential moves and inferior housing, drastically diminished or nonexistent funds for recreation and leisure, and intense pressures due to inadequate time and money. Financial hardships in turn cause social dislocation and a loss of familiar networks for emotional support and social services, and intensify the psychological stress for women and children alike. On a societal level, divorce increases female and child poverty and creates an ever-widening gap between the economic well-being of divorced men, on the one hand and their children and former wives on the other.[31]

Weitzman is writing about the United States, and California in particular. But similar conclusions can be drawn about the Canadian situation. To take one example, research in New Brunswick suggests that 95 percent of what Statistics Canada identifies as female-headed, single-parent families in the province are receiving social assistance.[32] Some of these are unmarried mothers who have chosen to keep their child, but the majority are separated or divorced. Like other provinces in the Atlantic region, New Brunswick is a "have not" province, so we might not expect the situation to be quite as severe elsewhere in Canada. However, as the Task Force on Child Care found, in 1983, some 49 percent of all female, single parents had incomes below the poverty line.[33] Similarly, my research on divorce and divorce mediation shows that 58 percent of women and children have incomes below the poverty line, compared to about 10 percent of the divorced or separated men.[34]

Parents have a legal obligation to support their children. While the present legislation in most provinces does not, as in the past, distinguish between fathers and mothers, virtually all child support and spousal support flows from the father to the mother. However, even if the maintenance payments are made in full, the amount of money men are ordered by the courts to pay is usually so low that most women and children will be living below the poverty line.[35] Inevitably, women must find other financial resources such as employment or social assistance. However, since women earn from 50 to 65 percent of male earnings, employment, even if available, may not be a realistic possibility for mothers of pre-school children. In many instances, the expense of unsubsidized child care may make it economically preferable to remain in the home and receive social assistance.

In any event, the size of the average award is rather irrelevant because, in a large proportion of cases, fathers default on their maintenance payments. For example, Weitzman reports that no American study has found a state or county in which even half of the fathers comply with court orders. The situation seems to be no better in Canada. An Alberta study showed that a full 80 percent of men have defaulted on their orders after five years.[36] Most of the evidence suggests a gradual process of disengagement whereby, over time, progressively more men fail to make payments or do so irregularly. It is for this reason that, along with the new *Divorce Act*, legislation was also enacted which will allow the federal and provincial governments to maintain a registry of people with support orders and to update it using various sources such as unemployment insurance, Canada Pension Plan, and drivers' licences, and to garnishee a number of income sources—tax rebates, unemployment insurance payments, even dividends on Canada Savings Bonds.

Failure to comply with a support order is an offense, punishable, ultimately, by imprisonment. In fact, however, few men are ever incarcerated for non-compliance and, when summonsed to court, are often forgiven their arrears or are allowed to pay them back over a very extended period of time. It goes beyond the scope of this chapter to look at why men do not pay and what should be done about the problem. It is worth noting, however, that there appears to be little relation between a father's level of income and his compliance with the support order. Nor, as the Alberta study found, is there a relationship between visitation and compliance. Men who see their children on a regular basis are about as likely to be in default as those who have little or no contact with them. For now, the critical point is that sexual inequality built into the occupational structure and between men and women within the nuclear family destines many children of divorce and separation to absolute and relative poverty. And, in turn, poverty has a number of objective, negative consequences for children.

CHILD CUSTODY AND THE LAW

Separation and divorce are essentially legal processes, so that what happens to children when a marriage ends is both directly and indirectly shaped by the legal system and legal conventions. This is not to suggest that all divorces involve endless litigation, but that the kinds of decisions people make, or are advised by lawyers and others to make, take place in the shadow of family law tradition and assumptions prevailing at particular times. So it is important to understand what that tradition is and how it is changing. Custody decisions are perhaps the most difficult that parents, lawyers and, above all, judges must make. As we will see, how a custody decision is reached may have as great a consequence for children and their adjustment as what decision is made.

TYPES OF CUSTODY DECISIONS

Before looking at alternative forms of custody, it is probably useful to see what is meant by custody. One judge defined it as:

> the full responsibility and control in providing physical nurture as well as mental and emotional nurture of children—for providing physical care, educational training and guidance in all matters that are considered of importance in the healthy rearing of a child.[37]

This definition emerged out of a case in which the mother, who had custody of the children, was raising them in the Roman Catholic faith. The father, who had access rights, was teaching them the beliefs of Jehovah's Witnesses when he visited or saw the children. The Court forbade him to do so on the basis that, as the non-custodial parent, he had no say over the religious training of the children.

In general, there are three alternatives available to the Court in deciding custody: sole custody to one parent, joint custody, and split custody. By far the most common choice has been sole custody awarded, as will be discussed, to the mother.

The growing concern that children should have continuing contact with both parents means that, invariably, custody awards also contain provisions for access of the non-custodial parent, or what in the United States are called "visitation" rights or privileges. Usually, access is left open or stated as "reasonable access," and it is left to the parents to work out what that will mean in practice. However, where either custody or access has been in dispute, the terms can be set out in minute detail. One can only imagine the amount of turmoil that preceded the following kind of order:

> Peter will have the children, Mary and James, every other weekend from 5:00 p.m. on Friday until 5:00 p.m. on Sunday. He will also have the children for one week during his annual vacation provided that he give two weeks notice to Elizabeth, the mother of the children, as to when he will be taking his vacation. He will also have the children from 5:00 p.m. on Christmas Eve until 12:00 p.m. on Christmas day and on alternate birthdays of Mary and James.[38]

Fortunately, these are the exceptions. But they do exist in the files of any Canadian family court.

In Canada, joint custody or, as it is sometimes called, "shared custody," has been such a rare concept that the Central Divorce Registry Forms for use with the Divorce Act, 1968, did not include this category. It appears that only about two percent of awards are for joint custody though, in practice, it is probable that some couples with a sole custody award act as if they had joint custody: both share in decisions about their children and there is shared parenting.

Proponents of joint custody cite evidence that a crucial factor in children's adjustment to their parents' divorce is the continuing involvement of both parents in parenting. There may also be direct benefits to children in that they receive better quality parenting when parenting responsibilities are shared.[39] One of the major stresses for post-divorce mothers with sole custody is that they often feel overwhelmed, overburdened, and imprisoned at the very time when they are attempting to become economically independent.[40] Recent legislation puts an onus on women to become economically independent whenever possible. But this also puts them into a double bind. On the one hand they are expected to look after the children like "good mothers," but they are also supposed to become, after some specified time, economically self-sufficient, capable of contributing as much as their former husbands to the maintenance of the children. Thus, as various studies show, one of the main advantages of joint custody *when* it involves joint parenting is that it allows both parents more time to pursue their own projects.

Nevertheless, until recently, Canadian judges have been extremely reluctant to make joint custody awards, and almost never use them as a way to resolve a custody dispute. Unless the parents have worked out such an arrangement and have shown an ability to co-operate with each other, few Canadian judges will consider this alternative, and even then, many are reluctant to make this kind of award.

Because there are so few joint custody awards, there is limited evidence as to how these work out in practice. What we do know suggests that they can take a variety of forms. While we are likely to think in terms of children moving, say, on a weekly basis between two residences: i.e., joint physical and legal custody, this may be the exception. Often there is joint *legal* custody, but with physical arrangements indistinguishable from sole custody to the mother. While both parents feel it important to have a say in matters related to the children's education, religious training, and so forth, it may be impractical or unfeasible for the children to live on an equal and alternating basis with both parents. Either the parents live too far apart or the children eventually find that the day-to-day stress of keeping track of their things is too much, so that they prefer to have one home as their base. Luepnitz found in her study that most children who were in joint custody arrangements liked it but, because of mundane problems like finding clean socks, preferred to think of one of their two homes as their permanent place of residence.[41]

Lenore Weitzman has studied the California divorce legislation which makes it mandatory for judges to give first preference to joint custody if either or both of the parents request it.[42] She finds that, in practice, the legislation has not had a major impact on the pattern of custody awards in California. While about 18 percent of awards are now joint custody awards, it appears that many of these are, in fact, joint *legal* custody awards with *physical* custody to the mother. Weitzman concludes that most men and most women do not want to share post-divorce parenting. Such arrangements require inordinate amounts of time, energy, and money, things that most couples cannot afford. She also found that while a minority of men want more involvement in the parenting of their children, the reality is that most men do not want custody of their children or more involvement with them. Her interview data show that 70 percent of men without custody would prefer to see their children *less* often, while 30 percent said about the same. None said that they would like to see their children more often.

Nor does joint custody necessarily lessen the conflict between ex-spouses. Jessica Pearson, who has carried out an extensive study of divorce mediation in Colorado, found that fully half of the joint custody awards had been changed because they were found to be unworkable.[43] These were awards worked out with the help of a mediator, and were not imposed by the Court. Similarly, Luepnitz found no difference in her sample in levels of conflict and hostility between couples with joint as opposed to sole custody.[44]

At the time the new divorce legislation was being debated, there was considerable presssure, especially from Fathers' Rights groups, for the Divorce Act, 1986 to follow the American lead and make it mandatory for judges to give preference to joint custody. However, partly on the basis of the American experience with joint custody, and partly because of the opposing pressure from various groups concerned with the status of women, the joint committee reviewing the proposed legislation rejected the notion of "presumed joint custody."[45] After considerable debate, the decision was to stay with the "best interests of the child" principle and to encourage settlements which maximize children's contact with both parents. While it remains to be seen how judges will interpret the provisions of the Act, there is nothing in it which precludes joint custody or other arrangements parents might reach prior to going to Court. The Committee debating the legislation seems to have recognized the growing consensus that one cannot legislate to make people co-operate and accept their parental responsibilities. Joint custody does seem like the most sensible arrangement for many divorcing families, and is probably the model one would like to see all divorcing parents aspire to. But one cannot, as it were, legislate an ideal.

Finally, in a very small number of cases, courts have awarded what is called "split custody." This seems to mean one of two things. First, there have been a few unusual situations in which legal custody is awarded to one parent and physical custody to the other. Second, and more commonly, split custody means that the children themselves are divided between the two parents, something which is more likely with older children. A boy, say, is given over to his father, and a daughter to her mother. While rare, this kind of decision does have merits, since there is some evidence that children living with the parent of the same sex are better adjusted than children living with a parent of the opposite sex.[46] Again, it should be emphasized that this is what is explicitly ordered by the Court. My present research shows that, while in most cases, custody of all of the children was awarded to one parent, usually the mother, one or more of the children were, in fact, living with the other parent who, to all intents and purposes, had legal as well as physical custody of the child or children living in his or her home.

HOW IS CUSTODY DECIDED?

Marital breakdown usually involves the legal system, but it is important to keep in mind that the law enters the picture only when there is a dispute about who should have the children or about money or property acquired during the marriage. In the overwhelming number of separation and divorce cases, people work out a settlement prior to going to court on their own or with the help of lawyers or other professionals. Judges are empowered to overturn or disregard these agreements if they appear to be harmful to the children, but they seldom do so. Sometimes, for religious reasons, or because they do not envision remarrying or because they basically trust one another to live up to the agreement, separating couples never go near the Family Court at all. Not infrequently, when people do change their minds and seek a divorce, the judge may not wish to tamper with an existing provincial order or a private separation agreement, and will say nothing about custody.[47]

What happens if parents cannot agree about custody? When couples separate or divorce, the laws in most provinces are quite explicit as to how family assets are to be divided. Recent legislation with respect to property generally requires that the property and assets acquired during the marriage be divided equally. Strangely enough, the law is nowhere as clear as to what should happen to the children when marriages break down. Rather, changes in what are called "presumptions" tend to mirror changes in conceptions of what is meant by a child and what a woman's rights are vis-à-vis her husband's. Since these are not entirely clear or fully accepted in all sectors of society, it is perhaps understandable why there is confusion and inconsistency as to what should be the basis for assigning the children to one parent or the other.

Indeed, the best we can say at this point is that the rules for determining custody have been in a state of flux over the past century. In the mid-to-late 19th century the traditional right of the father to custody gave way to preference for maternal custody for at least the

younger children. In turn, in this century, the notion of maternal preference was replaced by a supposedly gender-neutral rule based on
what is seen as being in the best interests of the child. At the same
time, there has also been some inclination towards the so-called "psychological parent." And, as just mentioned, there now seems to be an
increasing interest in joint custody. Indeed, some lawyers and social
scientists, concerned with family law reform, have recently argued
that, since the term "custody" seems more appropriate for peniten-
tiaries, it should disappear from our family legislation and be replaced with concepts such as "shared parenting" and "primary" and
"secondary" caretaker.[48]

It may clarify things somewhat to explain that a good deal of Canadian, British, and American law is based, not on legislation, but on
judges' previous decisions, which together make up the body of what
is called British common law. That is, in the absence of legislative
direction, judges tend to base their decisions on what judges decided
before them. Historically, British common law decisions held that children were the natural property of their fathers. Paternal preference
reflected both the fact that women did not have rights before the law
and the supposed need of fathers in pre-industrial societies for the
labour of their older children. Since Canada inherited British law and
legal institutions, we also inherited the notion of paternal preference.[49]
While American law is also based on British law, the presumption that
children should be "given" to their fathers was never as strong in the
United States.[50]

Gradually, under the influence of psychoanalytical theory and the
general recognition of children's and women's rights in the mid-19th
century, paternal preference was undermined by what came to be
called the "tender years doctrine." As child development theories
evolved which recognized children as developing personalities, there
was also growing concern with their emotional development and nurturance.[51] Increasingly, judgments came to be based on the assumption that, other things being equal, young children are better off with
their mother. At times judges have defended their preferences for the
mother in rather exaggerated and emotional terms. As recently as the
1950s one judge was moved to state in his decision:

> No father, no matter how well-intentioned or how solicitous for the wel-
> fare of (the) child, can take the full place of the mother. Instinctively, a
> little child, particularly a little girl, turns to her mother in her troubles,
> her doubts and her fears. In that respect, nature seems to assert itself.

The feminine touch means so much to a little girl; the frills and the flounces and the ribbons in the matter of dress; the whispered consultations and confidences on matters which to the child's mind should only be discussed with Mother; the tender care, the soothing voice; all these things have a tremendous effect on the emotions of the child. This is nothing new; it is as old as human nature and has been recognized time after time through the decisions of our Courts.[52]

The age at which children are no longer in their "tender years" has never been well-defined, and seems to have ranged from under age seven to under age 12. However, since there are often pre-school children in divorcing families and judges are loath to separate young children, maternal preference became, for a time, the rule rather than the exception.

BEST INTERESTS OF THE CHILD PRINCIPLE

Overlapping the "tender years doctrine" and what is now, in theory, the basis of all custody decisions, is what came to be called "the best interests of the child" principle. This principle is not easy to define but, as it has developed in various judgments, it appears to include such factors as the wishes of the parents, sometimes (but not often) the expressed wishes of the children, the child's relationship to his or her parent or parents, the child's adjustment, the length of time the child has lived with one parent, and the relative emotional and financial ability of each parent to raise the children. The conduct of the parent is also an important factor, especially if it can be shown to have relevance to the best interests of the child. Here, standards have changed. For example, not too long ago, an adulterous parent (particularly a mother) would have had almost no possibility of obtaining custody. It appears that for most judges this is no longer very relevant, though contesting parties do attempt to make it so. Clearly, a history of child abuse and addiction will be considered important in most cases.

A principle giving judges leeway to choose the parent best able to offer parenting in the interests of the child *should* mean that either parent is entitled to custody. In practice this is not the case. It seems that the "tender years doctrine" did not disappear but was simply subsumed under the "best interests of the child" principle. In other words, in applying this principle judges continue to base their decisions on implicit, if not explicit, assumptions about women. While it is unlikely that a judge today would make the kind of statement just quoted above, their judgments tend to reflect the belief that women are better able to nurture children; that, in most cases, a woman will be the best parent for the children; and that, in most instances, men are less capable of parenting.

In an influential but also controversial book, *Beyond The Best Interests of the Child*, Goldstein and his colleagues made a strong argument for decisions which do the least damage to the children's need for "unbroken continuity."[53] They introduce yet another concept into an already confused set of guidelines: that of the "psychological parent." Their argument is that custody decisions should be made quickly and permanently and that if it is difficult to choose between parents, it is better to "flip a coin" than put the children through a protracted custody dispute and an indefinite period of uncertainty. As Bala and Clarke put it, out of the "continuity principle the legal definition of the model parent has arisen, like a phoenix arising from the ashes of the common law."[54]

The "model" parent is, of course, the psychological parent, usually the parent who has been the primary caretaker of the child, and who can offer the most promise of unbroken continuity. The Goldstein argument is based, in part, on the premise that children's sense of time is quite different from adults. Where custody is in dispute, children will have to live for several months, perhaps for more than a year, uncertain as to who will be their permanent parent and where will be their permanent home. This is because contested custody cases take up an inordinate amount of court time and must usually be scheduled quite far into the future. Where a custody assessment is ordered, the time between actual petition and final hearing may amount to several months and as long as a year or more.

It is apparent that the continuity principle weighs strongly with judges, who will seldom upset an interim order or a *de facto* custody arrangement. In this rather messy business of custody disputes, the cliché, "possession is nine-tenths of the law" has real meaning. Lawyers are quite aware of this, of course, and when representing the parent who has the children will sometimes use any and all stalling techniques and strategies. Interestingly, the authors of *Beyond the Best Interests of the Child* do not make a special case for the mother nor, where the child has been in the care of another person, do they see either biological parent as necessarily the best choice or entitled to custody. However, the reality is that, in most instances, the mother will have been the "psychological parent." Maternal preference is now bolstered by a psychological theory of children's need for continuity in their lives.

While things may be changing, it seems evident that, in preferring the mother, judges are also reflecting what most people believe. Luepnitz, for example, in her study of divorced families, found that, where mothers had full custody, the usual response to how this came about was that "it was never in question; it was just assumed that I would have the children."[55] However bitter the dispute between the parents, most men also recognize how central children are to the lives of women, particularly those who have stayed at home. Traditionally, men's occupational role has been as important, if not more important, than their parental role. Separation and divorce do not change this. For women to lose custody of their children will often mean a drastic change in their lives. We should also keep in mind the different meanings giving up children have for men and women. Whereas there is little stigma attached to fathers who do not fight for custody of their children, women who relinquish custody or who prefer joint custody feel, or are made to feel, that they are unloving mothers. And, where women do agree to give up custody or "lose" in Court, they are likely to be seen as incompetent mothers or as in other ways at fault.

It is hardly surprising, then, that, despite the gender-neutral language of most legislation, about 86 percent of Canadian and about 90 percent of American custody awards are made in favour of the mother.[56] The small minority of men who have sought custody of their young children will usually have had to overcome the deeply rooted values, beliefs, truths, and stereotypes underlying the presumption of maternal preference. Something of the power of these assumptions and idealizations of the "mother" role can be seen in the fact that most men do not contest custody either because they, too, believe children should be with their mother, or because their lawyer advises that it will require an expensive and probably futile effort to do so.

The apparent bias in favour of mothers has led in recent years to the formation of "Fathers' Rights" groups which have argued that the underlying presumption of maternal preference is based on sexual stereotypes as limiting and unscientific as those which have barred women from equal access in the workplace, and which ignore the fact that some men are actively involved in parenting. In the United States these men have been challenging the constitutionality of the "tender years" presumption, and similar groups in Canada have recently been asking whether this principle violates the Charter of Rights and Freedoms.

What of the small number of cases where men do ask for custody? Despite the contention of Fathers' Rights groups that the Courts are biased in favour of women, it appears that when men in the United States do contest custody, they have a more than equal chance of "winning." Lenore Weitzman finds for her California sample that some 63 percent of men who requested custody were successful. In Canada, the "success rate" has been about 43 percent.[57] We must, of course, consider the reasons and circumstances which might lead men to break with the tradition of maternal preference. A study by Kellin Gersick of custodial and non-custodial fathers suggests that the former may be driven to seek custody because, for various reasons, the mother is incapable of parenting or does not want the children.[58]

At the same time, there is some evidence that men who have departed from traditional fathering and participated even to a limited extent in child care may be favoured by the Courts. This is the conclusion reached by Susan Boyd, a Carleton University law professor. She has examined Canadian custody decisions, and concludes that they reveal "an absence of discussion of primary responsibility for parenting, an attendant inclination to overemphasize fatherly involvement in child care and, overall, a tendency to penalize working mothers for the perceived instability of their lifestyles."[59] As Boyd notes, men who work full-time but show some interest in and involvement with parenting are viewed by the courts as dedicated fathers. Women who work full-time and do most, but not all, of the child care are considered "half" mothers and as uninterested in parenting. She also observes a recent tendency to award custody to the parent who can provide the greatest financial stability and highest standard of living. Given average differences between men's and women's earning power, it is evident that this would also tip the scales in favour of the father. And, finally, she detects some tendency for the courts to award sole custody to a father who has another woman to look after the children (a mother, an aunt, or a new partner).

In sum, while custody of the children is usually not at issue, it does appear that when men initiate the divorce, when they ask for or contest custody, when they have shown some prior involvement in parenting, and when they have an alternative "mother" available to look after the children, their chances of gaining custody are relatively good.

In the United States this has raised questions of whether gender-neutral legislation may not have the unintended consequence of terrorizing women into accepting inadequate and unfair financial settlements in order to avoid going through a costly custody battle and taking a risk of losing their children. As Nancy Polikoff, an American lawyer, has recently observed, "Women who are scared to death of losing their children will trade away anything else — child support, property, alimony — to keep it from happening."[60] Whether, in either the United States or Canada, this is a real or a potential problem remains to be seen. It does, however, reflect some of the difficulties and pitfalls which face anyone attempting to bring about changes in legislation which on the surface at least seem fairer and less sexist than previous laws.

CHILDREN'S RIGHTS

In bitterly contested custody disputes, a judge is likely to hear the testimony of parents and the arguments of lawyers as to why one of the contestants would be the better parent of the children. These will often be augmented by the professional advice of experts. Rarely, however, will the children be heard who are the subject of the dispute.[61] Should children have the right to be represented in court and to make their preferences known? While there are many who would say "yes," there are many others who would say "no." The most compelling argument against it is that it puts children into an intolerable situation, since preference for one parent is likely to be seen as rejection of the other. Nor do most children want that kind of responsibility. Luepnitz found in her study that children were relieved that they did not have to choose between their parents, or make the decision where they were to live. As one of her adolescent respondents put it:

> They didn't ask me and I'm glad they didn't. It would have meant hurting one of them. I'm close to both of them in different ways. I'm glad they didn't put that responsibility on me.[62]

Others, such as Robert Weiss, an American sociologist, have questioned whether children will necessarily be able to make a decision in their own best interests; the parent the child seems to prefer may not be the best parent. As he points out, children may act out of anger against the parent they see as having caused the breakup of the family. Yet they may have only partial or one-sided knowledge of what went wrong with their parents' marriage. Alternatively, their preferences may be shaped by a sense of guilt or responsibility to one parent who they feel would not be able to survive if they were not present. Finally, Weiss questions whether, even where preferences are not tinged with guilt and anger, children are necessarily competent to make this kind of decision.[63]

In any case it is not self-evident what we mean by "children's rights."

The evidence is overwhelming that what children want is for their parents to reconcile, to keep loving one another. And it is equally obvious that this is not what will happen. It is in this context that separation counselling and mediation which brings the whole family into the picture is a more likely way to include children's preferences in the final decision.

RESOLUTION OF CUSTODY DISPUTES

As we have seen, the majority of divorce and separation cases are settled out of court, so that the actual hearing is more or less a rubber stamping of what the parents have somehow worked out. What naturally receives most of the attention is the small proportion of cases where people caught up in the adversarial process turn the courtroom into a battleground. Ironically, two people who started out in love and harmony, who have lived in an intimate relationship, and who have created and raised children, now find themselves hurling accusatory charges back and forth. It is not surprising, therefore, that a few years ago, the Law Reform Commission of Canada depicted the adversarial system as "one of Canada's great self-inflicted wounds" and as an approach "inherently inconsistent with the harmonious resolution of family disputes. It should not, therefore, be available as an extension of the destructive capacity of spouses who disagree over their personal relationships."[64] In the Commission's view, the adversary approach is unable to contribute to a therapeutic or constructive resolution of marital and familial disputes; it does not serve the best interests of the children involved; it may sometimes intensify and exacerbate the trauma and suffering associated with marriage breakdown; and it is expensive both for the families involved and for the State.

Family law practitioners are proud of their record of avoiding courtroom battles through negotiation. Nevertheless, their primary responsibility is to get the best "deal" possible for their client. There is always the possibility that children will be used as "bargaining chips" to obtain a better and perhaps unequal financial settlement. Moreover, by definition, a lawyer does not have direct access to the other parent and must rely on a client's account and what the other lawyer conveys during negotiation. These may not be very accurate portrayals of the other person's ability as a parent nor of the circumstances surrounding the marriage breakdown. Most lawyers who choose to do family law are interested in working out a reasonable and fair settlement, and are genuinely concerned with the welfare of the children involved. However, people caught up in the bitterness, hostility, and trauma of marriage breakdown are not likely to be reasonable in their demands. As a result, lawyers may not be able to dissuade their clients from taking certain positions and making what, on the face of it, seem like unreasonable and irrational demands.

In any event, negotiated settlements are very much part of the adversarial process, and are not settlements which necessarily come from the parents themselves. In recent years, two closely related approaches to settling the most difficult of the issues, custody and access, have come into much greater use as alternatives or complements to the traditional adversarial approach. These are divorce mediation or conciliation counselling, and the use of custody assessments or investigations when the couple cannot agree on who should have custody of the children.

DIVORCE MEDIATION

Essentially, divorce mediation (or "conciliation counselling" as it was called until very recently) involves a third party counselling persons whose marriage is in trouble or has actually broken down. Howard Irving, the best-known Canadian proponent of this approach, suggests that it has a number of objectives:

> 1) reduce the level of real or perceived conflict between spouses; 2) facilitate communication between spouses, either in general terms or about specific issues problematic for them; 3) transform an amorphous problem into a resolvable issue; 4) suggest problem-solving strategies as a viable alternative to litigation; 5) provide the most efficient use of the legal system; 6) optimally help the spouses achieve a written agreement concerning one or more disputable issues or problems.[65]

At a time of intense emotion, confusion, and often ambivalence on the part of at least one of the spouses, mediation is meant to help people arrive at a decision that may include staying together as a couple and trying to rehabilitate their marriage. The logic underlying this approach is that mediated or conciliated resolutions are longer lasting and more likely to protect children's interests than are those imposed by the court or negotiated by lawyers. From the child's perspective, one hope is that, through mediation, parents will be better prepared to deal with the difficult problem of explaining the reasons for the breakup of the marriage and what will happen afterwards. Another is that parents will be led to recognize that, while the marriage has ended, their roles as parents continue, and that both have ongoing emotional and financial commitments to the children. As we have seen, most of the evidence suggests that children fare better in divorce when there is easy access to the non-custodial parent and when there is a post-divorce relationship between the mother and father that is relatively free of conflict. Thus, while some mediators do deal with financial matters, the focus is on custody and access arrangements that will reflect the child's need for continuing contact with both parents.

In Canada, divorce mediation is a relatively new approach to the resolution of family problems and is undergoing considerable change and development. Does mediation work? Is it intrinsically better than adversarial approaches? Despite the optimism of those advocating this approach, the evidence is inconclusive. Indeed, Kenneth Kressel, after a lengthy study of evaluation research, concludes that "it is a vehicle of social influence which is not inherently superior to any other method of conflict resolution.[66] However, there is other evidence that, at its best, mediation can have positive benefits for families undergoing marital dissolution, and is especially useful in helping people work out realistic and meaningful access arrangements as things change in their lives and their children's.

While mediation offers an alternative to the adversary approach, there remain some cases where the dispute over custody is so intractable that there is no other alternative but to have the matter settled in court. Increasingly, it appears that, in matters of custody, Canadian judges are less and less confident that the strictly adversarial approach will reveal the "truth" of who is the better or more suitable parent and what, in turn, will be in the best interests of the child. This is hardly surprising since, in many instances, either or perhaps neither parent would be suitable.

The result is that some judges frequently, and others invariably, request a custody assessment or, as it is sometimes called, a "custody investigation." Over roughly 40 hours, an independent professional, usually a social worker, makes an evaluation of both parents, visits and interviews the children in each of the parents' homes, talks with neighbours, teachers, ministers, or priests who have knowledge of the family, and eventually makes a recommendation to the judge. Sometimes, in the process of carrying out the assessment, the social worker may attempt to mediate a settlement of the dispute.

Although lawyers and, especially, judges are generally enthusiastic about this approach, existing research suggests that, far from being a panacea, custody assessments are a drastic last resort. Certainly, "consent" orders usually emerge, once the parents and their lawyers know the recommendations in the report, but parents denied custody on the basis of an assessment are often so embittered and shattered as to cut off all ties with the children. Often they are also humiliated to learn how others in the community assess their conduct and ability as a parent. In sum, while custody assessments arise out of the understandable desire to do what is best for the children, and have appeal because they remove some of the responsibility from judges who previously had to make these agonizing decisions, they do little to encourage the "losing" parent to maintain an ongoing relationship with his or her children.[67]

REMARRIAGE FAMILIES

Various sociologists have argued that divorce rates, rather than providing an indication of the declining importance of marriage and the family, simply show how important these institutions are to most people. As evidence, they cite the fact that most divorced people remarry. This suggests, then, that it is not marriage *per se* which is the problem, but a specific marriage. According to Statistics Canada, about 29.4 percent of all marriages performed in 1983 were remarriages. Throughout the century remarriage rates have been relatively high. But, as with marital dissolution, the pattern has shifted from remarriage following widowhood to remarriage following divorce. Thus, in 1983, in slightly over 90 percent of remarriages, either one or both partners had been divorced. Overall, it appears that within five years of divorce, about three-quarters of divorced men and two-thirds of divorced women will remarry.[68]

Many of these people will have children from the previous marriage and, as our opening vignette suggests, will have more from the second marriage. This raises a number of interesting questions about the role and situation of children in these "reconstituted families," and suggests that the breakup of the parents' marriage may only be one, and not necessarily the most difficult, aspect children must deal with. An additional problem is that divorce and remarriage may complicate and, in confusing ways, expand kinship relations and the kinship universe which the child perceives. If both parents remarry, children may, in effect, have four distinct sets of relatives and attachments. Thus, aside from the obvious problem of fitting into what will undoubtedly be a different family structure with different rules and expectations, many taken-for-granted assumptions about who is and who is not family may be challenged.

Penny Gross, who has recently focused her research on this very issue, points out that from the child's point of view:

> There is (following remarriage) a restructuring of the relationship with biological kin, between children and their non-residential parent, between children and their non-residential parent's kin, and possibly even between children and siblings because, often, they do not live together. With stepkin, there are additional relationships, those between children and stepparents, between children and stepsiblings and children and stepparent's kin. In addition there is another possible category, half siblings, who are half biological kin and half stepkin.[69]

The teenagers Gross studied varied considerably in their decisions about whom to regard as an actual parent. Some included stepparents, some did not, and some excluded one of their biological parents.

Research on what are variously called "reconstituted families," "remarriage families," and so on has only recently begun to appear, so that the effects on children are not known with any degree of certainty. However, as with the divorce process itself, there is every reason to believe that people, including children, do adjust. On the positive side is that remarriage will probably result in an improved standard of living for children, especially if they have been living with their mother. Second, much of the research on remarriage suggests that adults are satisfied with their second marriage, and think it to be far superior to their failed marriage. As we have seen, the consensus is that the most damaging situation for children is a home torn by habitual and sometimes violent conflict. The happier marital situation of the custodial parent is bound to have positive spin-offs for the children. To the extent that father absence is a factor detrimental to children's development and behaviour, remarriage should be beneficial to children in the long run.

On the negative side is that, as Longfellow concludes, "remarriage and the presence of a stepfather tend to create more problems than they solve".[70] Most studies she examined found no differences between children with no fathers and those living with stepfathers. Where differences have been observed, children living with their mothers and a stepfather are always the ones with more problem behaviours. In short, it remains to be discovered whether the economic and personal benefits the mother is likely to experience and which presumably are passed on to the children outweigh or offset the difficulties of adjusting to a new parent and a new family lifestyle.

CONCLUSION

Not long ago, textbooks on the sociology of family and marriage devoted only a short chapter and a few paragraphs to divorce and to remarriage families, respectively. Certainly, not everyone who marries divorces and not everyone who divorces remarries. But these are sufficiently pervasive and enduring phenomena as to force us to rethink what we mean by the concept of family, what we now mean by a kinship structure, and what it means to be a parent. While not everyone is directly affected by either divorce or remarriage, there are few people in North America who will not know someone who has gone through one or both of these experiences.

But, as we have tried to show in this chapter, marital breakdown and family dissolution are never normative or routine events to the persons most concerned. In the immediate aftermath of the decision to end the marriage, it seems to matter very little which of the parents initiated the process: both find their lives disrupted, and experience a variety of conflicting emotions ranging from feelings of rejection, anger, and bitterness to an ambivalent relief that an unhappy, perhaps intolerable, situation has ended.

For the parents, there is at least the compensation that at the end of the painful period of adjustment there may be some gains: independence, freedom from conflict and tension and possibly a new and, hopefully, better relationship. From the point of view of the children, however, there do not seem to be any similar compensations. From the child's perspective, there is nothing to be gained by marital breakdown except distress, confusion, loneliness, inconvenience, and probably a lower standard of living.

We should not be surprised that children in divorce are upset and that this may persist for a long time. What else would we expect? What is surprising is that most children do recover and adjust. With varying degrees of success, they do manage to cope with life in a single-parent family, with living their lives in two households, and with the remarriage of one or both of their parents. Indeed, the fact that most children of divorce are about as likely as children in intact families to grow up to be fairly normal members of society is testimony to the resiliency of children in the face of change and disruption.

While persons concerned with preservation of the sanctity of the traditional family and the effect of divorce on children call for more restrictive divorce laws, what in our view are wiser voices recognize that it is impossible to legislate marital harmony, and that forcing people to stay in intolerable (and often dangerous) marriages would be a greater injustice and even more harmful to the children caught up in the conflict. In any event, tightening or restricting the divorce law would simply mean that more people than do already would resort to desertion and informal separation. Moreover, as we have broadened our conception of family, we have come also to recognize that divorce, as well as being a disruptive process, can also be a constructive process for many people. While in the short run children may feel they are the losers, they may eventually benefit from a more stable and conflict-free home environment.

What recent research demonstrates is that though divorce may be as inevitable as death, the way it is dealt with and handled is a matter of choice. Where the law can play a role is in ensuring that parents who have decided that their marriage is ended have access to support systems, particularly counselling. At present, much of the focus is on finding ways outside of the courtroom to resolve intractable disputes about custody and access. But, as we have discussed, there is often comparable conflict in divorces which, on the face of it, and in terms of court time, are seen as routine and uncontested. And, even where there is little or no conflict, it is apparent that most divorcing parents find great difficulty in explaining to children what is, after all, usually a one-time occurrence in their lives. Yet children may fear the unknown far more than the known so, though saddened by the breakup of their family, they feel relieved to know what will happen to them. Parents and children undergoing divorce can benefit from the help of professionals who are better able to view divorce as a patterned and routine occurrence. There is, in short, a need not only for non-adversarial ways to resolve conflicts, but an even greater need for divorce and separation counselling and post-divorce counselling.

NOTES AND REFERENCES

1. D. C. McKie, B. Prentice, and P. Reed. *Divorce: Law and the Family in Canada*. Ottawa: Ministry of Supply and Services, 1983, p. 96 and p. 145. Margrit Eichler, in her book, *Families in Canada Today*, Toronto: Gage, 1983, suggests that about 55 percent of divorcing couples have dependent children.

2. In Canada, as a result of the B.N.A. Act, divorce is a federal matter. But, in all provinces, there has for decades been legislation which allows people to obtain an enforceable order specifying child and spousal support as well as custody and access. Prior to the 1968 divorce legislation, Acts such as the *Deserted Wives and Children's Maintenance Act* were the principal way people could seek a legal remedy for the issues which arise when a marriage breaks down. In a number of provinces the rather antiquated D.W.C.M.A., along with a number of other Acts relating to family and children, have been replaced by new family legislation which, among other things, is gender-neutral in its language and intent, in the sense that both parents are seen as equally responsible for the support of their children and for each other in the event of need. As well, people can simply work out a written separation agreement which, in some provinces, is enforceable. Should the couple later choose to divorce, both provincial orders and separation agreements will, in most instances, form the "minutes of settlement" in the divorce petition.

3. Wayne W. McVey and Barrie W. Robinson, "Separation in Canada: New Insights Concerning Marital Dissolution." *The Canadian Journal of Sociology*, vol. 6 (3) 1981: pp. 353–366.

4. Frank Furstenburg et al., "The Life Course of Children of Divorce," *ASR* 48 (5) 1983, p. 667.

5. Paul C. Glick, "Children of Divorced Parents in Demographic Perspective." *Journal of Social Issues* 1979 (35) : pp. 170–182.

6. Status of Women Canada, *Report of the Task Force on Child Care*, Ottawa: Supply and Services, 1986. pp. 12–14.

7. An excellent review of American research on the level of conflict in the uncoupling process itself and after the divorce settlement can be found in Kenneth Kressel's *The Process of Divorce*. New York: Basic Books, 1985, chap. 1.

8. An excellent review of this literature can be found in Ann Goetting, "Divorce Outcome Research: Issues and Perspectives," in Arlen and Jerome Skolnik, *Family in Transition*, 4th edition, Boston: Little Brown and Company, 1983.

9. Much of this literature is reviewed in Deborah Ann Luepnitz, *Child Custody: A Study of Families After Divorce*. Toronto: D. C. Heath and Company, 1982.

10. For a recent review of this literature, see Lenore Weitzman, *The Divorce Revolution*. New York: The Free Press, 1985.

11. In particular, see Judith Wallerstein and Joan Kelly, *Surviving the Breakup*. New York: Basic Books, 1980.

12. Wallerstein and Kelly, *Surviving the Breakup*.

13. Ann Goetting, "Divorce Outcome Research: Issues and Perspectives."

14. Peter Berger and Brigitte Berger, *The War Over the Family*. New York: Basic Books, 1983.

15. Paper presented by Joan Kelly at First Family Mediation Canada Conference, Toronto, November, 1986.

16. Frank Furstenburg et al., "The Life Course of Children of Divorce". *ASR* 48(5) 1983, pp. 656–667.

17. Christopher Lasch, *Culture of Narcissism*. New York: Harper and Row, 1982; Joseph Pleck, *Men's New Roles in the Family: Housework and Child Care*. Ann Arbor: Institute for Social Research, 1976.

18. Deborah Ann Luepnitz, *Child Custody: A Study of Families After Divorce*. Toronto: D. C. Heath and Company, 1982.

19. A personal communication to the author.

20. Ann Mitchell, *Children in the Middle*. London: Tavistock Publications, 1985, p. 177.

21. Latency refers to an individual's sexuality being "latent," i.e., held in reserve, during the years of childhood.

22. Judith Wallerstein and Joan Kelly, "The Effects of Parental Divorce: Experience of the Child in Later Latency." *American Journal of Orthopsychiatry*, vol. 46, No. 2 (April, 1976), p. 443.

23. S. Walczak and S. Burns, *Divorce: The Child's Point of View*. London: Harper and Row, 1984.

24. E. Mavis Hetherington, Martha Cox, and Roger Cox, "Effects of Divorce on Parents and Children." In Michael Lamb, ed. *Non-Traditional Families: Parenting and Child Development*. Hillsdale, New Jersey: Lawrence Erlbaum, 1982.

25. Elisabeth Kübler-Ross, *On Death and Dying*. New York: Macmillan, 1969.

26. Ann Marie Ambert, *Divorce in Canada*, Toronto, Longman, 1980. p. 10.

27. G. B. Spanier and R. F. Casto, "Attachment to Separation and Divorce: A Qualitative Analysis." In G. Levinger and O. Moles, *Divorce and Separation: Contexts, Causes and Consequences*." New York: Basic Books, 1979.

28. E. Mavis Hetherington, "Children and Divorce." In R. W. Henderson, ed., *Parent-Child Interaction: Theory, Research and Prospects*. New York: Academic Press, 1981.

29. Robert S. Weiss, *Marital Separation*. New York: Basic Books, 1980, p. 137.

30. This study is being carried out for the Department of Justice, Canada. At the time of writing, the research is still in progress.

31. Lenore Weitzman, *The Divorce Revolution*, p. 323.

32. New Brunswick Department of Social Services, *Unmarried Mothers*, 1983.

33. Status of Women, Canada. *Report of the Task Force on Child Care*, pp. 12–14.

34. C. James Richardson, *An Evaluation of Divorce and Family Mediation in Four Canadian Cities*. Ottawa: Department of Justice, 1987. It should be noted that about 40 percent of men with custody of their children also had incomes below the poverty line.

35. The divorce and family mediation study finds that, on average, men are ordered to pay about $380.00 per month, or about 18 percent of their gross income. It is also apparent that the amount ordered does not adequately take family size into account, so that as the number of children in the family rises, the amount per child declines.

36. *Matrimonial Support Failures: Reasons, Profiles and Perceptions of Individuals Involved*. Edmonton, Institute of Law Research and Law Reform, 1981, p. 22.

37. Nicholas Bala and Kenneth Clarke. *The Child and the Law*, Toronto: McGraw-Hill Ryerson, 1981, p. 44.

38. A fictional example based on research experience in various family courts.

39. There is now a large literature on joint custody. A good review of this literature can be found in H. Jay Folberg and Marva Graham, "Joint Custody of Children Following Divorce," in Howard Irving, ed. *Family Law: An Interdisciplinary Perspective*. Toronto: Carswell, 1981. Some recent Canadian data are reported in Howard Irving et al., "Shared Parenting: An Empirical Analysis Utilizing a Large Data Base." Family Process, 1984. An excellent summary of the feminist critique of joint custody can be found in Lenore Weitzman's *The Divorce Revolution*, chap. 8.

40. H. Jay Folberg and Marva Graham, "Joint Custody of Children Following Divorce." Also M. Roman and W. Haddad, *The Disposable Parent*. New York: Holt Rinehart and Winston, 1978.

41. Deborah Ann Luepnitz, *Child Custody*.

42. The California legislation would seem to empower judges to order joint custody even when neither parent wants it, but when, in the judge's view, to do so would be in the best interests of the children.

43. Jessica Pearson and Nancy Thoennes, "Child Custody, Child Support Arrangements and Child Support Payment Patterns." Paper presented at the Child Support Enforcement Research Workshop, August, 1984, Washington, D.C.

44. Deborah Ann Luepnitz, *Child Custody*, p. 147.

45. Careful inspection of American family law suggests that in only one state, Louisiana, is there actually a presumption of joint custody. In others, the legislation requires judges to justify why, when the couple request joint custody, it should not be granted. And, as noted above, in some states such as California, judges have the power in principle to make a joint custody award where it would be in the interests of the children to do so, regardless of the parents' wishes. In practice, there is no evidence that judges are, in fact, using this power. On the whole, it would appear that

feminist critiques of joint custody have exaggerated the extent to which there is now, in the United States, a joint custody presumption.

46. Andrew Cherlin, *Marriage, Divorce, Remarriage*. Cambridge, Mass.: Harvard University Press, 1981, p. 70.

47. See McKie et al., *Divorce: Law and the Family in Canada*, p. 207.

48. See, for example, Alastair Bisset-Johnson and David Day, *The New Divorce Law: A Commentary on the Divorce Act, 1985*. Toronto: Carswell, 1986, chap. 4.

49. As a famous legal case of the 1970s, Oakes vs Oakes, revealed, the presumption of paternal preference still held sway in at least one province, New Brunswick.

50. For a fuller description of changes in custody decisions, see Nicholas Bala and Kenneth L. Clarke, *The Child and the Law*. Toronto: McGraw-Hill Ryerson, 1981, especially chap. 3.

51. See H. Jay Folberg and Marva Graham, "Joint Custody of Children Following Divorce." In Howard H. Irving, *Family Law: An Interdisciplinary Perspective*. Toronto: Carswell, 1981.

52. Bell v. Bell, quoted in Bala and Clarke, 1981:55.

53. J. Goldstein, A. Freud and A. Solnit, *Beyond the Best Interests of the Child*. New York: Free Press, 1973.

54. Bala and Clarke, *The Child and the Law*, p. 53.

55. Deborah Ann Luepnitz, *Child Custody*, p. 23.

56. Statistics Canada's analysis of Central Divorce Registry data indicates that when women are the petitioner, they almost always receive custody (95.7 percent). When men are petitioners, they receive custody in 42.6 percent of cases. Since most petitioners are women, overall, women are awarded custody in 85.6 percent of the cases. See *Divorce: Law and the Family in Canada*, p. 207 and p. 211. American figures come from Lenore Weitzman, chap. 4.

57. L. Weitzman, pp. 231–235. See also Nancy Polikoff, *Why Mothers are Losing: A Brief Analysis of Criteria Used in Custody Determinations* (cited in Martha L. Fineman and Anne Opie, "The Uses of Social Science Data in Legal Policymaking: Custody Determinations at Divorce," paper presented at the Conference on Child Custody, Detroit, 1985.) For Canada, see Craig McKie et al.

58. Kellin E. Gersick, "Fathers by Choice: Divorced Men Who Received Custody of the Children." In G. Levinger and O. Moles, eds. *Divorce and Separation*. New York: Basic Books, 1979.

59. Susan Boyd, "The Ideology of Motherhood, The Ideology of Equality and Child Custody Decisions Concerning Working Mothers." *Socialization of Judges to Equality Issues Conference*, Banff, 1986.

60. Quoted in *The New York Times*, Sunday, April 6, 1986.

61. In recent years, especially with the shift away from maternal preference to the "best interests principle," there has been increasing pressure for

children to be consulted and perhaps represented by a lawyer or child advocate. In the United States it is, in fact, increasingly the case that judges are expected to honour the preference of older children (12 or older or 14 and older, depending on the state) in making their decision about awarding custody. In Canada there are no legal provisions for including children's preferences except, as we have seen, in the list of factors to be taken into account in determining what constitutes the best interest of the child. However, some judges do make it a practice to interview the children privately in their chambers. And, of course, where a custody assessment or investigation has been ordered by the court or requested by one of the lawyers, the children's views and preferences will indirectly emerge when the social worker's report is completed and he or she is asked to give testimony in the Court hearing.

62. Luepnitz, *Child Custody*, p. 27.
63. Robert S. Weiss, "Issues in the Adjudication of Custody When Parents Separate." In G. Levinger and O. Moles, *Divorce and Separation: Contexts, Causes and Consequences.*
64. Law Reform Commission of Canada, *Report on Family Law*. Ottawa: Ministry of Supply and Services, 1976, p. 16.
65. Howard H. Irving et al., "A Study of Conciliation Counselling in the Family Court of Toronto: Implications for Socio-legal Practice." In Howard Irving, ed. *Family Law: An Interdisciplinary Perspective*. Toronto, Carswell, 1981, p. 42. See also Howard Irving, *Divorce Mediation: The Rational Alternative*. Toronto: Personal Library Publishers, 1980.
66. Kenneth Kressel, *The Divorce Process*, p. 178.
67. C. James Richardson and Avrim Lazar, *Restructuring Family Law Administration: Unified Family Courts in Canada*, Ottawa: Department of Justice, 1983.
68. Ann Marie Ambert, *Divorce in Canada*.
69. Penny Gross, *Kinship Structures in Remarriage Families*. Ph.D. Thesis, University of Toronto, 1985, p. 12.
70. Cynthia Longfellow, "Divorce in Context: Its Impact on Children." In G. Levinger and O. Moles, eds. *Divorce and Separation: Context, Causes and Consequences*. p. 289.

CHAPTER 9

Violence in the Family

JANICE DRAKICH AND CONNIE GUBERMAN

There is no doubt that being assaulted or raped by a stranger in some
dark alleyway is frightening, humiliating, painful and perhaps fatal, but
are such things any less horrific if they happen within the home and at
the hands of a relative? The fact is that for most people, and especially
for women and children, the family is the most violent group to which
they are likely to belong. Despite fears to the contrary, it is not a stranger
but a so-called loved one who is most likely to assault, rape or murder
us (Dobash and Dobash, 1979:7).

INTRODUCTION

Violence is part of the human repertoire. War, capital punishment,
nuclear armament, corporal punishment, or murder, all are forms of
violence that society has sanctioned and that the state or individual
people have used to resolve conflict or bring about change (Straus and
Gelles, 1979). We have acquired a tolerance and acceptance of these
"legitimate" forms of violence. In some cases they even meet our
approval. Violence in the defense of country and home is socially
approved and rewarded. Violence as punishment for wrongdoing is
considered moral and just. The acceptance of violence in conflict resolution between countries, between the state and individuals, or
between individuals has been extended into the home, where the use
of violence between family members is tacitly sanctioned. In this chapter, we will examine the varieties of violence that occur within families,
provide explanations for them, and explore how "violence between
family members is a normal part of family life" (Straus and Gelles,
1979:549).

Violence in the family was kept behind locked doors until very recently. It was not the subject of sociological research. A review of the table of contents of *The Journal of Marriage and the Family* (an important journal for scientific research on the family) from its inception in 1939 through 1969 shows a total absence of the word "violence" from its table of contents (O'Brien, 1971). The lack of published academic work on family violence prior to 1970 does not indicate, of course, that violence did not occur, simply that it was not discussed. O'Brien (1971:696) states:

> During the same period [1939-1969], discussions and studies of 'conflict' in the family were quite common. But apparently violence, as such, was either assumed to be too touchy an issue for research or else thought to be [so] idiosyncratic as to be unimportant as a feature of 'normal' families.

The evidence presented by the contributors to *Violence in the Family* (Steinmetz and Straus, 1974), the first book published on the subject, unequivocally demonstrated the pervasiveness of family violence and alerted the academic community to the need for research into it. Yet social scientists neither accepted the challenge nor acknowledged the prevalence of family violence. A survey by Eichler (1983) in the 70s indicated that violence in the family continued to be ignored by social scientists. She found that, of 18 textbooks on the family either published or reprinted in the 1970s, only three mentioned family violence. The other 15 texts had no reference to it in either their table of contents or their index. Even with the increasing proliferation of popular articles and more open discussion of family violence, it was acknowledged neither by the academic community nor the general public. But why? Why has it taken so long to recognize and study the fear and pain that so many people suffer within this sacred institution?

Norms of family privacy, coupled with the sensitive nature of the issue, prohibited public investigation and permitted society to turn a blind eye to reality. It was generally believed that family violence did not routinely occur. If it did occur, it was considered to be the result of mental illness or violent personalities. For the most part, family violence was and still is viewed as a consequence only of deviance in family structures, family histories, or family members. Thus, any evidence of violence within families was treated as an aberrant case. Even today, while the existence of violence has become more visible, it has not yet been acknowledged as the widespread phenomenon it is, and, though family violence is now condemned, the following statement, published in 1886, could be said to state explicitly what members of our society felt implicitly in 1987. Not much has changed in 100 years:

> If no permanent injury has been inflicted, not malice nor dangerous violence shown by the husband, it is better to draw the curtain, shut out the public gaze, and leave the parties to forgive and forget.
> North Carolina Court, 1886 (Martin, 1979:47).

The purpose of this chapter is to examine the dark side of family life — the violence that occurs within it. What follows documents the incidence of violence in the family, identifies the forms of family violence, and discusses the various psychological and sociological explanations for it.

We know that violence in the family is neither a recent nor a rare phenomenon (Pleck, 1979); it has been approved and sanctioned in our cultural tradition. Throughout the history of Western civilization there has been a tradition of family relations where men — husbands and fathers — were the absolute and undisputed heads of the home. Both in law and in tradition, men have often held complete and unquestioned authority over their wives and children. Roman law of 753 B.C. proclaimed that husbands were to rule their wives as possessions and that a married woman was to obey the wishes of her husband. He was given the legal right to punish his wife for any misbehaviour including adultery, drinking wine, attending public games without permission, or appearing unveiled in public. Under English common law, "the wife came under control of her husband and he had the legal right to use force against her in order to ensure that she fulfilled her wifely obligations" (Dobash and Dobash, 1979:60). Under this law, women lost all of their civil rights. Wives had no separate legal status, and they became the chattel of their husbands. Even when the common law was changed to the newer civil law, men were allowed under certain circumstances and conditions to beat and punish their wives severely.

Legal systems and community norms of Europe, England, and North America sanctioned the husband's right to beat his wife (Dobash and Dobash, 1978). Just in the last hundred years has woman-battering been considered a problem at all. Dobash and Dobash (1978:428) sum up how wife assault has been viewed in the western world since the days of the Roman Empire:

> It has only been a hundred years since men were denied the legal right to beat their wives in Britain and the United States [and Canada]. Prior

to the late 19th century it was considered a necessary aspect of a husband's marital obligation to control and chastise his wife through the use of physical force. The legal prescriptions which once supported this practice no longer exist yet the behaviour continues unabated. Behaviour which was once legally condoned is now proscribed by law, yet cultural and normative prescriptions still support such practice and it is only mildly condemned, if at all, by law enforcement and judicial institutions.

Violence among family members is not an atypical deviation. Sociologist Margrit Eichler (1983:55) estimates that at least 50-60 percent of Canadian families experience some form of familial violence. The editors of *The Social Causes of Husband-Wife Violence*, a comprehensive volume on family violence, conclude that:

> . . . the family is the predominant setting of every form of physical violence from slaps to torture and murder. In fact, some form of physical violence in the life cycle of family members is so likely that it can be said to be almost universal . . . . If this is indeed the case, then violence is as typical of family relationships as is love (Hotaling and Straus, 1980:4).

While it is no longer legally permissible for men to beat their wives or children, and women now have equal rights under the law, the prevailing circumstance in our society has been one of inequality between men and women. Men have held a position of power and privilege both inside and outside the home.

Although family violence is not limited to wife assault and the sexual abuse of children, it is women and children, those in the weakest positions, who are most often the victims of abuse. The figures that show this are overwhelming. One out of every two women will suffer some form of violence at some time in her life (Lenore Walker, 1979:61). One-fifth to one-third of all women are sexually assaulted in childhood (Finkelhor, 1985:21). Psychologist Lenore Walker estimates that in 99 out of 100 cases of spousal abuse it is the husband who beats the wife. The incidence, frequency, and severity when men are beaten are minimal in comparison to wife abuse (Walker, 1979:59-60). The methods of violence used by men and women are different, also. Men usually use physical force, such as hitting or choking; women are more likely to throw objects such as kitchen utensils (Steinmetz, 1977). Social scientist David Finkelhor estimates that 85-95 percent of perpetrators of sexual abuse are men. While women are also guilty of behaviour that has a sexually traumatic effect on children, "women do not seem to use children for their own direct sexual gratification to anywhere near the same extent that men do" (Finkelhor, 1985:22).

Evidence from clinical and non-clinical studies, from random and national surveys, and from case studies and police records shows overwhelmingly that men are the abusers and women are the victims in the areas of family violence. The use of violence is encouraged by the widespread belief in the superior status of men, the equation of dominance and physical power with masculinity, and the assumption that physical force and intimidation are proper means of solving disagreements. These are the three fundamental parts of traditional male socialization that encourage the continuation of the use of violence (Carlsson, 1977). Men find a lot of social reinforcement for their abusive behaviour. They are socialized to be aggressive and dominant; they learn to protect their authority and control by using force. Men are more likely than women to be taught the skills related to physical force and are more likely to use them (Dobash and Dobash, 1977-78:150).

Women's socialization is in sharp contrast to men's. They are trained to be non-aggressive and non-assertive. For their adult roles of wife and mother, women are taught to be nurturant, co-operative, tender, self-denying, empathetic, helpless, and dependent. Women are socialized from childhood towards powerlessness and helplessness, and to accept their position of dependence on and subordination to men. To do otherwise would be unfeminine, unmotherly, unwifely. "Many recent feminists [sic] theorists have said that society, by teaching women to deny [their] own needs, makes us behave in ways that can be misconstrued as a wish to suffer" (Caplan, 1986:44).

Men, on the other hand, are implicitly and explicitly assigned the job of maintaining and perpetuating the hierarchical family structure.

> In our research, it was the real or perceived challenges to the man's possession, authority and control which most often resulted in the use of violence. A late meal, an unironed shirt, a conversation with any man no matter how old or young, all served as 'justification' for beatings; many of the precipitating factors were exceedingly innocuous and would appear inexplicable without an understanding of the context of authority, subordination and control in which they occurred (Dobash and Dobash, 1978:438-439).

But it is necessary also be understand why men are the most frequent perpetrators of sexual as well as physical abuse. Finkelhor (1985:26) suggests three explanations, all of which address the differences between male and female socialization. First, women learn how to express affection in a non-sexual way. Men are not comfortable with non-sexual affection. Physical affection is withheld from boys at an early age, and only allowed them much later in adolescence through sex. As a result, it is in sex that men tend to seek fulfillment of their affectionate and nurturant needs. Second, men are socialized to separate their sexual arousal from the context of the relationship in which the sexual act takes place.* This makes it easier for men to sexualize relationships with children. Third, Finkelhor suggests that men are trained to be attracted to those who are younger, smaller, and weaker, while women are trained to be attracted to someone older, bigger, and more powerful than themselves.

THE NATURE OF FAMILY VIOLENCE

Wife Assault

Violence against wives is not a new phenomenon in our culture. One author has pointed out that "wife beating is a matter of historical record" (Davidson, 1980:99). Although husbands are no longer legally allowed to chastise wives, the toleration of wife assault is built into patriarchal social attitudes and social arrangements.

In the last 15 years, studies conducted throughout Canada, the United States, and Great Britain have shown that violence against wives is a fact of family life. Despite a lack of uniformity in data collection, it is currently estimated that at least one Canadian woman in ten, living with a man, is assaulted by her partner (MacLeod, 1980).†This estimate is considered conservative by many working in the field. The FBI estimates that a women is severely beaten in the United States every 18 seconds (Sinclair, 1985).

Wife assault is rarely a single, isolated event. Data from the National Crime Survey, conducted by the Bureau of Justice Statistics in the United States, shows a high risk that, once battered, women will be beaten repeatedly (Goalkasian, 1986). A Canadian study showed that women were beaten as many as 35 times before they made contact with the police (Jaffe and Burris, 1982).

---

*This is analyzed by Mary di Michele in the poem "Hunger," in her book, *Immune to Gravity*. Toronto: McClelland and Stewart, 1986.

†We use the terms "husband" and "wife" interchangeably with "partner." These terms reflect an intimate relationship between a man and a woman whether they are legally married or not (Sinclair, 1985).

A Scottish study by the well-respected team of Dobash and Dobash found that 76 percent of all physical attacks in the family setting were directed at wives by their husbands. Children were victims in 10.7 percent of cases, while assaults by wives against husbands constituted 1.1 percent of incidents (Dobash and Dobash, 1979). In a study of calls for help to the Hamilton police force, made in 1974, Dr. Jack Byles found that, in 95 percent of the calls, women were the victims (Sinclair, 1985).

> Females, whether they may be sisters, mothers, wives or daughters, are more likely to be subject to control through the use of physical force than are male counter parts—it is [in] their capacity as wives that the risk is the highest (Dobash and Dobash, 1978:437).

In the majority of cases, the victims of assault between spouses are wives. Twenty-one percent of a random sample of 644 ever-married women reported that they had been beaten by their husbands. In this study the women themselves defined violent behaviour as being slapped, hit, or beaten. Other degrees of force such as being pushed, held down, or shaken were not defined as violent behaviours (Russell, 1982). Based on estimates from her own experience as a counsellor, Lenore Walker suggests that one out of every two women—or 50 percent—are beaten at some point in their lives by a man within the context of an intimate relationship (Walker, 1979:61).

Women are hit in the head and the face, assaulted with weapons such as stove burner coils, broken bottles, knives, and guns. Assaults result in bruises, broken bones, internal injuries, and even death. Statistics from 1982 show that one-fifth of all Canadian homicides derive from wife assault. Over half (60 percent) of all female homicide victims in Canada are killed in a family context: this is more than double the number of male victims killed in similar situations (Statistics Canada, 1982). Twenty percent of visits to emergency medical services are the direct result of wife assault (Stark and Fillitcraft, 1982). Pregnant women are especially vulnerable to violence. Forty percent of wife assaults begin during the woman's first pregnancy (Education Wife Assault Fact Sheet, 1985). This phenomenon is explained by a pregnant woman's more limited access to resources and the greater dependency on her partner that results. (Sinclair, 1985)

Sexual, psychological, and emotional abuse often accompany physical beatings. Sexual abuse may involve forced intercourse after a beating, having pain inflicted during intercourse, or being forced against her will to take part in sex acts like those portrayed in violent pornographic magazines. Nowadays, a man can be charged with abusing his wife sexually, but prior to January 1983 it was not an offense for a husband to rape his wife.

Psychological and emotional abuse can take various forms, such as forcing a woman to do degrading things like breaking her favourite vase or licking the dishes clean, making threats to harm the victim or her loved ones, attacking her personality and belittling her, or terrorizing her by tying a noose around her neck, or driving through red lights. This psychological torture renders a woman in a constant state of fear for her safety (Sinclair, 1985).

Much previous research on wife assault has assumed that violent behaviour arose from the psychopathology of the woman who was beaten, the man who did the beating, or the marriage in which the violence occurred. Wife assault has sometimes been explained as an example of a dysfunctional family, or the woman is blamed for being masochistic, for provoking the violence, and for staying in the violent relationship. Yet both these theories place too much responsibility for the violence on the beaten woman herself.

Why do men assault their wives? Are men who batter mentally ill? Are they economically impoverished? Are they ignorant? Are they violent because they are addicted to drugs or alcohol? Do they batter because there is too much stress in their lives?

The answer to all of these questions is a definite "No." Many people are under great stress, yet don't resort to violent behaviour. While many batterers do abuse alcohol and drugs, many others do not. Research has shown that batterers come from all walks of life. They represent all ages, all education levels, all ethnic and religious groups, and all socio-economic classes, and are found in both urban and rural communities (Walker, 1979; Moore, 1979).

Most obviously, men are violent toward their wives because they are allowed to be. As has been discussed, violence is a cultural style in our society. And it is a cultural style belonging particularly to men (Cole, 1985). Men are socialized to believe that they are superior and that they have a right to dominate and control. They are taught that physical power equals masculinity: ". . . violence used by men against women in the family . . . attempts to establish or maintain a patriarchal social order" (Dobash and Dobash, 77–78:150). This violence is positively reinforced by our social structure.

Moreover, men assault their wives because violence is a highly effective method of controlling behaviour (National Institute of Justice, 1986). To avoid further beatings, a woman will spend a great deal of energy trying to stay out of her husband's way and anticipating his needs and desires. Abusive men often explain their violence by insisting that they have a right to control "their" women. Violent behaviour is a way of coercing their wives to do what they want them to do.

Who is the battered woman? The demographic profile of the assaulted woman looks very similar to that of the man who beats her. She can be any age, comes from all ethnic and cultural backgrounds, from all socio-economic groups; she lives in the city and she lives in rural areas. She very likely holds traditional notions of male and female behaviour: that the family is sacrosanct, that her husband is the head of the household, and that she must be supportive to him, even if it means being beaten. (Moore, 1979). Women who are beaten by their husbands almost always believe that it is their fault, that they deserve to be beaten.

> Battered women tend to internalize blame and assume responsibility for the violent encounters. They believe their actions provoked and, in some way, justified the abusive action. A woman who argues with her husband or refuses an order may believe that she has thereby provoked and consequently deserved the violent response. . . . Victims tend to be far more passive than assertive in their interpersonal relationships. They frequently play down the seriousness of a particular beating and are protective and defensive of the men who beat them. This inappropriate denial is a major means by which they cope with their own anxiety and fear about abuse (Pressman, 1984:27). [Pressman makes the point that these traits describe women during their abusive relationships. They do not necessarily describe women before the relationships.]

A woman often thinks she has caused the beating because she did something wrong. But the violence has little to do with her behaviour or her personality. Women grow up believing it is their responsibility to make a marriage work and that if it doesn't, somehow it is their fault.

Why do battered women stay in the home? There is no simple answer. They do not stay because they ask for, or deserve, to be beaten. They stay with or return to abusive relationships for many reasons which include economic dependence, ambivalence, hope, fear, disbelief, and low self-esteem. Few women have the financial independence to leave their marriages. Battered women are not always being abused, and their partners are not always violent. Batterers often become kind, loving, and contrite after an attack. They often promise the beatings will never happen again (Walker, 1979). Women want to believe the promises. They want the violence to end, not the marriage. Besides, many battered women stay in abusive relationships out of fear. They are afraid of staying and afraid of leaving. Loneliness, financial devastation, a sense of failure, the possible loss of family and friends, and fear of the unknown are very real. Leaving is "a very drastic and lonely move for her to consider. After all, if the one who loves you treats you like that, what might the rest of the world do to you?" (Moore, 1979:22). These feelings are intensified by the many messages women receive from our society which reinforce their inferiority. "The woman who has little support in challenging the traditional female role is most vulnerable to remaining in an abusive relationship" (Sinclair, 1985:34). When a woman has been beaten repeatedly, her self-esteem and her belief in her self are shattered. The more severe the abuse and the longer it has continued, the poorer self-image she will have (Sinclair, 1985:35).

Despite these dynamics, many abused women try to end their abuse by seeking outside help. But pleas from battered women often go unanswered. Public institutions and professionals (doctors and hospital staff, welfare officials, clergy, and mental health professionals) have often failed to provide needed support and assistance (Goolkasian, 1986). Traditional training in these areas is reflected in a bias toward keeping the family together at any cost.

Domestic violence is not merely an interaction between two people, however. The sheer number of violent relationships in our society indicate that wife assault can no longer be treated as a private or personal dilemma. It is a major public and social concern.

The Sexual Abuse of Children

The sexual abuse of children is a much greater problem within our society than previously thought possible. A national survey conducted in Canada in 1984 reported that one in every two females, or 53.5 percent, had experienced unwanted sexual acts (defined as exposure, threats, touching, and attacks). Slightly fewer than one in three males (30.6 percent) had been a victim. About one in five (22.3 percent) of the female victims reported experiencing two or more sexual offenses, while only about one in 15 males (6.6 percent) had been involved in two or more incidents (Badgley, 1984:179-180).

The study also found that about three out of four people who had been sexually assaulted for the first time as children were females (71.8 percent) and that about one in four (28.2 percent) were male. Many other studies showed that a far greater proportion of girls was abused than of boys—estimates range from three in five to nine in ten. A report prepared in 1982 for the Metropolitan Toronto Special Committee on Child Abuse concluded that almost all victims of child abuse are girls: "Since the overwhelming number of child sexual abusers are male (97 percent) and their victims female (90 percent), [they chose] to refer to female "victims" and male "offenders" (Badgley, 1984:197).

Our assumption in this society is that most sexual abuse of children is perpetrated by individuals who are strangers to them, persons outside of the family. But this is not necessarily the case. Child sexual abuse is also inflicted by family members and within the family setting. Defining sexual assault as "any type of sexual touching of the child by another person" (Badgley, 1984:195), the Badgley Report found that well over half (55.4 percent) of the incidents occurred in the homes of victims or perpetrators (Badgley, 1984:201). Home is a place we have traditionally considered safe, and which is normally closed to scrutiny by the public. Yet most perpetrators of sexual abuse live under the same roof as their victims. In a study of incest experiences reported by 152 sexually abused women, social scientist Diana Russell learned that 95 percent of the victims were living with their parents when the abuse occurred (Russell, 1986:101). In over two-thirds of the cases (68 percent), the sexual abuse occurred in the home of the victim, the offender, or both. It took place in the home shared by the offender and the victim in 38 percent of cases; in the victim's home in 18 percent of the cases; and in the offender's home in 12 percent of the cases (Russell, 1986:101).

The word commonly used to describe sexual relations within the family is "incest." Dictionaries generally define "incest" as sexual intercourse between closely related people where marriage is forbidden either by law or taboo (Funk and Wagnall's *Standard College Dictionary*). In the last decade, researchers, social scientists, and counsellors (Russell, 1982; Butler, 1978; Herman, 1987; Berliner, 1977; and Finkelhor, 1979) who have studied the particular problem of the sexual abuse of children have found this definition too restrictive. First, it refers only to sexual intercourse. Second, it assumes that there is consensus between adults (i.e., a brother and sister) and among children who engage in sexual play or experimentation. Third, it ignores the severe trauma that children often suffer as the after-effect of sexual relations with adults. Finally, the term "incest" does not reflect the power dynamic involved in the incestuous relationship.

In 1978, Sandra Butler was one of the first who looked at the phenomenon of child sexual abuse within the family from the perspective of the victim. In her ground-breaking book, *Conspiracy of Silence*, she describes the exploitative nature of sexual abuse, and the power dynamic involved in it.

> Incestuous assault is any manual, oral or genital sexual contact or other explicit sexual behaviour that an adult family member imposes on a child, who is unable to alter or understand the adult's behaviour because of his or her powerlessness in the family and early stage of psychological development. This type of incest is non-consensual because the child has not yet developed an understanding of sexuality that allows him or her to make a free and fully conscious response to the adult's behaviour (Butler, 1978:4–5).

Russell also works with a redefinition of the meaning of incest. In her studies, she defines sexual abuse in the home as

> any kind of exploitative sexual contact or attempted contact that occurred between relatives, no matter how distant the relationship, before the victim turned 18 years old. Experiences involving sexual contact with a relative that were wanted and with a peer were regarded as nonexploitative and hence nonabusive (Russell, 1986:41).

Russell and Butler both use the terms "incestuous assault," or "sexual abuse" rather than "incest," to reflect the broader definition of incestuous behaviour. The acts associated with incestuous assault are not always genital, and the experience is not always physical. Legal definitions have usually been limited to penile-vaginal sexual intercourse, but the current definition includes a range of behaviours from voyeurism, exhibitionism from which adults get sexual satisfaction, fondling, touching, kissing, mutual masturbation, hand-genital or oral-genital contact, to sexual intercourse (Russell, 1986:96). Most often, an adult coerces, seduces, or intimidates a child into co-operating.

Studies which have examined the rate of incidence of child sexual abuse are useful for having kept track of the number of cases coming to the attention of social service professionals and agencies. But they do not reflect the true scope of the problem. According to Finkelhor and Hotaling (1983) "most cases of sexual abuse do not come to the attention of any child welfare agency or any professional. The nature of the problem — its secrecy and shame, the criminal sanctions against it, and the young age and dependent status of its victims — inhibits discovery and discourages voluntary reporting."

Current research on the prevalence of sexual abuse starts from the assumption that most of it is never officially reported. Because of this lack of information the most valid measure of the scope of the problem of incestuous assault must come from either the offenders or the victims themselves. Russell's survey, undertaken in 1978, was the "first to study incest victims identified through interviews with a large representative sample of women" (Russell, 1986:9–10).

Russell's random sample showed results which support those of the Badgley Report. Of the 930 women interviewed, Russell (1978:60–62) found that 54 percent (504 women) reported at least one experience of incestuous and/or extra-familial sexual abuse before they reached the age of 18. Forty-eight percent (450 women) reported at least one abusive experience before they reached 14. Twenty-six percent of the sample reported at least one experience of incestuous abuse before the age of ten. And 19 percent reported being sexually abused by someone in the family at least once in their lives.

The implications and the impact of these findings when extrapolated to the population at large are astounding. According to Russell,

> it means that approximately one in six women are incestuously abused before the age of eighteen and one in approximately eight are so abused before the age of fourteen. It means in addition that over one-quarter of the population of female children have experienced sexual abuse before the age of fourteen, and well over one-third have had such an experience by the age of eighteen years (1986:74).

The violence of incestuous assault can no longer be viewed as a problem that involves only a few particularly disturbed offenders. It reveals an immense trouble in the contemporary family.

Social scientists currently doing work in the field of incestuous abuse repeatedly report that between 92 and 95 percent of the victims are female and that 97 to 99 percent of the offenders are male (Berliner, 1977; Burgess et al., 1977; Giaretto, 1976). The fact that the greatest amount of sexual abuse within the family is perpetrated by males, and that the majority of victims are younger females, suggests that we must look at this problem as one of extreme inequality between genders and generations (Russell, 1986:11). The theory that violence occurs between persons at extremes of power within the family holds true in this example.

Children are powerless to protect themselves from unwanted behaviour, to avoid their abusers, or to stop their abuse. Having been taught to obey their parents and to be polite to all adults, children frequently consent to behaviour, sexual or otherwise, when the request or order comes from an adult. In our society, obedience and deference to older family members is generally both expected and rewarded (Russell, 1986:54). Incestuous assault fits into our earlier analysis of the family and the power that the husband or father has within it. It is the abuse of power. It cannot be reduced to an aberrant act out of a "particular configuration of family interaction or personality types," nor does it occur when families become dysfunctional (Butler, 1980). Such an analysis serves to excuse offenders. "To assign each family member a role in causing the incestuous assault is to imply that whatever happens to women and children in [their] homes can be traced back to something that is [the women's] fault" (Butler, 1980:49).

Elder Abuse

Our population is aging, and the percentage of older people in the population is increasing. Less than 10 percent of the population in Canada was elderly in 1976, but it is estimated that, by 2031, 20 percent of the population will be over 65. In the United States, the total population has increased 300 percent since the turn of the century, while the population of people aged 65 years and over has increased almost 800 percent (U.S. Bureau of the Census, 1979, in Pagelow).

The majority of the aged are women. Life expectancy for Canadian females is 77 years—seven years longer than the average life span of a man. More than a million women in this country are over 65, and it is projected that, by 1996, there will be two million women over 65 years of age, half of them over 75. It is estimated that by the turn of the century there will be twice as many women as men over the age of 75 (Women and Aging Fact Sheet, #2, Canadian Advisory Council on the Status of Women, based on 1976 statistics).

In Canada, the majority of single elderly parents are women; first, because they live an average of seven years longer than men; second, because women have tended to marry men older than themselves. In addition, men of 65 who are widowed or divorced remarry at a rate seven times that of women of the same age. American figures show 77 percent of elderly men living with their wives, with only 36 percent of elderly women living with their husbands (U.S. Bureau of the Census, 1979).

Where and how do the majority of these older women live, if 64 percent of them do not live with their husbands? Contrary to popular belief, fewer than five percent of the elderly population live in institutional settings such as nursing homes, though approximately 75 percent of people 65 or older are both physically and financially dependent. Thus about 20 percent of the elderly population live in some kind of family setting with varying degrees of dependency on adult care-providers (C. M. Long, 1981:124). It is these people, the older people who live in some kind of household or family setting, and who depend on a related adult to provide care, who are at the greatest risk of becoming victims of abuse in the family context.

What is elder abuse? Like other forms of abuse in the family, it can take many forms. It may include financial exploitation, where pension cheques or other monies are taken; physical injury including beatings or restraints; threats, ridicule, insults, humiliation, and imposed isolation (both physical and social); or a forced change in living arrangements. Neglect is elder abuse, and so is refusing or failing (whether intentionally or unintentionally) to provide food, health care, or aid. Elder abuse usually follows a chronic or repetitive pattern in which the older parent is malnourished or dehydrated, in which personal hygiene is ignored, or medications are administered or withheld in order to keep the older person "manageable."

The problem of elder abuse in institutional settings was exposed years ago, but the abuse of elderly parents by their adult children is just now coming to public attention. Awareness of the issue is at the stage where awareness of wife assault was, ten years ago. For example, before 1980, the topic of geriatric abuse had not been indexed in the American literature relating to social sciences, health care, criminal justice, or gerontology. It is likely that the public attention now given to elder abuse is an outgrowth from the exposure that other forms of family violence have received in the last two decades.

The subject is so new that there are almost no researchers or social scientists who have studied the area and are willing to estimate the extent of the problem. When studies do develop, they will confront the same methodological difficulties that researchers into all other areas of family violence have had to deal with—penetrating the barriers of family privacy, gaining access to victims, and lack of agreement on concepts and definition. There will be considerably more difficulty in identifying victims of elder abuse, as they are often more cloistered within the family than are women and children who have regular contact with doctors, teachers, and other adults. However, certain things about elder abuse can be said, based on a few studies conducted in the last decade.

These studies conclude that older women, not older men, are the major victims. This is not surprising, since women are over-represented among the elderly and the elderly poor. Older women are often dependent on their families financially. One in two Canadian women over the age 65 lives at or below the level of poverty (Poverty Profile 1985, National Council of Welfare, October, 1985). A Manitoba study (Shell, 1982) found that two-thirds of the victims were women who had lived with their families for at least ten years. The women were most frequently between 80 and 84 years old. Three-quarters of the abusers were family members, 60 percent of them male. The son was found to be the most likely abuser, followed by the daughter and then the spouse. Many of the care-givers were over 60 years of age themselves.

One thousand professionals who come in contact with the elderly were questioned about their caseloads in a Massachusetts study conducted in 1979. Fifty-five percent of them reported that they were aware of clients who had been abused within the previous 18-month period, 80 percent of them older women who had been abused by people they live with. The study also found that 85 percent of the victims were related to their abusers.

An earlier study conducted in Cleveland in 1978 found that, out of 404 cases of elderly abuse, 76 percent concerned older women who had at least one major physical impairment (Cohen, 1984:98). Another study, conducted in 1979 by the Center on Aging at the University of Maryland, attempted to identify the victims and the kind of abuse they suffer. Although it was based on only 26 case studies, the researchers were able to draw some conclusions. They learned that the abusers of the elderly were adult children, spouses, grandchildren, and other relatives. The victims were on the average 84 years old and were generally in poor health and unable to carry out certain tasks by themselves. Eighty-one percent of the abused were female, and they were white, middle-class, and disabled.

Documenting the incidence of abuse is difficult, because, first of all, observable signs of physical abuse such as breaks and bruises can easily be attributed to falls and injuries that frequently happen to older people anyway. Second, it is difficult to document elder abuse, because our society stereotypes older people as prone to forgetfulness and confusion; if the aged report their abuse, they leave themselves open to having their credibility questioned. Third, elder abuse is currently reported under the generic heading of "domestic violence." It does not have a category of violence of its own. Last, older people are reluctant to report abuse because they have no other choice for shelter, they are afraid of being placed in nursing homes, they lack support services, they fear retaliation, they want to avoid the humiliation and embarrassment of being abused and of not being able to take care of themselves, or they are ashamed that they raised a child who now abuses them. Elder abuse is bound to become more common in the future (simply because of the increase in the number of elderly people) unless society provides the needed support services for caring for the old and aging.

THE MEASUREMENT OF FAMILY VIOLENCE

The family today is far from the "haven in a heartless world" which it is often idealized to be. Violence inside the family home takes a variety of forms and occurs in an astounding number of families. It ranges from child neglect, child sexual assault, child battery, sibling violence, sexual abuse of wives, spouse abuse (usually wife abuse), and the abuse of elderly parents by their children, to infanticide and homicide. Research has attempted to investigate the nature and extent of these various forms of family violence. This has not been an easy task, however. Statistics on family violence are difficult to collect. Certainly there are methodological problems common to all studies of human behaviour, but there are unique problems inherent in the study of violence in the family. Because of the shame and stigma that surround it, victims, offenders, and their families are neither eager nor co-operative research subjects. And, until recently, as has been stated above, the police, medical practitioners, the legal profession, and social service agencies have kept inadequate records for study. It is only in the last 15 years that data have been collected.

Collecting data has been hindered significantly by the attitude that the family is private territory. Along with the social need to maintain an image of the family as loving, caring, and safe goes the cultural assumption that the family is a private area that must be protected from outside intervention or intrusion.

A prevailing attitude in our society is that the state has no right to interfere in the private lives of its citizens, and that any one who violates the sanctity of the home is "anti-family." The inscription over the doors of the New York Family Court which reads "The Sanctity of the Home and Integrity of the Family" exemplifies the ideal of the family as a unit separate unto itself.

In Canada, the state's distinction between a private dilemma and a public social issue can be highlighted by comparing the police response to drug trafficking to their response to wife assault. When the police suspect that there are illegal drugs in a private home, they have the power, either by Writ of Assistance or a warrant to go into the home. But, until 1983, the law was both confusing and restrictive in its policy regarding domestic assaults. In the case of wife assault, the police did not believe that they had the right to enter a private home, even if they had been told a "wife" had been assaulted. And while the presence of illegal drugs is sufficient grounds for making an arrest, police rarely lay a charge of wife assault unless they have seen the offense being committed. The crime of assault against women is still seen as primarily a problem between husband and wife, not as a violation of the law. When the law was changed in 1983, it abolished the term "common assault." It is now illegal for a man to assault his wife sexually, and police have been instructed to lay charges in cases of wife assault, just the way they would in non-family assault. But many officers still regard wife assault as a private matter between husband and wife.

A study conducted on behalf of the solicitor general of Canada in the first six months of 1979 demonstrated this point (Jaffe and Burris, 1981). It reveals that the police laid a charge of assault in only three percent of cases of family violence, even thought they had advised 20 percent of the victims to seek medical attention. One of the causes of this reluctance on the part of the police is the traditional attitude that wife abuse is a private family matter, that females are the legitimate victims of abuse, and that violence is a normal male response to stress. By not arresting or charging the batterer, police implicitly give him the message that he has a right to hit his partner and that he will not be held responsible for his own behaviour (Jaffe and Burris, 1982).

The techniques for gathering data commonly employed by researchers of violence are survey and ethnographic research. The problems attached to collecting generalizable data are twofold: (1) gaining access to victims and perpetrators of violence; and (2) the validity of the data obtained. In 1976, Straus, Gelles, and Steinmetz interviewed a representative sample of 2,143 intact American families. Surprisingly, the study was successful in getting people to talk about violence in their families. However, the information provided may not have revealed its actual nature and extent. Gelles (1985) speculates that data collected through surveys and interviews under-represent the reality of family violence because they are based on information that respondents willingly provide. Family violence may recently have become more visible, but neither its victims nor its perpetrators may want to be visible, themselves. The information they give, if they give it at all, is under their control, and thus they may not reveal the totality or severity of the violence.

Official figures more seriously under-represent the occurrence of violence, because they are obtained by recording the number of cases actually reported. Only a small percentage of cases is ever brought to the attention of a public agency. The abuse may not be severe enough to require medical attention, and thus never becomes public. Or teachers, doctors, friends, and relatives may be reluctant to report cases they know of, because of the stigma attached to the act of reporting and the consequences of being reported. To report on "private" family business jeopardizes their relationship with relatives, friends, or acquaintances. Moreover, the perception of abuse is affected by assumptions about the abuser. A study conducted in the United States presented pediatricians with cases of child abuse (Turbett and O'Toole, 1980). The pediatricians were asked to review children's medical files (which included social and medical information on each child and its family), to assess the information, to indicate whether or not the cases before them were child abuse cases, and to recommend whether or not they should be reported. Unbeknownst to the doctors, the researchers had manipulated the variables of occupation and race of the children's fathers, all other information being standardized. The results of the study indicated that the doctors were less likely to report the abuse of an injured white child or of a child whose father was a professional.

The problem of bias in reporting abuse is problematic to the study of family violence. Although we have come to know that violence in the family cuts across all boundaries of race, economic class, religion, education, and geography, there is a widely-held assumption that violence chiefly occurs in lower-class families. This assumption could stem from the different ways violence is reported, depending on class background. Middle- or upper-class families have greater access to support services such as private psychiatric therapy. The violence committed within these families is less likely to come to the attention of public authorities. Families less privileged socially and economically are more likely to call the police after an incident of violence, or to seek the help of public agencies. In doing so, they become more subject to the scrutiny of social workers, doctors, the police, and the courts. Data collected from their records reflects a skewed portion of the total population of victims.

Do available statistics and research indicate an increase or decrease in family violence? This is a difficult question to answer. While reports of family violence including sexual victimization, wife assault, elder abuse, and child battery have increased dramatically in the last decade, the true incidence of violence in the family is difficult to determine, because statistics on family violence have not been collected routinely. The following case is an example of how a change in recording methods can greatly alter the data as to the increase or decrease of abuse. In 1967 there were no official cases of child abuse in the state of Rhode Island. But by 1977 there were more than 1,500 cases reported. On the surface it appears that there had been an overwhelming increase in the incidence of abuse, but what had changed in fact was the system of reporting and recording. Residents of the state thought there was an epidemic of child abuse; it was simply that, prior to 1967, the problem of child abuse was invisible, and mandatory laws for reporting it were not in place. Therefore the absence of reported child abuse cases in 1967 reflects only the social conditions for reporting abuse, not the reality of its incidence (Gelles, 1985). Most researchers in Canada and the United States believe a revolution in awareness is underway. Because of changed mores, professionals (and the public) are more sensitive to the instances of abuse, victims are more willing than ever before to seek help, and there are more services in place to provide help (Finkelhor, 1979:132).

EXPLANATIONS FOR VIOLENCE IN THE FAMILY

Explanations for violence in the family range from blaming the individual to placing responsibility on the social structure. Four theories are discussed in the following section. The first, Violence as Individual Pathology, deals with the psychopathological model of violence from both the biological and psychological perspectives. The second, Violence as a By-Product, looks at the association of violence and stress and violence and drug or alcohol abuse. The third, Violence as Learned Behaviour, explores how individuals learn violent behaviours, and examines the cycle of family violence. The fourth, Society Constructs Family Violence, pulls the argument together that we have made throughout this chapter: that family violence is best understood in its historical, cultural, and structural context.

Violence as Individual Pathology

Historically, the treatment of violence in the family has been the focus of medical and mental health professionals. The professional training and experience of these practitioners directed their analysis of family violence to biological and psychological anomalies which produce and characterize perpetrators of violence. The medical model, also known as the "pathological model," proposes that individuals who assault members of their family physically or sexually possess distinguishing personality characteristics that reflect some form of mental illness or pathology. This notion fits in neatly with the general diagnostic framework of practitioners and the commonly held beliefs of the general public. Steele and Pollock (1968), Bennie and Sclare (1969), and Kempe and his associates (1962) believe that abusers are psychopathological: who other than a sadist or pervert would have sexual intercourse with his daughter or break his wife's arm? That an abuser is sick is often the public's perception as well. In a trial of a man accused of killing his wife and chopping up her body with an axe, the defense counsel argued:

> it stretches the imagination to suggest that the husband is faking the depth of his mental problems. Nearly everyone would consider the husband 'nuts' for what he did. You don't need a psychiatric degree to come up with that (*The Toronto Star*, March 7, 1987, p. A8).

The psychopathological model has been approached from biological and psychological perspectives. These perspectives share the definitions of pathology, but differ in their explanations of the causes. According to the biological perspective, violent behaviour is the effect on a person's physiological makeup as a result of (1) bad genes (Ellis, 1982; Hutchings and Mednick, 1977); (2) hormonal imbalances (Jeffrey, 1980); (3) nutritional factors; or (4) exposure to physiological stress (Humphrey and Palmer, 1982). In the psychological perspective, defective personality structures result in individuals who are impulsive, unable to control their emotions or behaviour, immature, depressed, and insecure. In this view, individuals who are violent toward other family members are seen as incapable of love or of forming empathic attachments or nurturing characteristics (Helfer and Kempe, 1968). However, researchers have not been able to develop a personality profile that identifies abusers or potential abusers. Research has looked at mentally ill individuals for evidence of violence and looked for mental illness in the perpetrators of violence, only to find that personality disorders occur no more often in perpetrators of violence than in the general population (Straus, 1980; Steele, 1978; and Gelles, 1974; 1983). Straus (1980) claims that mental illness or personality disorders would be found in fewer than 10 percent of perpetrators of violence. (The section, Violence as Learned Behaviour, will look at how an "ordinary" member of society can become a perpetrator of violence.)

By locating the characteristics of abusers in mental illness, clinical studies provide both an explanation for violent behaviour and, insofar as individuals are not held accountable for what they do, an excuse.

Violence Viewed as a By-product of Alcohol, Drugs, and Stress

In this view of family violence, the perpetrator remains the primary source of violence, but is considered to have been pushed to it by external factors of stress and alcohol or drug abuse.

The popularity and pervasiveness of stress as an explanation for family violence are reflected in the family texts of Skolnick and Skolnick. In 1977 they stated that family violence seems to be a product of psychological tension and stresses. Ten years later, and in the face of evidence supporting explanations for family violence as a product of social arrangements (Finkelhor, 1983), this explanation was repeated:

> What happens to the child in the course of a day often seems to be a by-product of what happens to the parent in his or her adult life outside the realm of parenthood—a fight with the spouse, troubles with the boss, money worries, the household workload, illness (Skolnick, 1987:98).

The family is a receptacle for both inside and outside stresses. Farrington (1980:113), in his development of a general stress model for family violence, states that "violence occurs so often in the family setting because (1) the family encounters a high amount of stress; (2) it tends to be poorly equipped to handle stress; and (3) there is thus a great potential for frustration within the family." Researchers have indeed found evidence of violence associated with stress. Among some of the stresses related to violence are pregnancy (Gelles, 1975), poverty (Gil, 1971), and failure to achieve economic reward (O'Brien, 1971). That stress exists in the family or that it may precipitate violence cannot be denied; however, attention must extend beyond the precipitating factor of stress to such social factors as implicit norms which allow men to release stress and tension through violence directed toward family members.

We all experience varying degrees of stress at home, at work, or at school, but most of us do not respond to the stress with violence. Considering the stress generated in the workplace, we would expect a high frequency of violence on the job. But, although there appears to be no literature or research on violence in the workplace, it is unlikely that we would find much violence there, because norms and laws prohibit the slapping, punching, beating, or sexual assault of one's boss or co-workers. The consequences of engaging in violence at work are serious. Victims have a formal avenue of redress through company rules, union grievance procedures, or the legal system, which could lead to loss of employment for the perpetrators, to criminal charges, or incarceration. Obviously, stress by itself does not explain violence. A further explanation is needed, in addition to identifying stressors and their presence in the family. If the family had prohibitive sanctions like the workplace, violence would probably occur less often. As it is, violence in the family remains hidden from public accountability.

Another factor commonly used as an explanation for violence is the abuse of alcohol and/or drugs. Langley and Levy (1977) suggest that alcoholism is present in 49 to 95 percent of cases of wife abuse. Fagan, Stewart, and Hansen (1983) found in their study of 270 wife-assault victims that alcoholism was involved in more than half of the cases and drugs in one-fourth. Okum (1984:57–58) conveniently summarizes the results of a number of studies: "Gelles found alcohol abuse in 48% of his violent couples, Gayford in 52% of his cases, Carlson in 60% of her sample of couples, and Einsenberg and Micklow in 70%. Roy found that 85% of batterers in her sample were also substance abusers." The contribution of alcohol or drugs to incidents of violence cannot be denied; yet it would be illogical to conclude that substance abuse is the *cause* of violent behaviour. Gingold (1976) suggests that alcohol abuse is a "disavowal technique" which releases the individual from feeling responsibility for violent behaviour. Research shows that people do get drunk and beat up their wives and children (Langley and Levy, 1977; Hilberman and Munson, 1977; Gelles, 1974). Yet they do not abuse because of the alcohol, but drink to supply the abuse with an explanation.

Stress, drugs, and alcohol may facilitate violent behaviour; but these external factors do not address the central questions of why violence is the way to release tension in response to these factors. Later, we will examine why violence is most likely to be used as a response within the family.

Violence Viewed as Learned Behaviour

According to social learning theory, violence is learned in interaction with others. Through observation of violence between parents, or between sisters and brothers, children may learn that violence is useful for achieving one's goals, for gaining power, or for controlling and manipulating others. As victims of violence, children learn that violence goes unpunished as a form of interpersonal behaviour. In other words, it is socially acceptable. Thus, not only are the acts of violence learned, so are the family's attitudes to violence and their acceptance of it.

Steinmetz and Straus (1974) devote an entire section of their book to the family as a training ground for violence. Another chapter in this book describes how the family is a primary agent of socialization; its impact on our development is perhaps greater than any other social contact we have in our lifetime. In the family we learn the appropriateness and inappropriateness of our behaviour, our roles in the family and in society, and expectations for ourselves and others. Several social scientists (Bandura, 1973; Owens and Straus, 1975) argue that, since we learn so many things in the context of the family, violence is simply another skill that we acquire. In this way, the family is appropriately labelled "the cradle of violence" because it is in the family context that individuals are most likely to first experience it.

Straus (1978:47) states that "learning violence begins with physical punishment." Most of us as children have been spanked or slapped for our behaviour, and the research indicates that physical punishment is commonplace in families. Gelles (1979:74) states that studies of physical punishment indicate that 84 to 97 percent of parents punish their children physically. In his own study (1979) he found that 71 percent of parents slapped or spanked their children, 46 percent pushed or shoved their children, and 20 percent hit a child with something. Steinmetz (1977) found that, in 63 to 70 percent of the families in her study, physical violence was used by brothers and sisters to resolve conflict. The prevalence of physical punishment is not surprising when we consider that 20 to 25 percent of all Americans approve of slapping their spouse on appropriate occasions (Stark and McEvoy, 1970). Straus, Gelles, and Steinmetz (1980:55) found that most parents feel that spanking and slapping a twelve-year-old child are good, normal, and necessary forms of punishment. From research on attitudes and behaviour, it would seem that cultural norms do not preclude the use of physical punishment or force in resolving conflict with loved ones or as a disciplinary technique. These "minor" forms of physical punishment are commonly perceived as normatively legitimate, and as having little relevance for violent behaviour. However, Straus (1983:229) argues that "widespread use of physical punishment is one of the factors accounting for the high rate of child abuse and wife battery."

While the old adage, "Spare the rod and spoil the child," embodies the principle that physical punishment will teach children appropriate behaviour, the use of punishment teaches children other things as well. Straus (1978:45) states that children learn that violence is appropriate with those we love. Moreover, the moral rightness of physical punishment is established by being used to teach acceptable and correct behaviour.

According to social learning theory, physical punishment provides a model of aggressive behaviour which the individual imitates in interaction with others. The propensity to repeat violent behaviour is influenced by success or failure which is, in turn, dependent on the reaction or outcome to the behaviour. If the behaviour is successful, the individual will repeat it; if it proves unsuccessful, it will be discarded. (Bandura, 1973).

Straus (1983:229) found that the more violent parents are to their children, the more violent these children are to their siblings; the more violent the husband is toward the wife, the more violent the wife is toward her children. This suggests that victims of violence perpetuate rather than prevent this behaviour. Many argue that victims of childhood abuse recreate the familial context of their upbringing in their own homes. This latter point has been extensively studied, and has come to be known as "the intergenerational transmission of violence." That is, the violence experienced and learned in the family of origin is perpetuated in the family of procreation. Steinmetz (1977) reports on a number of studies which found that a proportion of perpetrators of violence suffered from or observed violence in their families of orientation (Gaylord, 1975; Owens and Straus, 1975; Silver, Dublin, and Lourie, 1969). In lay terms, "violence breeds violence." Numerous studies support this assumption. Adults who were physically abused as children are more likely to abuse their own children than are adults who were not abused as children (Kalmuss, 1984; Straus et al., 1980; Steinmetz, 1977; Gelles, 1976; Spinetta and Rigler, 1972). Kalmuss (1984) studied the effects on the subsequent generation of being a victim of family violence and observing family violence including marital abuse. She found that observing parental hitting had more of an influence on future violent behaviour toward a spouse than being a victim of parental abuse. The reason she offers for this is that, in addition to learning that violence is acceptable between their mothers and fathers, children generalize that aggression between husbands and wives is acceptable. Children learn that physical strength and power are the appropriate means of controlling behaviour.

Another factor that plays a part in the future use of violence is that the more violence children are exposed to, the greater the chances of their using violence in the future. Yet, although the studies we have referred to indicate that children from violent homes are more likely than children from non-violent homes to be perpetrators of violence as adults, Steinmetz (1977) cautions the reader in the interpretation of the evidence. While there are data supporting the intergenerational transmission of violence for some of the perpetrators of violence, there is also evidence that many victims of abuse do not abuse in adulthood. In fact, in a national study of violence in the United States, Straus, Gelles, and Steinmetz (1979) found that being abused as a child did not directly lead to abusive behaviour, and that not all abusers were abused as children. As in the case of the relationship of mental illness to violence, the connection is possible, rather than inevitable.

We have now looked at the more commonly known explanations for violence in the family, the pathological model, explaining violence in terms of personality dysfunctions, the by-product model, which identifies drugs, alcohol and stress as precursors to violent acts, and the learning model, which indicates that violence is learned behaviour. These perspectives provide explanations of how individuals learn to be violent, and identify factors that facilitate violence, but they do not tell us *why* individuals are violent in the family. Further, these explanations obscure our understanding of violence by locating the responsibility for abuse with the individual alone, and by emphasizing the pathology of the individual. When the individual is blamed, society and the structure of the family are absolved of any responsibility. However, the pervasiveness of family violence, and the fact that women and children are overwhelmingly the targets of violence, cannot be explained by pathology, substance abuse, or stress, nor by examining an individual's behaviour apart from the setting of the family. The social learning model directs us implicitly to take the social context into account; as suggested earlier, violence is encouraged, supported, and rewarded by the social system. It is learned in interaction with others. The structure of the family, and the relative position of men, women, and children within it, is a most useful focus for an analysis of the occurrence of family violence. The next section summarizes our position that violence in the family is socially constructed and maintained.

SOCIETY CONSTRUCTS VIOLENCE IN THE FAMILY

Violence is built into the hierarchical structure of the family. Goode (1971) argues that the maintenance of the family structure rests to some degree on force or threat, and that the preservation of family roles or family structure would not be possible in their absence. Force or threat, according to Goode, are legitimate uses of violence, beneficial to the functioning and maintenance of the family. That violence in the family is socially approved, and that it routinely occurs, is interpreted by Straus and Gelles (1979:549) as indicative that violence is not an outgrowth of social of psychological pathology but, rather, "is a normal part of family life in most societies" for resolving conflict and maintaining the viability of the social unit.

There are three factors common to all experiences of domestic violence. These include power differentials, social isolation, and psychological abuse.

Power Determines Abuse

Power is common to all forms of violence. The perpetrators of violence and their victims usually occupy differential positions of power. That is, the ones who are stronger or bigger, the ones with greater access to important resources, and the ones who are culturally defined as being dominant are the ones who can impose their wills on others who are smaller, weaker, lacking resources, or culturally defined as subordinate. Finkelhor (1983:17–18) states that the common patterns of violence "are not merely for the more powerful to abuse the less powerful but for the most powerful to abuse the least. This is an interesting commonality: Abuse tends to gravitate to the relationships of greatest power differential." Finkelhor continues by using sexual abuse as an example. The most commonly reported form of sexual abuse involves adult males in positions of authority abusing girls in subordinate positions. Even though incest does not usually involve violence in the form of a physical attack, it always involves an abuse of power.

All family members do not have equal status. Status depends on sex, age, roles, physical strength, financial resources, and access to other resources. Some adult males may be in subordinate, powerless positions compared to others in society as a whole, but within the family unit they often have ultimate power. Thus it is important to consider power differences within the family and society. Studies have shown that the less power the wife has — when she is not in the paid labour force, when she is excluded from family decision-making, and when she has less education than her husband—the more her husband is likely to abuse his greater power (Finkelhor, 1983). On the other hand, as a woman earns a wage or salary of her own and gains some economic independence from her husband, the husband loses some of his power over her (Eichler, 1983:188-189).

> . . . whereas the working wife may be characterized as more assertive than housewives, husbands of working wives can be characterized as less assertive and less concerned with power and authority than husbands of housewives (Burke and Weir, 1976:457).

A power imbalance is also an important factor in the abuse of an elderly parent. The more self-sufficient and able the elderly parent is, the less likely she is to be abused by her caretakers.

Social Isolation Encourages Abuse

Another recurring factor in family violence is that of social isolation. Evidence shows that the family's condition as a private institution makes it prone to violence (Gelles, 1979). Sandra Butler (1978), in *The Conspiracy of Silence: The Trauma of Incest*, refers to the social isolation commonly found in abusive families:

> A factor discouraging aid to troubled families is that we tend to consider the nuclear family's isolation and self-imposed privacy to be a valuable source of strength. We believe that the family needs to be shielded and protected from the prying eyes of the larger community. Keeping family secrets from outsiders, teaching our children that 'blood is thicker than water' and that outsiders are not to be trusted, we reinforce an unhealthy isolation of the nuclear family unit.

This isolation is social, not necessarily geographic. It includes isolation caused by poverty, unusual social values, or family disorganization (Finkelhor, 1979). Isolation in this case refers to the insulation of the family from the rules of the larger society. Gelles (1978) also noted that, as privacy increases, the level of social control decreases. It has been found that most father/daughter incest occurs in families which are isolated and dominated by the father in the exteme (Herman and Hirschman, 1980). Family isolation, combined with a social attitude that parents own their children, makes it difficult for any outside prevention or intervention in cases of sexual abuse (MacFarlane and Lieber, 1978:88). The family is not obliged to explain its behaviour inside or outside the home. Studies of wife abuse show that many of the women are isolated in the home, while their husbands have many social contacts and friendship networks outside it (Dobash and Dobash, 1979). This is also the case with abused elderly people, especially when their mobility is restricted and contact with people outside of where they live is limited. When they are unable to get out of the house and maintain their friendship networks, they increasingly come under the control of their caretakers. If they have moved into their child's home, neighbours often don't know they even exist.

Psychological Abuse

A third common factor is that victims of all types of family violence share a sense of humiliation and low self-esteem. The terrible shame and sense of worthlessness that a women feels when she has been beaten by her husband is also felt by the child who has been sexually molested or by the elderly parent who has been mistreated. Each form of physical abuse is accompanied by psychological abuse; Finkelhor (1983:17–18) writes about this psychological abuse and its effects on victims:

> All forms of family abuse seems [sic] to occur in the context of psychological abuse and exploitation, a process victims sometimes describe as 'brainwashing.' Victims are not just exploited or physically injured, but their abusers use their power and family connection to control and manipulate victims' perceptions of reality as well. . . . This 'brainwashing' that occurs along with family abuse is potent because families are the primary group where most individuals construct reality. Family members often do not have enough contact with other people who can give them countervailing perceptions about themselves.

As we have shown, historical antecedents and other aspects of the social structure support the direction of violence from men to women and children. The family is a hierarchically organized social unit with some of its members having more power, more status, and more privileges than others. The grounds are age and gender, with men in positions of power over women and children and parents in positions of power over children. To trace this development historically is beyond the scope of this chapter. Suffice it to say that economic and social conditions contributed to the establishment of the patriarchy which permeates the social and structural relationships in the family. The first legal sanctioning of men's power in the family occurred around 753 B.C., when men were vested with paternal power and the rights of life and death over their wives and children (Okum, 1986:2). Not only was physical punishment a male prerogative, but so also was the right to murder one's wife (Okum, 1986:3). While men's violence toward their wives and children is no longer legally sanctioned, vestiges of this male prerogative in the family remain. This is not surprising, considering the differential status and power of men and women in society and in the family. Practices of socialization and the ideologies of gender still sanction male dominance, female subordination, and men's aggressiveness.

Violence is the overt manifestation of inequalities of gender and power. It is an extension of men's power over women and children or, more generally, an extension of power over the powerless. Violence itself is not the problem. The problem is embedded in the power relationships of social structures. Gender socialization trains men to be violent or aggressive. First, it teaches them that they are the dominant members of society, and then gender roles encourage them to live up to their cultural attributes. Differential power permits men to perpetrate acts of violence upon women and children.

Any analysis of violence in the family is complex. We have situated our argument in those historical, cultural, and structural contexts of the family by which relationships of power and ideologies of gender legitimate and perpetuate violence. Through social learning processes we develop the knowledge of and readiness to be violent that can be brought to the surface by drugs, alcohol and stress. In the majority of cases, violence is carried out by normal men who are living up to what they've learned they can do within a male role.

Dobash and Dobash (1979:8) state that, "[i]n order to provide the foundation upon which meaningful proposals for solutions might be based, it is necessary to develop an explanation and to have an understanding of violence. . . ."

CONCLUSION

This chapter has dealt chiefly with the sources of violence in the family. But placing them within historical structures and assumptions does not mean that we think this violence is inevitable or incurable: the fact that violence is being discussed, researched, and written about helps to educate members of society. Certain changes have to be made, however. To gain a sense of their power, women must become economically self-reliant: the government's response regarding equity in employment is one positive step. Moreover, the legal system must establish barriers to family violence as potent as the inhibitors of violence in the workplace.

If it is true that violence in the family is a complex phenomenon involving personality, substance abuse, and the way the family is set up, it is also true that even without the precipitating factors of drugs, alcohol, and mental illness, the structure of family violence remains. Unless the historical, cultural, and structural contexts of the family are altered, and the legitimating ideologies of power and gender that accompany them, violence in the family won't go away.

REFERENCES

Badgley, Robin F. 1984. *Sexual Offences Against Children.* Vol. 1, Ottawa: Ministry of Supply and Services. Canadian Government Publishing Centre.

Bandura, Albert. 1973. *Aggression: A Social Learning Analysis.* Englewood Cliffs, N.J.: Prentice-Hall.

Bennie, E. and Sclare, A. 1969. "The Battered Child Syndrome." *American Journal of Psychiatry*, 125:7, pp. 975–979.

Berliner, Lucy. 1977. "Child Abuse: What Happens Next?" *Victimology* 2:2, pp. 327–331.

Burgess, Ann W., Holmstrom, Lynda L., and McCausland, Maureen P. 1977. "Child Sexual Assault by a Family Member: Decisions Following Disclosure." *Victimology* 2:2, pp. 236–260.

Burke, Ronald J. and Tamara Weir. 1976. "Some Differences Between Members of One-Career and Two-Career Families." *Journals of Marriage and the Family*, 38: p. 3.

Butler, Sandra. 1978. *The Conspiracy of Silence: The Trauma of Incest.* San Francisco: Volcano Press.

———. 1980. "Incest: Whose Reality, Whose Theory?" *Aegis*, Summer/Autumn, pp. 48–55.

Canadian Advisory Council on the Status of Women. 1979. *Women and Aging Fact Sheet #2.* Ottawa: Advisory Council on the Status of Women.

Caplan, Paula. 1985. *The Myth of Women's Masochism.* Toronto: Fitzhenry & Whiteside.

Carlsson, M. 1977. "Equality Between Men and Women in Sweden." In L. Carter, et al., eds. *Women and Men: Changing Roles, Relationships and Perceptions.* New York: Praeger. pp. 245–270.

Cole, Susan. 1985. "Child Battery." In Connie Guberman and Margie Wolfe, eds. *No Safe Place. Violence Against Women and Children.* Toronto: The Women's Press, pp. 21–40.

Cohen, Leah. 1984. *Small Expectations: Society's Betrayal of Older Women.* Toronto: McClelland and Stewart.

Davidson, Terry. 1980. *Conjugal Crime.* New York: Ballantine Books.

Dobash, R. Emerson and Russell P. Dobash. 1977–1978. "Patterns of Violence in Scotland." In Richard J. Gelles and Claire Pedrick Cornell, eds. *International Perspectives on Family Violence*. Lexington Books, 1983.

———. 1977. "Wives: The 'Appropriate' Victims of Marital Violence." *Victimology*. 2:3/4, pp. 426–442.

———. 1979. *Violence Against Wives: A Case Against the Patriarchy*. New York: The Free Press.

Education Wife Assault. 1985. *Fact Sheet*. Toronto: Ontario Women's Directorate. (revised by N. Crook).

Eichler, Margrit. 1983. *Families in Canada Today: Recent Changes and Their Policy Consequences*. Toronto: Gage Publishing.

Ellis, L. 1983. "Genetics and Criminal Behaviour." *Criminology*. 20, pp. 43–65.

Fagan, J. A., D. K. Stewart, and K. Hansen. 1983. "Violent Men or Violent Husbands? Background Factors and Situational Correlates." In David Finkelhor et al., eds. *The Dark Side of Families*. Beverly Hills: Sage Publications, pp. 49–67.

Farrington, K. M. 1980. "Stress and Family Violence." In M.A. Straus and G. T. Hotaling, eds., *The Social Causes of Husband-Wife Violence*. Minneapolis: University of Minnesota Press.

Finkelhor, David. 1979. *Sexually Victimized Children*. New York: Free Press.

———. 1983. "Common Features of Family Abuse." In David Finkelhor, et al. eds., *The Dark Side of Families*. Beverly Hills: Sage Publications.

———. 1985. "Sexual Assault and Physical Abuse: Some Critical Differences." In Eli H. Newberger and Richard Bourne, eds. *Unhappy Families. Clinical and Research Perspectives on Family Violence*. Litlleton, Mass.: PSG Publishing Company.

Gayford, J. J. 1975. "Wife Battering: A Preliminary Survey of 100 Cases." *British Medical Journal*, 1 (January), pp. 194–197.

Gelles, Richard, J. 1974. *The Violent Home. A Study of Physical Aggression Between Husbands and Wives*. Beverly Hills: Sage Publications.

———. 1975. "Violence and Pregnancy: A Note on the Extent of the Problem and Services Needed." *The Family Coordinator*, 24: pp. 81–86.

———. 1979. *Family Violence*. Beverly Hills: Sage Publications.

———. 1983. "An Exchange/Social Control Theory." In David Finkelhor, et al., eds. *The Dark Side of Families*. Beverly Hills: Sage Publications, pp. 151–165.

Gelles, R. J. and C. P. Cornell. 1985. *Intimate Violence in Families*. Beverly Hills: Sage Publications.

Gelles, R. J. and Murray Straus. 1976. "Determinants of Violence in the Family: Toward a Theoretical Integration." In Wesley R. Burr, et al. *Contemporary Theories About the Family*. Vol. 1. New York: The Free Press, pp. 549–81.

Giaretto, Henry. 1976. "The Treatment of Father-Daughter Incest: A Psycho-Social Approach." *Children Today*, 34: July–August, pp. 2–5.

Gil, D. 1971. "Violence Against Children." *Journal of Marriage and the Family*, 33; November, pp. 637–648.

Gingold, Judith. 1976. "One of These Days—Pow—Right in the Kisser." *Ms. Magazine*, August, pp. 51–52, 54, 94.

Goode, W. 1971. "Force and Violence in the Family." *Journal of Marriage and the Family*, 33:4, pp. 624–636.

Goolkasian, Gail A. 1986. "Confronting Domestic Violence. The Role of Criminal Court Judges." *National Institute of Justice: Research in Brief.* U.S. Department of Justice, pp. 1–8.

Helfer, R. E. and C. H. Kempe, eds., 1968. *The Battered Child.* Chicago: University of Chicago Press.

Herman, Judith. 1981. *Father-Daughter Incest.* Cambridge, Mass.: Harvard University Press.

Herman, Judith and Lisa Hirschman. 1980. "Father-Daughter Incest." In Kee MacFarlane, et al., eds. *Sexual Abuse of Children: Selected Readings.* Washington, D.C.: Government Printing Office. Dept. of Health, Education, and Welfare.

Hilberman, Elaine and Kit Munson. 1977. "Sixty Battered Women." *Victimology*, 2:3–4, pp. 460–471.

Hotaling, Gerald T. and Murray A. Straus. 1980. "Culture, Social Organization and Irony in the Study of Family Violence." In Murray A. Straus and Gerald T. Hotaling, eds., *The Special Causes of Husband-Wife Violence*. Minneapolis: University of Minnesota Press. Chapter 1.

Humphrey, J. A. and S. Palmer. 1982. *Stressful Life Events and Criminal Homicide.* Paper presented at The National Conference on Social Stress Research, Durham, N.H.

Hutchings, B. and S. A. Mednick. 1977. "Criminology in Adoptees and Their Adoptive and Biological Parents: A Pilot Study." In S. Mednick and K.O. Chistiansen, eds. *Biosocial Bases of Criminal Behaviour.* New York: Gartner Press, pp. 127–141.

Jaffe, Peter and C. A. Burris. 1982. *An Integrated Response to Wife Assault: A Community Model.* Ottawa. The Solicitor General of Canada.

Jeffery, C. R. 1980. "Sociobiology and Criminology: The Long Lean Years of the Unthinkable and the Unmentionable." In E. Sagarin, ed. *Taboos in Criminology.* Beverly Hills: Sage Publications.

Kalmuss, Debra. 1984. "The Intergenerational Transmission of Marital Aggression." *Journal of Marriage and the Family*, 46:1 (February), pp. 11–19.

Kempe, C. H., Silverman, F. N. et al. 1962. "The Battered Child Syndrome," *Journal of the American Medical Association*, 181: pp. 107–112.

Langan, Patrick A., and Innes, Christopher A. 1986. *Special Report: Preventing Domestic Violence Against Women.* Washington, D.C.: Bureau of Justice Statistics.

Langley, R. and Levy, Richard C. 1977. *Wife Beating: The Silent Crisis.* New York: E. P. Dutton.

Lincoln, Alan J. and Kirkpatrick, John T. 1985. "Criminological Theory and Family Crime." In Alan Jay Lincoln and Murray A. Straus, eds. *Crime and the Family*. Springfield: Charles C. Thomas Publisher.

Long, C. M. 1981. "Geriatric Abuse." *Issues in Mental Helath Nursing* 3: pp. 123–135.

Martin, Del. 1979. "What Keeps a Woman Captive in a Violent Relationship? The Social Context of Battering." In Donna M. Moore, ed. *Battered Women*. Beverly Hills: Sage Publications, pp. 33–58.

MacLeod, Linda, 1980. *Wife Battering in Canada: The Vicious Circle*. Canadian Government Publishing Centre. Ottawa: Minister of Supply and Services Canada.

MacFarlane, Kee, and Lieber, Leonard. 1978. *Parent Anonymous: The Growth of an Idea*. Washington, D.C.: Department of Health, Education, and Welfare.

Moore, Donna M. 1979. "Editor's Introduction. An Overview of the Problem." In Donna M. Moore, ed. *Battered Women*. Beverly Hills: Sage Publications, pp. 7–31.

National Council on Welfare. 1985. *Poverty Profile*. October 1985. Ottawa: National Council on Welfare.

O'Brien, John E. 1971. "Violence in Divorce-Prone Families." *Journal of Marriage and the Family*. November, pp. 692–698.

Oakes, Gary. 1987. "Wife's Axe-killer Lying about Illness to Get Off, Court Told," *Toronto Star*, March 7, A-10.

Okum, Lewis. 1986. *Woman Abuse*. Albany N.Y.: State University Press Albany.

Owens, David and Straus, Murray A. 1975. "Social Structure of Violence in Childhood and Approval of Violence as an Adult." *Aggressive Behaviour*. 1:3, pp. 193–211.

Pagelow, Mildred, Daley. 1984. *Family Violence*. New York: Praeger Publishers.

Peters, S. D. et al. 1986. "Prevalence" in David Finkelhor, ed. *A Sourcebook on Child Sexual Abuse*. Beverly Hills: Sage Publications, pp. 15–60.

Pleck. E. 1979. "Wife Beating in the 19th Century." *Victimology*, 4; pp. 60–74.

Pressman, Barbara. 1984. *Family Violence: Origins and Treatments*. Guelph, Ont.: The City of Guelph Children's Aid Society and Family Counselling Services and the University of Guelph.

Russell, Diana E. H. 1982. *Rape in Marriage*. New York: Macmillan.

———. 1986. *The Secret Trauma: Incest in the Lives of Girls and Women*. New York: Basic Books.

Shell, Donna 1982. *Protection of the Elderly: A Study of Elder Abuse*. Winnipeg: Manitoba Association of Gerontology.

Silvers, L. et al. 1969. "Does Violence Breed Violence? Contributions from a Study of the Child Abuse Syndrome." *American Journal of Psychiatry*, 126: pp. 404–407.

Sinclair, Deborah. 1985. *Understanding Wife Assault: A Training Manual for Counsellors and Advocates.* Toronto: Ontario Ministry of Community and Social Services, Family Violence Program.

Skolnick, A. 1987. *Intimate Environments.* Boston: Little, Brown and Co. Limited. 4th edition.

Small, Shirley Endicott. 1980. *Wife Assault: An Overview of the Problem in Canada.* Toronto: Education Wife Assault.

Spinetta, J. and Rigler, D. 1972. "The Child Abusing Parent: A Psychological Review." *Psychological Bulletin,* 77: pp. 296-304.

Stark, Even and Filitcraft, A. 1982. "Medical Therapy as Repression: The Case of the Battered Woman." *Health and Medicine,* Summer/Fall.

Stark, R. and McEvoy, J. 1970. "Middle Class Violence," *Psychology Today,* 4: pp. 52-65.

Statistics Canada 1982. *Homicide in Canada: A Statistical Synopsis.* Ottawa: Justice Statistics Division.

Steele, B. F. 1978. "The Child Abuser." In I. Kutash, et al. eds. *Violence: Perspectives on Murder and Aggression.* San Francisco: Jossey-Bass, pp. 285-300.

Steele, B. F. and Pollock, C. 1968. "A Psychiatric Study of Parents Who Abuse Infants and Small Children." In R. Helfer and C. Kempe, eds. *The Battered Child.* Chicago: University of Chicago Press, pp. 103-47.

Steinmetz, S. 1977. *The Cycle of Violence: Assertive, Aggressive, and Abusive Family Interaction.* New York: Praeger Publishers.

———. 1977. "Wifebeating, Husbandbeating—A Comparison of the Use of Physical Violence between Spouses to Resolve Marital Fights." In Maria Roy, ed. *Battered Women.* New York: Van Nostrand Reinhold.

———. 1977. "The Battered Husband Syndrome." *Victimology,* 2: 3/4, pp. 499-509.

Steinmetz, S. and Straus, Murray, eds. 1974. *Violence in the Family.* New York: Harper & Row.

Straus, Murray A. 1983. "Ordinary Violence, Child Abuse and Wife Beating: What Do They Have in Common?" in David Finkelhor, et al. *The Dark Side of Families.* Beverly Hills: Sage Publications, pp. 213-234.

———. 1980. "A Sociological Perspective on the Causes of Family Violence." In M. R. Green, ed. *Violence and the Family.* Boulder: Westview Press, pp. 7-31.

———. 1978. "Wife beating: How Common and Why?" *Victimology* 2: 3/4 pp. 443-458.

Straus, Murray A., Gelles, Richard, and Steinmetz, S. K. 1980. *Behind Closed Doors: Violence in the American Family.* Garden City: Doubleday.

Turbett, J. P. and O'Toole, R. 1980. "Physician's Recognition of Child Abuse." Paper presented at the annual meeting of the American Sociological Association, New York.

Walker, Lenore E. 1979. *The Battered Woman.* New York: Harper & Row.

CHAPTER 10

Thinking About the Future

MEG LUXTON

INTRODUCTION

There is no question but that families are now in a state of very rapid
transformation. Since the early 1960s there have been dramatic
increases in divorce rates, the number of single-parent families, teenage pregnancies, individuals co-habiting without getting married,
openly lesbian and gay couples, the ages at which people are having
their first child, the number of people having only one or two children,
and married women's employment. All of these changing statistical
patterns reflect profound changes in people's experience of daily
life. As a result, much effort is devoted to the task of interpreting the
significance of these changes. Why are they occurring? Will they
continue to occur, and will they in turn provoke further, as yet unanticipated, changes? What will the consequences be? All of these
changes raise important questions about the future of families.

These questions get raised in a range of different ways, from individuals contemplating their personal future to government legislators
and policy analysts designing legislation that can shape the course of
an entire nation for several generations. So these are not abstract academic issues but life-and-death concerns affecting everyone. Questions
that are asked about what is happening to families today and what
such changes will mean for the future reflect both deep confusion
about what is possible and profound social disagreement about the

I would like to thank Leslie Coates and Ester Reiter for their help with this
chapter.

way society *should* be organized. Contending visions are at stake, of how we want our future to be.

In this concluding chapter I explore a number of questions about family life in the future. Because the shape of the future results from developments in the present, I argue that in thinking about families of the future, we must determine first what we include in the concept of "family." Then we can assess what currently exists, what the trends are, and where they might lead. We can uncover varying visions of the future, and anticipate what the world might look like if those visions came to pass.

THE IDEOLOGY OF "THE FAMILY"

One of the reasons why it is so difficult for people to discuss visions of future family life is that there is little consensus about what "the family" actually is. As Michele Barrett and Mary McIntosh (1982) have shown, to understand "the family" we have to differentiate between *ideology* and the actual ways in which people interact, co-reside, have sexual relations, have babies, marry, divorce, raise children, and so on. In other words, "the family" exists in two quite distinct forms: as "familialism," a widespread and deeply embedded ideology about how people *ought* to live; and as economic and social groups which in fact organize domestic and personal life (Gittins, 1985). The ideology of "familialism" is a belief system which argues that the best way for adults to live is in nuclear families; that is, as a socially and legally recognized heterosexual couple (a woman and man) who normally expect to have children (Rapp, 1978). The ideal way for children to be raised is in such a family, according to this belief system (Bloom 1976; Blumenfeld 1976), the nuclear family being thought to provide the most stable, intimate, loving environment possible (Spock, 1968). The more people live in ways that deviate from this idealized model, the less likely they are, again according to this ideology, to get intimacy, love, and stability, and the more likely they are to be in some way socially unstable (Riley, 1983). This ideology also assumes that the prevailing organization of family life profoundly affects the total organization of society. Thus, it is argued, the more that people deviate from the nuclear family, the more the fundamental organization of contemporary society is undermined.

Basic to the ideology of familialism are patriarchal definitions and ideals of how men, women, and children should behave. While men are defined primarily by their occupation (the origin of many surnames, e.g., in English, Smith, Taylor, Steward), women and children have for centuries been defined by their relation to the kinship system through men (taking the surname of their fathers and husbands) (Gittins, 1985:35). Because "the family," by definition, has referred to the authority of the male head over his wife and children (see Anderson, this volume), the ideology of the nuclear family implies male power over women and children and a wife's subordination to her husband (Weber, 1967).

This ideology about the way we *should* live shapes our lives profoundly. First, most individuals carry some form of that belief system around with them throughout their lives, and it affects the way they assess their own circumstances (Barrett and McIntosh, 1982). Too often, people marry and have children, not because they are certain that is what they want, but because they feel they should. Other people who have clearly chosen a different route are still affected by this ideology, and may have residual anxieties about whether their decision was actually the right one.

Second, the ideology of familialism permeates the assumptions made about and for other people. So young women will be asked by their well-intentioned relatives whether they have found "Mr. Right" yet, and young men will be asked when they are going to find a nice "girl" and settle down. A daughter's husband whom she has married after a short acquaintance will be much more welcome at family gatherings than another daughter's female lover and companion of 20 years. Someone in hospital for a major illness is permitted to have "immediate family" visit, while friends are excluded, even though these friends may in fact provide the only real love and caring in the patient's life and the "proper" family may be estranged and uncaring. In schools it may be assumed that children who do not live in nuclear families will be less able to perform well and more likely to present behaviour problems. Children who actually do have problems may find them attributed to their "abnormal" domestic situation rather than to perceptual difficulties (Griffiths, 1983).

Third, the ideology of familialism has shaped social policy and government legislation for much of the 20th century (Eichler, 1983, and this volume). For example, in many workplaces employees are able to obtain benefits for spouses of the opposite sex but not for those of the same sex. Women can get maternity leave if they give birth or adopt but not if their woman partner gives birth and both are going to be closely involved in raising the child. Married individuals cannot obtain a mortgage without their spouse's involvement, even when the couple keep entirely separate finances. Income tax laws are similarly based on certain assumptions about family. Neighbourhood zoning laws and building codes, as well as the types of housing constructed, impose material constraints on domestic arrangements (Hayden, 1981). For example, in certain areas, *by law*, only people legally related to each other are allowed to share a house. Though a married woman and man and their children can share a dwelling in such areas, three friends cannot.

CONTROVERSIES ABOUT "THE FAMILY"

The prevailing ideology of familialism, or the concept of "the family," has recently become a centre of major controversy. The most serious challenge to it comes from reality—the way people actually organize their domestic and personal lives. Yet, while we have quite exact figures on the number of people employed in the labour force and what their earnings are, we have very little information about the actual relations between co-habiting individuals (Rubin, 1976), about how housework is done, or who pays for what in a household (Luxton, 1980; Luxton and Rosenberg, 1986). Precisely because such information on how people actually live is so difficult to obtain, the myths about family life are hard to challenge. However, increasing evidence reveals that, while it is most likely that the greatest number of people will live in a nuclear family for some part of their lives, they may well do so for only a few years; at any given time the majority of the population does not live that way.

Another challenge to the prevailing ideology has emerged with the revelation that the nuclear family is often not the centre of love and security its proponents claim. For example, one of the most prevalent myths about "the family" is that young children grow best when raised exclusively by their (biological) parents and that other ways of raising children, in group daycare, for instance, are only second best. And yet there is no evidence to support this myth at all (Gallager Ross, 1978). Indeed, the few studies that have been done suggest that daycare is excellent for children (Zigler and Gordon, 1983); and there is evidence to show that the nuclear family is too often the site of violence against children, of sexual assault and psychological deformation (Guberman and Wolfe, 1985). Similarly, the idea that women will find their greatest pleasure and satisfaction as wives and mothers has been undermined by women articulating needs for additional sources of self-worth (Friedan, 1963), and is overtly contradicted by the evidence of violence against women in the home (MacLeod, 1980) and by married women's persistent economic vulnerability (Wilson, 1986).

Another powerful challenge to the prevailing family ideology comes from increasing numbers of women who, in their personal lives, have challenged the authority of patriarchal ideology and domination and are insisting on their rights to equality both in the paid workplace and within their families (FitzGerald et al., 1982; Briskin and Yanz, 1983). Collectively, the feminist movement has played a part in revealing the differences between the ideology of the ideal family and the lived reality of daily life (Luxton and Rosenberg, 1986:10-11). Feminists demand that society as a whole provide quality social services (such as health care and childcare) for all people, rather than expecting individuals or families (usually, in practice, women) to bear these costs themselves. Many feminists demand that the term "family" be stretched to include any adult-child groupings such as single parents, lesbian or gay parents, and all intimate co-habitating or self-consciously committed support groups including childless couples, communes, or networks of friends. Such demands raise the issue of public legitimization for people whose existence in the past was always private, sometimes secret. All of them challenge the concept of family which dominates ideologically.

In reaction, conservatives have organized to defend the legitimacy of familial ideology and to attempt to enforce conformity to it. These anti-feminist "backlash" movements, the so-called "pro-family" movements (such as REAL Women), derive some popular appeal from fears evoked by the new definitions of the family, especially as most people's experience with these ideas come through the media's distorted images.* But today's anti-feminism (like its earlier versions) is also closely linked with hostility to the principle of government provision of social services; it disguises a call for cutbacks by claiming that "the family" (meaning unpaid women) is the best group for providing care. They oppose government intervention in business decisions (e.g., regarding affirmative action and equal pay, health and safety) and in education; they are even averse to the promotion of sexual and racial equality. Indeed, conservatives have used family politics to call for a re-privatization which is a wholly political project, and which demonstrates the links between support for private property and free enter-

---

*For a critique of media representations of the women's movement, see the 1981 video *Rising Up Strong* by Lorna Weir and Linda Briskin, DEC Films, Toronto.

prise on the one hand, and support for the nuclear family's structure of breadwinner husband/dependent wife on the other. It includes not only bolstering the authority of the husband/father as family head, but also increased autonomy for corporate heads—whose control over their private domains in each case has been in dispute for at least a decade (Gordon and Hunter, n.d.).

It is worth nothing that, though current, conservative politics of "the family" are not new. Concerns about the future of the family are often used to mask various political intentions. They have reappeared with regularity in the history of Western Europe, the United States, and Canada, especially at times when "underclasses" (such as women, working-class people, socialists or communists, blacks, or people of the First Nations in Canada) are perceived as politically mobilized and therefore dangerous. The discontent of such groups is often attributed to failures in their family life, rather than to the material conditions that motivate their rebellion. In the past several centuries there has been constant flux in *all* social institutions, including families. Equally constantly, community leaders, both religious and secular, have worried about the implications of aspirations for change, and have predicted general doom as a result.*

At present, a dual concern, about the apparent "crisis of the family" and about the "future of the family," prevails in much of contemporary political discourse. The Canadian government formally recognized the importance of this controversy in the 1986 Speech from the Throne, which promised to place "the family" on the formal political agenda. "The family" is at the centre of a major social controversy, as various interest groups compete to ensure that their model of the family wins widespread acceptance and is legislated into social policy. The future of "the family" depends on the outcome of their struggles.

SOCIOLOGY AND THE FUTURE OF THE FAMILY

Sociology is a science which studies human interaction, social organization, and social structure. It provides both an analytic framework and methods of study which can interpret the influence of the past in shaping the present, analyze the present, identify and assess current developments, and project their potential consequences. In this way

---

*For a powerful fictionalized projection of that position into the future, see Margaret Atwood's novel, *The Handmaid's Tale*. Toronto: McClelland and Stewart, 1985.

sociology can help in the combined effort to both predict the future and formulate realistic visions of what it might be.

However, "the family" is one of the most problematic and difficult areas to study (Morgan, 1975). First of all, families are relatively private, and it is very difficult for an investigator to study what actually goes on in family relationships. Whereas a researcher can get hired on in a factory and learn fairly accurately on the job what that work experience is like (Westwood, 1984), her colleague hoping to study families will have to rely on interviews in which people describe their family life (Rubin, 1976). The discrepancies between what people say about their families (and often even genuinely believe) and the actuality of family life may never be caught by the research (Luxton, 1980:142).

Second, everyone has had an experience of family life, and therefore each of us brings a certain expertise to the topic. Because family experiences are so important and the emotions generated by them are so deeply felt, people often find it very difficult to separate their personal experiences and feelings from their analysis of "the family." While individuals may be very clear that their experiences with paid work are quite specific, and that it is not possible to generalize to all paid work situations from that one particular experience, they may find it much more difficult to remember when talking about families that generalizing from their own family life is not appropriate in that case, either. Individual sociologists are just as vulnerable as everyone else to the myth of "family," and that vulnerability can affect their analysis. As Karen Anderson and Margrit Eichler have demonstrated (this volume), instead of investigating the reality of "family" life, historians and sociologists have all too often developed contending theories of the family which correspond to the contending popular ideologies (Segal, 1983).

These problems become even more difficult when sociology tackles the future. The task requires cutting through the ideology of familialism, dispelling the myths surrounding "the family," and holding our personal dreams and fears in careful perspective as we investigate current trends and their implications for the future.

DEFINING "THE FAMILY"

Before we can begin to think about the future of families, we must determine how to think about the differences between myth and reality, between how we think people should live and how they actually do. Once we have some sense about what "the family" actually is and why it is that way, we can begin to assess the implications of the competing models of family currently advocated and begin to develop realistic visions of what it might be. Central to that task is the problem of clarifying what is meant by "the family." In everyday language, the term "family" is used variously to refer to a number of different groupings. A "single-family dwelling" is intended for a married woman and man and their children; when a university student living in residence says he is going home to his family at Thanksgiving, we usually assume he means his parents; when a mature adult talks about missing her family she is probably referring to her grown-up children. But when someone says that most of her family were killed in the holocaust, she is referring to a wide range of extended kin; and when a man invites a group of friends to celebrate his success and he tells them they are his real family, he means those from whom he receives loving support and encouragement.

The flexibility with which the term "family" is used in regular conversation reflects the complexity of social relations and activities which are commonly included in the term. What is assumed in these usages are notions of "blood" or kinship and strong emotional bonds; family is associated with belonging—those people who have to take you in no matter what.

In academic discourse, "the family" is a term used widely and often uncritically. There are several problems with it. First, it assumes that there is, and has been, and in the future will be one single phenomenon that can be called "the family." So adult sexual and emotional relations get lumped with parent-child relations, or kinship is merged with emotional caring. And it is assumed, despite profound historical changes in all those relationships (Anderson, this volume), that there is something common to all of them throughout time.

Second, it presents a variety of different family forms as though they were really the same thing. For example, an extended matrilineal kin network of immigrants from the Carribean is equated with a white, middle-class, nuclear family from Ottawa, and both are seen as being the same as a Métis kin group in Saskatchewan; a wealthy factory owner and his heirs in Vancouver are considered in the same light as a single welfare mother in a fishing village in Nova Scotia. Third, the notion of "the family" tends to assume that all individuals within "the family" are in a similar situation sharing similar resources and life chances (despite extensive research which shows that men and women, boys and girls, do not have equal access to family resources, nor do they share equal life chances). Assuming one identical family form throughout denies important differences based on class, race, ethnicity, age, and gender (Thorne and Yalom, 1982). Finally, such usage tends to imply that the model of the nuclear family represented by familial ideology is normative, and actually exists in real life. As a result, other family forms and relationships appear to be deviant. Thus the term "the family" both obscures reality and contributes to the maintenance of familial ideology, instead of recognizing the multiplicity of relationships and activities that are actually subsumed by the term (Collier, Rosaldo, and Yanagisako, 1982).

Analytically, sociologists include within the definition of family such relations and activities as kinship and marriage, economic inheritance, pooling and sharing, conceiving and bearing children, raising children, domestic labour, sexuality, love and caring, and forms both of power and domination and of intimacy. So, when people talk about the future of the family, they are actually discussing the ways in which that whole range of relations and activities might be organized. And when others advocate that certain legal and social practices be implemented in relation to any one of those items, they are shaping the future of families in Canada.

KINSHIP AND MARRIAGE

Throughout the history of capitalist societies, kinship and marriage have decreased in importance as primary forms of social organizing. Increasingly through the 20th century, adult men have been able to arrange their lives independently of kin and marriage relationships (Ehrenreich, 1983). More recently, increasing numbers of women have also been able to get jobs which pay enough to allow them to live independently as well. However, kinship and marriage still form the basis for one of the main ways in which groups or networks of people are organized. Kinship is a system which demarcates socially recognized and legitimated relations between people. Marriage is a legal relationship which links two different kinship groups and regulates gender relations between men and women. Together, kinship and marriage operate on a number of somewhat distinct levels.

For many people, their kinship and marriage connections form an extended family from which they receive an important sense of identity and belonging. The vast majority of children are raised by kin, and those relationships are among the most significant in their lives. For many adults, the commitment represented by marriage signifies a dedication to the partner greater than any an individual is willing or able to make to other people. For many people, kinship and marriage are the main, most stable, enduring, and committed of relationships. As a result, many people hold a very strong attachment to family and are very suspicious of any criticisms raised over it.

For subordinate social groups, extended family ties are often the means by which cultural, political, religious, and language traditions are maintained and preserved (Stack, 1974; Lamoureux, 1987). When such groups are subject to discrimination or persecution, extended family ties may provide a basis for defence and resistance (Caulfield, 1974).

Politically, kinship and marriage systems are one of the most important ways by which nation states — national governments — control and regulate individuals. First and foremost, kinship establishes an individual's right to citizenship and hence to access to national resources, (rights which vary enormously from country to country but in Canada include such things as the right to seek paid employment; access to social security benefits like unemployment insurance, mother's allowance, old age pensions and welfare; the right to certain legal protections; and the right to vote). The legal citizenship of the newborn child is derived from its kin, that is, from the citizenship of one or both of its parents. While immigration laws determining which adults can acquire Canadian citizenship are constantly changing, kinship or marriage ties are usually regarded as the significant grounds for admitting immigrants.*

The regulation of marriage is one way the state exerts social control over individuals. Legal marriage both enforces and privileges heterosexuality and regulates interpersonal relationships. The legal structure of marriage traditionally has reinforced male power and privilege over women and, although in recent years pressure from feminists has forced certain legal changes in family law which gesture in the direction of equality in marriage, its current structure is still fundamentally unequal. More significantly, marriage and kin relations are used by the state to hold certain individuals economically and socially responsible for others (i.e., their family) as a way of avoiding demands that the government provide adequate social services for everyone.

Kinship and marriage are also central to the ways in which individ-

---

*One terrible exception to this rule occurs when women (usually non-white women) are admitted as domestic workers and are expressly forbidden to bring their children, even after they have established themselves in Canada (Brand, 1984).

uals have access to and are required to provide certain kinds of economic resources. On a more structural level, kinship and marriage relations are fundamental to the organization of certain kinds of property relations and, consequently, as will be seen in what follows, are the chief way in which classes and class hierarchies are maintained and reproduced.

FAMILY ECONOMICS: INHERITANCE, POOLING AND SHARING

Because family is one way to organize access to economic resources, family patterns vary by class. One of the features of a capitalist economy is that wages or salaries are paid to individuals and legally belong to those individuals. Similarly, investment income is usually owned either by large corporate organizations or by individuals. However, there are well-established patterns of pooling and sharing by which wealth owned privately is redistributed among kin and household relations.

The economic resources of their family of birth largely shape the opportunities available to children, and therefore profoundly influence their class location as adults. Children from well-off families will have a much easier time establishing themselves as well-to-do adults than will the children of poor families (Porter, 1965). Class privilege and class disadvantage are seen most clearly with the passing of wealth from one generation to the next through inheritance. For poor working-class families, the wealth may be simply some jewellery or treasured mementoes; for better-off working-class families it may be a house or a nest egg sufficient to provide the heir with a down payment. Within the ruling class, an individual's inheritance may be the ownership of a business or controlling shares in a multinational corporation.

For many people, the economics of daily subsistence are organized through families. A family is a pooling, sharing group through which individuals obtain much of their food, clothing, and shelter. Legal obligations, cultural values, and common social practices assume that the economic support for individuals unable to support themselves should come from "their family." So governments resist giving greater access to welfare or social services, on the grounds that families have the "real responsibility" for such care. One of the most common of such patterns is found in the particular family form advocated as ideal by familial ideology; that is, a family in which the male is the breadwinner who takes on financial responsibility for the other members of his nuclear family and the female is the housewife-homemaker who takes responsibility for domestic labour including the raising of the children. Under the law the man is required to share his (privately owned) income with his wife and their children.

The fact that women are supposed to be wives and mothers supported by their husbands has been used since the 19th century to justify excluding women from many paid jobs, particularly the most skilled and best paid (Armstrong and Armstrong, 1983; Connelly, 1978). Young women are discouraged from obtaining the education and training that would enable them to qualify for such work, on the grounds that their main occupation will be as wife and mother (Russell, 1987). Jobs held primarily by women (especially in clerical work, sales, and services) are systematically paid less than jobs which require the same or even less training but are held predominantly by men; this discrimination is explained by claiming that women are secondary wage earners (Abella, 1986).

This economic discrimination in the paid labour force provides a major economic compulsion on the part of women toward marriage. Because they are unlikely to earn enough to support themselves very well, and definitely cannot support children on a typical woman's wages, women need marriage to provide them with basic economic resources (Ehrenreich, 1983). As a consequence, married women, whether they are employed or not, are economically dependent on their husbands. If the marriage is a loving and co-operative one, this economic dependency may seem insignificant, but the minute the marriage breaks down, through death, separation, or divorce, the economic consequences reassert themselves. Many women living comfortable lives have suddenly found themselves plunged into poverty when their breadwinner is gone. It is this economic inequality which results in the harsh reality of contemporary Canadian life that poverty is female; the vast majority of poor people in this country are either women with young children to support or older women trying to get by on their old-age pensions (Canadian Advisory Council on the Status of Women, 1983; National Council of Welfare, 1979).

The major social change of the last 20 years has been the dramatic increase in married women's participation in the paid labour force. In 1970 38.3 percent of women were in the labour force, and constituted 33.6 percent of it. By 1980, 50.4 percent of women were in the labour force, and they constituted 40.1 percent of the total. By (December) 1986 this had increased to 55.1 percent of women, becoming 49.7 percent of the total (Labour Force Annual Averages, Statistics Canada Catalogue 71-001; Historical Labour Force Statistics, Statistics Canada Catalogue 71-201). Most significantly, the greatest increase of women in the labour force has been amongst women with pre-school age children, 58.2 percent. While such shifts mean that women have some independent income, which begins to alleviate the negative consequences of their economic dependency on men, their lower incomes mean that the problem still remains.

This economic basis for family relations means that the future of family life depends more than anything else on what happens economically. Changing patterns of male and female employment will have profound economic consequences for households. As long as women are unable to earn enough to support themselves and their children, they will be subject to strong economic pressures to marry and thus to be dependent on and hence subject to men. Only when women have equal training, equal access to all jobs, equal pay, and equal pay for work of equal value will they be able to genuinely choose whether or not to marry. Hours of work, levels of pay, parental-leave benefits, security of employment, childcare arrangements, and access to housing all affect the way people organize their personal lives and their ability to care for children. So debates about the economy (on issues such as free trade, unemployment insurance, "acceptable" levels of unemployment, a guaranteed annual income, and a shorter work week) and about government spending (who should provide economic support for those unable to support themselves: children, the disabled, the elderly, the ill, and the unemployed) are also debates about family life. At the heart of those economic debates are contending visions of how social life "should" be organized; more than anything else, future economic developments will shape constraints and possibilities for future families.

CONCEIVING AND BEARING CHILDREN

While conceiving and bearing children appear to be private individual actions, rooted in biological processes, they are in fact profoundly social. Individual women have children for a variety of reasons, but in so doing they are reproducing the human species and their own particular population. The proportion of women who have children, and the numbers of children they bear, are determined by numerous complex social forces (Gittins, 1982), and in turn shape the population profile of the next generation (Seccombe, 1983).

Familial ideology has prescribed and proscribed appropriate behaviour for conception and child bearing. Fundamental to familial ideology is the assumption that adults marry to have children and that children should only be born to married couples.

> Heterosexuality, marriage, and having children are thus all part of the western partriarchal parcel of rules for appropriate sexual relations and behaviour between men and women. Indulging in one without accepting the rest of the "parcel" has been, and still is, widely condemned (Gittens, 1985:92).

Until recently, because women's economic survival depended on marriage, and because of male power over women's sexuality, having children was, in part, a price women paid for economic security. However, as increasing numbers of women have gained relative economic independence from men, it has become possible for them to exercise greater control over their biological reproduction. This control has been dramatically increased by developments in medical knowledge and reproductive technology.

Relatively effective (though not entirely safe nor cheap) birth control and abortions have made it possible for those fertile women who have access to them to choose when and if to have children. Increasing knowledge about human fertility has increased the chances of conceiving and carrying a pregnancy to term for people who might previously have been unable to do so. Childbirth itself, which was often extremely dangerous for both mother and child is now, for those who have access to modern medical knowledge and technology, much safer (McLaren and Tigar McLaren, 1986). Amniocentesis, genetic testing, fetal monitoring, and *in utero* surgery provide enormous possibilities for control over the types of children who are born.

The new knowledge and the reproductive technology which accompanies it has opened up tremendous possibilities for the future. What is at present completely unclear, however, is what that future might look like. On the one hand, these new developments have offered great hope for people previously unable to have children. On the other hand, a preference for male children has prompted the abortion of some female babies, a practice which could result in dramatic imbalances in future populations (Mies, 1986). While genetic testing and manipulation have eliminated for some parents the grief of producing genetically abnormal children, the various drugs and surgical techniques connected with this research are often tested on poor, immigrant, black, native, or third-world women before they are deemed safe for white, middle-class, Western women (Melrose, 1982). For some lesbians, the new knowledge has permitted them to use donated sperm to impregnate themselves without either having intercourse or seeking the intervention of the medical profession. Some people have called for the creation of a "super" population, and have established sperm banks to preserve the genes of (usually white) middle-class professional men. On the other hand, some women have become concerned that, with surrogate mothering, women will be reduced to being merely egg farmers (Murphy, 1984).

At present we simply do not have enough experience to know what the future consequences of such developments might be, but a number of issues have already emerged. There is a complex politics which determines what kind of research gets done and what does not get done. Evidence indicates that the large pharmaceutical companies determine what research is done into birth control, because they fear the loss of their profits if cheaper, more effective methods were to be found. Some of the recent research into genetic engineering was prompted by military strategies for limited nuclear war. At present this knowledge, and control over access to it, is in the hands of the medical profession, a predominantly white, male, middle-class group. They can decide what kinds of people receive certain medical treatment. So, for example, most of the doctors currently able to do artificial insemination insist that prospective parents be a heterosexual couple. Infertile women unattached to a man are refused assistance. The type of genetic counselling offered to parents whose fetus has been shown to have abnormalities varies according to the race and class of the parents (Rapp, 1987).

Concerns about the future consequences of these developments have prompted some people to call for a moratorium on reproductive research. The Roman Catholic Church has declared all aspects of reproductive technology unacceptable for its members. In contrast, feminist groups have called for increased access for all, and have challenged the control of the medical profession, advocating clinics under the control of the community.

The larger question underlying all these debates is who should have the right and the power to make decisions about if, when, and how women give birth (Petchesky, 1985; Gavigan, 1987). Do individual (white male) doctors have the right to decide which women can benefit from medical reproductive techniques? Should governments have the right to legislate (as China does currently) the number of children women can have? Should religious organizations have the right to impose compulsory motherhood on their members? Should individual women have the right to abort a fetus because they don't like its sex? Does anyone have the right to force women to have babies if they do not want to—the logical extension of making abortion illegal or restricted. At present, there are major political struggles over these questions, with some people arguing that the medical profession, the churches, the government, or some combination of all three have the right to determine and control women's biological reproduction. Others argue instead that, as it is individual women whose bodies are involved, and whose lives are most profoundly affected by pregnancy and birth, they must be the ones to make the final decisions. At issue are contending visions of women's place in society and opposing concepts of future family life.

RAISING CHILDREN

The bottom line in debates about the future of family life is always the question, "But what about the children?" The promoters of the ideology of familialism respond to proposals for alternative family forms by arguing that only the nuclear family can provide the best environment for raising children, and that mothers are the best caregivers for infants and young children. In practice, lived experience and systematic research (Zigler and Gordon, 1983) demonstrate over and over that this is not necessarily the case.

In the same way, women are not innately more skilled at childcare than men, nor are biological parents automatically good parents. What all the research shows is that many different forms of childcare can be equally effective. What matters is that the child is both emotionally and physically nurtured and stimulated, and that the caregivers are not isolated and lacking in support. What we know is that making mothers primarily responsible for their children without providing supporting social services such as daycare renders those women vulnerable to poverty (because they cannot take paid work), extraordinary stress (when they take paid work and juggle two jobs while worrying about childcare), and burnout from bearing too much responsibility in isolation (Rosenberg, 1987).

A current political issue revolves around the question of who should bear the costs of raising children. On the one hand, feminist and daycare activists call for free, universal daycare funded by the government and controlled by the parents, the staff, and the community. They argue that childcare is a social responsibility to be shared by all. In contrast, conservatives insist that the costs of caring for young children should be born by the individual parents. The outcome of this struggle could result in a continuation of current practices of ad hoc, unregulated, and often unsatisfactory childcare arrangements whose cost may keep a couple from having more children; or, on the other hand, if a system of quality daycare centres were to become available across the country, parents could have a much wider range of options available to them.

The question of who cares for the children is a much larger one than that, however. It is really about whether children are the private property and responsibility of their individual parents or whether a larger community of involved and concerned adults will share the work, the responsibility, and the joy of them. Why, for example, should people only have intimate access to children if they are their actual parents? Can we imagine a future society where the choice about who cares for children (and by extension, all those needing special care such as the handicapped, the ill, and the elderly), is not restricted to either their "family" (read "woman") or an institution (the horrors of which have been well documented) but is shared collectively by their community?

DOMESTIC LABOUR

Domestic labour is the work of looking after the home and the people living in it (which is one reason why it is so easily assumed that anyone primarily responsible for domestic labour will provide caregiving to all who need it). It includes housework (activities such as cooking, cleaning, and laundry), childcare, care of disabled, sick, or elderly people, and a whole series of vital but intangible loving and nurturing tasks which go into "making a home." Overwhelmingly, domestic labour is primarily a woman's responsibility (Oakley, 1974, 1976; Luxton, 1980). It is usually private, individual, and unpaid.

The ideology of familialism offers an explanation for why domestic work should be done on a private, volunteer basis by individual women in their own homes. Because it claims that the best family form is a combination of a male, breadwinner husband/father and a female housewife/mother, it implies that women are "naturally" the best qualified to do domestic labour, and argues that the home and the activities which go on inside it are a world apart from the spheres of economics and politics. To reinforce that argument, this ideology claims that women have always worked in the home and that home-making is women's "traditional" occupation.

That myth obscures the reality that the work done in the home for "love" rather than pay is indeed influenced by economic pressures and political decisions. Sociologists have shown that the structure of private family households and all the work activities which have historically gone on inside them have been transformed by corporate decisions made to ensure profitability (Strasser, 1982). For one thing, production and marketing strategies developed by the manufacturers of household items affect the work done in the home. Moreover, future changes in tax structures, social service provisions, housing policies, and in the relative wages of women and men will all combine to profoundly affect the supposedly private sphere of the family household.

INTIMACY AND SEXUALITY

In contemporary Canadian society "family" is at the heart of emotional life and is understood to be the centre of personal life. Family life establishes our expectations and promises to fulfil our deepest, most fundamental needs. As a result, family relations are among our dearest and most important. At the same time, precisely because of the way familial ideology results in privileging one type of social relationship—the nuclear family—over any others, it is very difficult for people to get intimacy elsewhere and, when they do, it is hard for them to get those alternative relationships validated or supported. As Barrett and McIntosh point out:

> It is the overvaluation of family life that devalues these other lives. The family sucks the juice out of everything around it, leaving other institutions stunted and distorted (1982:78).

Because family relations are supposed to provide love and intimacy, and because it is so difficult to get these elsewhere, family relations give us strength and undermine us simultaneously. The contradictory nature of the demands placed upon family life mean that those dynamics are also often the most harmful and damaging (Wilson, 1983). When family relations cannot provide what the ideology claims they should, when families are the site of violence, murder, sexual assault, or psychological terrorism, the disappointment generated may be nearly as damaging as the violence itself.

Familial ideology restricts sexuality to the heterosexual adult relations of marriage, claiming that other types of sexual relations are immature, inappropriate, or degenerate. Such notions first of all deny the reality experienced by, on the one hand, thousands of people who enjoy alternative sexual practices. On the other hand they also deny the misery and pain experienced by those people who remain in heterosexual marital relations because they believe they must. Such compulsory heterosexuality is essential in maintaining the nuclear family form in which men control women's sexuality and children are identified as the "property" of particular individuals (something that is absolutely critical in societies where wealth is redistributed through kin-based inheritance).

So, when thinking about the future, we need to focus on how people can best be assured of getting the secure, long-term, committed relationships they need. What the sociological evidence shows is that by restricting sexuality and intimacy to a small family group, and

> . . . in privileging the intimacy of close kin, it has made the outside world cold and friendless (Barrett and McIntosh, 1982:80).

By undermining the potential for community-based love and caring, the pressures on the individual family are enormous and the potential for pain and disappointment great. This suggests that unless other kinds of relations are strengthened and given legal, economic, and social support, "the family" will continue to appear to be a "haven in a heartless world" (Lasch 1977), an appearance which masks the actual extent to which "the family" is anti-social:

> Caring, sharing and loving would be more widespread if the family did not claim them for its own (Barrett and McIntosh, 1982:80).

The way society is currently organized, many needs formerly provided by communities are now offered for sale: childcare, therapy, even giving birth and affection. At the same time, anything which is wanted but is outside of a cash nexus or cannot be afforded is now redeposited in "the family." So "the family" is simultaneously the place where one gets what is not available elsewhere and a structure which prevents people getting those things elsewhere except for payment.

DEVELOPING NEW VISIONS: STRATEGIES FOR CHANGE

The activities, needs, and satisfactions that are usually embodied in the term "family" — security, affection, sexuality, love, parenting, who we live with and how our households are managed — are centrally important aspects of life. But, as I have tried to suggest, the ways they are actually met at the present time is highly problematic. Some people respond to these problems by reinforcing familial ideology and attempting to compel uniform social compliance to that ideology (Harding, 1981). Arguing that the family is in crisis and that the future of the family is threatened, they urge total social compulsion, from individual behaviour through to government legislation. They are particularly threatened by efforts to legitimize alternative sexual, emotional, economic, and parenting practices.

But attempts to impose universal conformity to an idealized model of how "the family" should be will not solve the problem, precisely because the source of the problem lies in the ideology of familialism and the way its associated practices restrict and limit how needs for love and sustenance are met.

Instead, we must develop a vision of the future in which more people can more easily rely on having those needs met regularly. However, our capacity to envision such a future is shaped and limited by our present experience. Because "the family" is currently one of the few places where people can hope to find security, love, intimacy, and so on, people tend to cling to it tenaciously, fearing that to let go would be to usher in something far worse — a cold, unfeeling, individualized, and competitive world. An analysis of familial ideology and of current practices of family life suggest that:

> . . . the iniquities of the family and its appeal are closely related — they are two sides of the same coin. The benefits of family life depend upon the suffering of those who are excluded. The ideal of the family life brings in its train many a bitter marriage and disappointed parents. If the family were not the only source of a range of satisfactions, were it not so massively privileged, it would not be so attractive (Barrett and McIntosh, 1982:133).

So what does an analysis of the present suggest for strategies of change for the future? First, it illustrates the problems inherent in familial ideology and the social practices that go with it. Compulsory conformity to a single model creates situations where people cannot ensure that their needs are met. Instead, we need multiple options which permit people to make real choices about how they will live their lives, and which allow people to live differently at different times of their lives. And those options need to be based on collectivities or communities, networks of people living and working together who can contribute, collectively, to the support needed by each of them.

Second, such an analysis suggests that we need to appreciate that social change occurs in many ways, and that families are changed by forces which may appear to be quite remote. And yet human agency, the actions of individuals organizing together, can play a major role in shaping how that change occurs. Social change involves the complex interaction of many forces, of which a good number are unintentional, but it can also be affected by deliberate intervention such as social policy legislation or political organizing by special interest groups. For example, economic forces lead to changing patterns in labour force participation for women and men; developments in science and technology such as birth control or abortion affect biological reproduction; new ideologies, social norms, and expectations can lead to new practices (for example, the growing involvement of men in the care of young babies); the underlying assumptions shaping various legislative policies can profoundly affect family life (for example, through income taxes, zoning laws, and building codes); and, finally, large social movements and organized political campaigns can either win new possibilities or constrict and limit them (for example, the inclusion of sexual orientation in the human rights code or the current battle over whether to remove abortion from the Criminal Code). The point is that social change occurs; our only hope for shaping a future we want to live in will come from committing ourselves to understanding the implications of contemporary issues and acting on that understanding.

REFERENCES

Abella, Rosalie. 1984. *Equality in Employment: A Royal Commission Report*. Ottawa: Minister of Supply and Services Canada.

Anderson, Karen. 1987. "A Gendered World: Women, Men, and the Political Economy of the Seventeenth Century Huron." In *Feminism and Political Economy: Women's Work, Women's Struggles*, Heather Jon Maroney and Meg Luxton, eds. Toronto: Methuen Publications.

Armstrong, Pat and Hugh Armstrong. 1983. *A Working Majority: What Women Must Do for Pay*. Ottawa: Canadian Advisory Council on the Status of Women.

Barrett, Michele and Mary McIntosh. 1982. *The Anti-Social Family*. London: Verso.

Bloom, Lynn. 1976. " 'It's All For Your Own Good': Parent-Child Relationships in Popular American Child Rearing Literature, 1820–1970." *Journal of Popular Culture* 10.

Blumenfeld, Emily. 1976. "Child Rearing Literature as an Object of Content Analysis" *The Journal of Applied Communications Research*, November.

Brand, Dionne. 1984. "*A Working Paper on Black Women in Toronto: Gender, Race and Class*." Fireweed *No. 19 Summer/Fall:* 26–43.

Briskin, Linda, and Lynda Yanz, eds. 1983. *Union Sisters: Women in the Labour Movement*. Toronto: The Women's Press.

Canadian Advisory Council on the Status of Women. 1983. *As Things Stand*. Ottawa: Canadian Advisory Council on the Status of Women.

Caulfield, Mina. 1974. *"Imperialism, the Family and Cultures of Resistance."* Socialist Revolution 4, No. 20, October.

Collier, Jane, Michelle Rosaldo and S. Yanagisako. 1982. *"Is There a Family? New Anthropological Views."* In Thorne and Yalom, *Rethinking the Family*. New York: Longmans.

Connelly, Pat. 1978. *Last Hired, First Fired: Women and the Canadian Work Force*. Toronto: The Women's Press.

Ehrenreich, Barbara. 1983. *The Hearts of Men: American Dreams and the Flight from Commitment*. London: Pluto.

FitzGerald, Maureen, Connie Guberman and Margie Wolfe. 1982. *Still Ain't Satisfied: Canadian Feminism Today*. Toronto: The Women's Press.

Friedan, Betty. 1963. *The Feminine Mystique*. New York: Dell.

Gallager Ross, Kathleen. 1978. *Good Day Care: Fighting for It, Getting It, and Keeping It*. Toronto: the Women's Press.

Gavigan, Shelley. 1987. "Women and Abortion in Canada: What's Law Got To Do With It?" In Heather Jon Maroney and Meg Luxton, eds., *Feminism and Political Economy: Women's Work, Women's Struggles*. Toronto: Methuen Publications.

Gittins, Diana. 1982. *Fair Sex, Family Size and Structure in Britain, 1900–39*. London: Hutchison.

———. *The Family in Question: Changing Households and Familiar Ideologies*. London: Macmillan, 1985.

Gordon, Linda and Allen Hunter. 1978. *Sex, Family and the New Right: Anti-feminism as a Political Force*. Somerville, Mass.: n.d. (reprinted from Radical America, Nov. 1977–February 1978.)

Griffith, Alison. 1983. "Skilling for Life, Living for Skill: The Social Construction of Life Skill in Ontario Schools," unpublished Ph.D thesis, University of Toronto, Toronto, Ontario.

Guberman, Connie and Margie Wolfe, eds. 1985. *No Safe Place: Violence Against Women and Children*. Toronto: The Women's Press.

Harding, Susan. 1981. "Family Reform Movements: Recent Feminism and its Opposition." *Feminist Studies*, vol. 7, No. 5:57–75.

Hayden, Delores. 1981. *The Grand Domestic Revolution: A History of Feminist Designs for American Homes, Neighbourhoods and Cities*. Cambridge: MIT Press.

Lamoureux, Diane. 1987. "Nationalism and Feminism in Quebec: An Impossible Attraction." In Heather Jon Maroney and Meg Luxton, eds. *Feminism and Political Economy: Women's Work, Women's Struggles*. Toronto, Methuen Publications.

Lasch, Christopher. 1977. *Haven in a Heartless World*. New York.

Luxton, Meg. 1980. *More Than Labour of Love: Three Generations of Women's Work in the Home*. Toronto: The Women's Press.

Luxton Meg and Harriet Rosenberg. 1986. *Through the Kitchen Window: The Politics of Home and Family*. Toronto: Garamond.

Maroney, Heather Jon and Meg Luxton, eds. 1987. *Feminism and Political Economy: Women's Work, Women's Struggles*. Toronto: Methuen.

McLaren, Angus and Arlene Tigar McLaren. 1986. *The Bedroom and the State*. Toronto: McClelland and Stewart.

Meis, Maria. 1986. *Patriarchy and Accumulation on a World Scale: Women in the International Division of Labour*. Atlantic Highlands, New Jersey: Zed Books.

Melrose, Dianna. 1982. *Bitter Pills: Medicines and the Third World Poor*. Oxford: Oxfam.

Morgan, D. J. H. 1975. *Social Theory and the Family*. London: Routledge & Kegan Paul.

Murphy, Julie. 1984. "Egg Farming and Women's Future." In *Test-Tube Women*, Rita Arditti, Renate D. Klein, Shelly Minden, eds. New York: Methuen Publications.

National Council of Welfare. 1979. *Women and Poverty: A Report*. Ottawa: National Council of Welfare.

Oakley, Ann. 1974. *The Sociology of Housework*. Bath: Martin Robinson.

———. 1976. *Women's Work: The Housewife Past and Present*. New York: Vintage Books.

Petchesky, Rosalina. 1988. *Abortion and Women's Choice*. Boston: Northeastern University Press.

Porter, John. 1965. *The Vertical Mosaic: An Analysis of Social Class and Power in Canada*. Toronto: The University of Toronto Press.

Rapp, Rayna. 1987. "Moral Pioneers: Women, Men and Fetuses on the Frontiers of Reproductive Technology," lecture at York University, North York, Ontario, February 25.

———. 1978. "Family and Class in Contemporary America: Notes Toward an Understanding of Ideology," *Science and Society* 42 Fall, pp. 278–301.

Riley, Denis. 1983. *War in the Nursery: Theories of the Child and the Mother*. London: Virago.

Rosenberg, Harriet. 1987. "Motherwork, Stress and Depression: The Costs of Privatized Social Reproduction." In Heather Jon Maroney and Meg Luxton, eds. *Feminism and Political Economy: Women's Work, Women's Struggles*. Toronto: Methuen Publications.

Rubin, Lilian. 1976. *Worlds of Pain*. New York: Basic Books.

Russell, Susan. 1987. "The Hidden Curriculum of School: Reproducing Gender and Class Hierarchies." In Heather Jon Maroney and Meg Luxton, eds. *Feminism and Political Economy: Women's Work, Women's Struggles*. Toronto: Methuen Publications.

Seccombe, Wally. 1983. "Marxism and Demography." *New Left Review No. 137*. pp. 22–47.

Segal, Lynn, ed. 1983. *What Is To Be Done About the Family?* Harmondsworth: Penguin.

Spock, Benjamin. 1968. *Baby and Child Care*. Reprint. Markham, Ontario: Simon and Schuster of Canada.

Stack, Carol. 1974. *All Our Kin: Strategies for Survival in a Black Community*. New York: Harper & Row.

Statistics Canada Catalogue 71-529: 71-201.

Strasser, Susan. 1982. *Never Done: A History of American Housework*. New York: Pantheon.

Thorne, Barrie and Marilyn Yalom, eds. 1982. *Rethinking the Family: Some Feminist Questions*. New York: Longmans.

Weber, Max. 1967. *The Protestant Ethic and the Spirit of Capitalism*. London: Allen and Unwin.

Westwood, Sallie. 1984. *All Day Every Day: Factory and Family in the Making of Women's Lives*. London: Pluto.

Wilson, Elizabeth. 1983. *What is to be Done About Violence Against Women?* London: Penguin.

Wilson, Sue. 1986. *Women, the Family and the Economy*. 2nd edition. Toronto: McGraw-Hill Ryerson.

Zigler, Dr. Ed and Edmund Gordon, eds. 1983. *Daycare: Scientific Issues and Social Policy*. Dover, Mass.: Auburn House.

Index